Creativity and Innovations in ELT Materials Development

NEW PERSPECTIVES ON LANGUAGE AND EDUCATION

Series Editors: Professor Viv Edwards, *University of Reading, UK* and Professor Phan Le Ha, *University of Hawaii at Manoa, USA*

Two decades of research and development in language and literacy education have yielded a broad, multidisciplinary focus. Yet education systems face constant economic and technological change, with attendant issues of identity and power, community and culture. This series will feature critical and interpretive, disciplinary and multidisciplinary perspectives on teaching and learning, language and literacy in new times.

All books in this series are externally peer-reviewed.

Full details of all the books in this series and of all our other publications can be found on http://www.multilingual-matters.com, or by writing to Multilingual Matters, St Nicholas House, 31–34 High Street, Bristol BS1 2AW, UK.

NEW PERSPECTIVES ON LANGUAGE AND EDUCATION: 58

Creativity and Innovations in ELT Materials Development

Looking Beyond the Current Design

Edited by
Dat Bao

MULTILINGUAL MATTERS
Bristol • Blue Ridge Summit

DOI https://doi.org/10.21832/BAO9696
Library of Congress Cataloging in Publication Data
A catalog record for this book is available from the Library of Congress.
Names: Bao, Dat editor.
Title: Creativity and Innovations in ELT Materials Development: Looking Beyond
   the Current Design/Edited by Dat Bao.
Description: Bristol; Blue Ridge Summit, PA: Multilingual Matters, 2018. |
   Series: New Perspectives on Language and Education: 58 | Includes bibliographical
   references and index.
Identifiers: LCCN 2017049307| ISBN 9781783099696 (hbk : alk. paper) |
   ISBN 9781783099719 (epub) | ISBN 9781783099726 (kindle)
Subjects: LCSH: English language--Study and teaching--Foreign speakers. | Language
   teachers--Training of.
Classification: LCC PE1128.A2 C6955 2018 | DDC 428.0071--dc23
LC record available at https://lccn.loc.gov/2017049307

British Library Cataloguing in Publication Data
A catalogue entry for this book is available from the British Library.

ISBN-13: 978-1-78309-969-6 (hbk)

Multilingual Matters
UK: St Nicholas House, 31–34 High Street, Bristol BS1 2AW, UK.
USA: NBN, Blue Ridge Summit, PA, USA.

Website: www.multilingual-matters.com
Twitter: Multi_Ling_Mat
Facebook: https://www.facebook.com/multilingualmatters
Blog: www.channelviewpublications.wordpress.com

The policy of Multilingual Matters/Channel View Publications is to use papers that
are natural, renewable and recyclable products, made from wood grown in sustainable
forests. In the manufacturing process of our books, and to further support our policy,
preference is given to printers that have FSC and PEFC Chain of Custody certification.
The FSC and/or PEFC logos will appear on those books where full certification has
been granted to the printer concerned.

Typeset in Sabon and Frutiger by R. J. Footring Ltd, Derby.
Printed and bound in the UK by the CPI Books Group Ltd.
Printed and bound in the US by Edwards Brothers Malloy, Inc.

Contents

Contributors

Alan Maley has lived and worked in 10 countries worldwide for over 50 years, including China, India, Singapore, Malaysia and Thailand. He has published over 40 books and numerous articles on ELT, most recently *Creativity in the English Language Classroom*, co-edited with Nik Peachey (British Council, 2015), *Integrating Global Issues in the English Language Classroom*, co-edited with Nik Peachey (British Council, 2017) and *Creativity in English Language Teaching: From Inspiration to Implementation*, co-authored with Tamas Kiss (Palgrave Macmillan, 2018). His main interests are in creativity and literature.

Brian Tomlinson has worked as a teacher, teacher trainer, curriculum developer, film extra, football coach and university academic in Indonesia, Italy, Japan, Nigeria, Oman, Singapore, the UK, Vanuatu and Zambia, as well as giving presentations in over 70 countries. He is Founder and President of MATSDA (the international Materials Development Association), an Honorary Visiting Professor at the University of Liverpool, a Professor at the Shanghai International Studies University and a TESOL Professor at Anaheim University. He has over 100 publications on materials development, language through literature, the teaching of reading, language awareness and teacher development, including *Discover English* (with Rod Bolitho), *Openings, Materials Development in Language Teaching, Developing Materials for Language Teaching, Research for Materials Development in Language Learning* (with Hitomi Masuhara), *Applied Linguistics and Materials Development* and *SLA Theory and Materials Development for Language Learning*. He has recently co-authored with Hitomi Masuhara *The Complete Guide to the Theory and Practice of Materials Development for Language Learning* (Wiley, 2017).

Dat Bao has worked with Leeds Metropolitan University in the UK, National University of Singapore, Cornell University in the US and Assumption University of Thailand, and is currently Senior Lecturer at Monash University in Australia. His expertise includes curriculum development, intercultural communication, classroom silence, creative pedagogy and visual pedagogy. He has conducted research in Australia, China, Indonesia, Japan, the Philippines and Vietnam. He has published poetry and also worked as a coursebook artist. He is the author of *Understanding Silence and Reticence: Ways of Participating in SLA* (Bloomsbury, 2014).

Flora Debora Floris is Senior Lecturer at the Petra Christian University, Surabaya, Indonesia, where she teaches general English and language teaching methodology courses. She has given talks at international conferences in Malaysia, Singapore and Thailand. She has written numerous journal articles and books, including *English for Academic Purposes* and *English for Occupational Purposes* (Graha Ilmu, 2007). Her research interests include materials development, language acquisition and teaching methodology and the use of ICT in language teaching. She actively manages an online teacher professional development forum called Teacher Voices (https://www.facebook.com/groups/teachervoices).

Hae-ok Park is Associate Professor in the Department of English Materials Development at the International Graduate School of English (IGSE), Seoul, where she teaches graduate courses such as 'Drama Techniques and Language Learning' and 'An Introduction to English Materials Development'. She is also the Director of the IGSE Education Center, where various ELT-related courses are run both online and offline. Hae-ok has a PhD in English materials development using process drama from the Leeds Beckett University in the UK. Currently, she is interested in using process drama techniques in flipped learning, CLIL and text-driven approaches.

Hosne Ara Begum is a Professor at the Institute of Education and Research at the University of Dhaka, Bangladesh. Currently, she is involved in teaching educational research (quantitative–qualitative) and assessment and supervision of students' work (Med, MPhil, PhD). Her research interests include teacher professional development, classroom assessment and inclusive practices concerning issues related to primary and post-primary education. Her ongoing project includes designing and implementing school- and classroom-based assessment methods and tools in 12 subjects, including English for students in grades I–V, which is supported by UNICEF and the Directorate of Primary Education of the government of Bangladesh.

Md Zulfeqar Haider is a PhD candidate at the Faculty of Education, Monash University, Australia, where he did his MEd-TESOL in 2003. He joined the Bangladeshi Civil Service in 1993 and has worked for a number of government organisations and projects as an English language teacher, teacher trainer, curriculum developer and textbook writer. He is the co-author of the six English textbooks for Bangladeshi secondary schools in the series 'English for Today'. His research interests include language testing and assessment, cultural representation in the EFL curriculum and textbook, teachers' professional development and teachers' educational and learning capitals.

Mohammod Moninoor Roshid is an Associate Professor at the Institute of Education and Research (IER), University of Dhaka, Bangladesh. He also closely works as a consultant with the British Council, UNICEF and the Ministry of Education. Recently he has been awarded PhD in TESOL at Monash University, Australia. His PhD study focuses on university–industry relationships in the development of graduates' English as an employability skill for international business communication. He has a published number of articles, book chapters and conference papers. His research interests include English for employability, English for international business, language skills development, university–industry partnership, and intercultural communication.

Paul Hullah is Associate Professor of British Literature at Meijigakuin University, Tokyo. He is a co-founder of Liberlit, an international forum for 'Discussion of the Role of Literary Texts in English Curricula' (http://www.liberlit.com) and has published and presented internationally in literary studies and TEFL. Publications include: 14 textbooks for EFL learners; *Rock UK: A Sociocultural History of British Popular Music* (Cengage, 2013); and *We Found Her Hidden: The Remarkable Poetry of Christina Rossetti* (Partridge, 2016). In 2013 he received the Asia Pacific Brand Laureate International Personality Award for 'paramount contribution to ... education of students in Asia'. He has published seven collections of poetry, most recently Climbable (Partridge, 2016).

Rajeevnath Ramnath teaches in the School of Education, Nottingham University, Malaysia. He gained his PhD in English Language from the National University of Singapore (NUS) after graduating with BA, MA and MPhil degrees in English language and literature from the University of Madras, India. He has published in several international journals, presented papers and conducted workshops in many prestigious ELT conferences around the world. Ramnath has supervised 30 theses at the master's level and has taught a range of MA courses in the past decade. His teaching and research interests are in materials development, reading and writing, language-through-literature, world Englishes and creative writing.

Ranran Liu is a graduate scholar in the Faculty of Education at Monash University. With experience and training in early childhood and primary education, she enjoys researching into child play in education, communication in the early years, as well as linguistics and sociocultural competence in children. She holds a bachelor's degree in English language education and upon completing her master's degree in early childhood education she is planning to pursue a doctoral degree with a focus on creativity in child play within the context of education.

Willy A. Renandya is a language teacher educator with extensive teaching experience in Asia. He currently teaches applied linguistics courses at the National Institute of Education, Nanyang Technological University, Singapore. His latest publications include *Simple, Powerful Strategies for Student Centered Learning*, co-authored with George Jacobs and Michael Power (Springer International, 2016) and *English Language Teaching Today: Linking Theory and Practice*, co-authored with Handoyo P. Widodo (Springer International, 2016). He actively manages an online professional development group called Teacher Voices (https://www.facebook.com/groups/teachervoices).

Tan Bee Tin currently teaches at the University of Auckland. She has published in the areas of materials development for language teaching, studies of academic discourse, the role of creativity and interest in language learning, and teaching English in peripheral contexts. Her research on creativity and second language learning has been published in international journals such as *Applied Linguistics*, *ELT* and *Innovation in Language Learning and Teaching*. Her work on the role of interest in language learning had been published as a monograph titled *Stimulating Student Interest in Language Learning: Theory, Research and Practice* (Palgrave Macmillan, 2016).

Xiaofang Shang holds a master's degree in early childhood education from Monash University, Australia. She is a second language teacher to a diverse group of learners in Melbourne. She also works as a registered kindergarten teacher with children from multilingual and multicultural backgrounds. Inspired by her field of work and motivated by the enthusiasm in second language teaching and learning, she has researched the perspectives of parents and teachers on materials to inform scaffolding strategies for second language learners.

Preface

This book recruits and showcases innovative voices in language curriculum issues. Some of those issues are insufficiently addressed in current debates and might need richer engagement; others remain less noticeable and thus less exploited in academic practice despite their significant potential. The volume brings together 14 academics in ELT materials development. Some are renowned scholars, the authors of profound publications that have shaped the field; others have recently joined the discipline with something new to say. We value all voices and refrain from listening solely to the dominant discourse, believing that sometimes an unusual thought might be worth noticing for disturbing current knowledge and revealing common practice as improvable.

Key issues discussed in the book include why commonly used language tasks should be challenged, what pedagogical choices accelerate creativity, why learners need more flexible activities, what types of task nurture children's creativity, how constraints promote innovations, whether imaginary content can merge with authentic materials, what place literature occupies in a multicultural context, whether technology can shape pedagogy, how classic SLA theories support creative digital learning, how teachers can be involved in developing materials, why learners' creative work should enter into task construction and how teacher perception helps adjust the sociocultural content of a coursebook. Although the authors may or may not address all of these questions to readers' full satisfaction, we raise these concerns in the hope of expanding current practice in coursebook design. Despite decades of scholarly research there remain gaps and unresolved issues, and scholars in this field never cease to challenge the dominant discourse in order to advance theorisation in ELT materials.

The book falls into three parts. Part 1, 'Improving ELT Materials Through Creative Pedagogies', discusses how innovative task-writing ideas can make materials more original and inspiring. Part 2, 'Improving ELT Materials Through Specific Resources', suggests how different forms of arts and technology can be used to craft innovations in coursebooks. Part 3, 'Improving ELT Materials Through Teacher and Learner Involvement', portrays how teachers and learners can participate in materials writing and negotiate ways to personalise learning. Together, the three parts of the book identify areas of debate in materials developing strategies, present critical views on various components of the coursebook and make recommendations on how to engage students in more fruitful and novel ways of learning.

The chapters invite readers to reflect on areas of contemporary materials development that can be enhanced through empirical research and pedagogical conditions for creative learning. One important message conveyed in this volume as a collective voice is that English course materials in today's local and global context need to become more inclusive and inspiring, by utilising all the artistic, cultural, theoretical and technological resources that we have. With rich materials at hand, learners not only learn better but also discover more diverse means to become linguistically innovative and culturally open-minded.

Dat Bao
Melbourne, 2018

1 Expanding the Discourse in ELT Materials Development Through Creativity and Innovation

Dat Bao

This chapter provides an overview of how ELT materials can be improved through creative mindsets and innovative efforts, as well as through materials personalisation and localisation. It is not, however, a review of current approaches to the ELT curriculum but mainly offers innovative insights to enrich current ways of developing course materials. It addresses the three main areas covered by this book, namely creativity, innovations and teacher–learner involvement in coursebook design.

One important obligation in the quest for successful English language education is to create and apply new experience in course materials. As the theme of this book indicates, materials writers are constantly challenged by the need to produce novel ideas (creativity) and implement them via coursebook design (innovation). Innovation in general refers to new procedure (Markee, 1992) and untried methodology (Hutchison & Torres, 1994) that bring about improvement (Nicholls, 1983).

Innovators are often defined as agents of change (Hall & Hewings, 2001) and for change to happen, materials developers need to understand the learning process. Although this book is about materials, it places the learner at the heart of much of the discussion. As Hae-ok Park highlights in Chapter 7, learners are active participants in research and in the practice of innovative problem solving. The implementation of creative elements, or innovation, can be understood in two ways. One is that materials themselves need to be creative in taking novel content from diverse resources such as literature, drama, poetry and multimedia resources. The second is that materials need to be innovatively employed through flexible tasks, original combinations and multiple options.

This introductory discussion is written to interact with the chapters in the book not only by capturing the essence of what is being raised but also by commenting on those issues. Although readers can interpret every topic in each chapter by themselves, the commentary below might provoke further thoughts and trigger more in-depth reflection. The key arguments in the contributing chapters somehow defy current practice in order to bring about positive transformation in materials development.

Part 1: Improving ELT Materials Through Creative Pedagogies

Part 1 identifies a number of pedagogical areas in second language materials which could be further enriched. Having problematised current practices, the contributors propose ways to improve them. Chapter 2 expresses dissatisfaction with a number of conventional activities as they offer little stimulus and low pedagogical value to the learner. Chapter 3 redefines the essence of creativity and suggests ways to implement it in task modification. Chapter 4 challenges common ways of understanding creativity via a constructivist lens and proposes strategies to enhance task quality. Chapter 5 explores the discourse in children's creativity and based on such understanding builds a framework for creative activities at primary level. Chapter 6 plays with the effect of constraints on creativity and connects that understanding to learner autonomy.

By and large, the chapters are written to refresh certain areas of theorisation that have not been sufficiently deployed in L2 curriculum development. They share the recognition that learners' inspiration and optimal output are often restricted by the presence of many mundane, uncreative and inflexible pedagogies in current task design. In doing so, the chapters address the following questions:

- What is problematic with typical language tasks?
- What pedagogical choices accelerate creativity?
- Why do learners need more flexible materials?
- What types of task nurture creativity in young learners?
- Do constraints impede or facilitate the innovative mind?

I shall re-articulate the authors' insights below and interact with them as a way of keeping the dialogue open, bearing in mind that no answers to academic enquiry should be theoretically conclusive but need to stimulate further debate.

Rethinking typical language activities

To resist routine is to take one step towards creativity. Incompetent teachers treat all students alike, and ineffective textbooks tend to provide mostly typical tasks, assuming that all learners will accept them and will not ask for more. Typical activities, as a matter of fact, offer little room for learners' personalised participation. For tasks to be inspiring, they need to stimulate improvisation among students so that they become more active in applying what they are learning (Cakir, 2006). Unfortunately, such activities need to be thoughtfully designed rather than purely reliant on the availability of real-life resources. This is because not all authentic materials facilitate learning if the content seems too ordinary. ELT discourse has highlighted occasions on which the typical choice of natural, native-context texts might lead to boredom and unproductive learning, simply because there is nothing exciting that stimulates the desire to learn (see, for example, Timmis, 2005).

Brian Tomlinson in Chapter 2, based on his own research, cautions us against routine-oriented, demotivating materials that restrict input, reduce emotion, produce little learning and hinder authentic language use in the real world. From a creative point of view, being typical amounts to being average and short of uniqueness, which is unacceptable, or even humiliating, as it suggests a lack of achievement. When learners are exposed to typical materials, their curiosity switches off and their learning capacity is narrowed down. The author not only criticises typicality but more importantly proposes a range of strategies to improve on mediocrity and inspire learning. He also adds illuminating examples to assist those who wish to try fresh ways of adapting materials. The examples might look simplistic but are powerful in helping teachers escape boredom and routine practice, to move into enjoyment and real-world communication. Both Brian Tomlinson in that chapter and Alan Maley in Chapter 3 propose ways to make such transformation possible, and give personalised and stimulating demonstrations of how upgraded tasks produce a more novel learning impact.

Redefining creative materials

Alan Maley in Chapter 3 refreshes our conceptualisation of creativeness by looking into whom creativity serves and the quality of learning it might bring. In other words, creativity itself does not have value in materials design unless it makes a change, by fostering creativity in teaching and learning. Thus, we are invited to problematise the construct creativity in ELT materials design. First of all, scholars' appeal for creativity has been so frequent that it risks becoming commonplace; moreover, when one attempts to be different without being able to enhance learning by much, creativity turns into a tedious responsibility. Secondly, creativity often means freedom, but whose freedom, and what for, are questions we must consider. Suppose textbook writers utilise freedom to develop original tasks that learners do not find useful for learning: such activities look fancy but turn out to be useless. The fundamental argument here is that trying to be creative and trying to be effective may not denote the same pedagogical intention.

Based on this understanding, the most important aspect of creativity in language instruction, as implied in the chapter, is the need for it to be well associated with positive learning impact. In reading the chapter, we are provoked to reassess the significance of creative effort: it is only worthwhile if we look into what a task eventually does for the learner rather than what it looks like to the reader.

One example of effective creativity in materials is the introduction of a variety of ways to perform the same task and allow learners to make their own choices of what suits them best. Another example is the 'marvel effect', as suggested by Schmidhuber (2006), which taps into learners' curiosity and inspiration for learning. Along these lines, Alan Maley offers a range of ideas to guide creative efforts in materials development, in order to produce a social effect on learners and enable them to connect, engage, control, enjoy and interact in their own optimal ways.

The appeal for materials to be more flexible

A coursebook to some extent should represent its immediate users rather than stay outside of their world and tell them what to learn. It is therefore important to raise the awareness that teachers and students can take control of material content through negotiation with it. Dat Bao in Chapter 4 argues that creativity does not grow in the independent mind but interacts with facilitating resources, a process which leads to the point where both coursebook users and the coursebook itself co-construct learning. To make this possible, the author appeals for materials to take on qualities such as novelty, openness to multiple responses, and challenge to learners' cognition and emotion, as well as to provide conditions for adaptation, contextualisation, choice and respect for cultural diversity.

The chapter provides an example of a flexible task that allows learners to give a positive, non-biased interpretation of events, reduce over-simplification of non-English-speaking cultures, share cultural information and lessen stereotypes imposed on them. Such negotiation with material content is important, in view of research into cultural values in ELT materials that has indicated that many coursebooks are filled with cultural stereotyping that distorts reality (Ndura, 2004), simplifies many cultures (Skopinskaja, 2003) and marginalises less privileged social groups (Sherlock, 2016).

Types of task that nurture children's creativity

There is presently a strong tendency for children to start learning English at an earlier age than ever before, which has come as the result of education reform around the world. Because of this, the teaching of English to young learners is becoming a field of study in its own right. While there is little SLA evidence that supports the superiority of an early start, when it comes to creativity or creative learning, educators and scholars in early childhood education tend to agree that the earlier the better. The flexibility of the young mind, which applies to learning in any field, needs a foundation of early learning for children to continue being creative when growing into adulthood.

Unlike many adults, children come into the learning environment with a great deal of inherent curiosity, physical vitality, the passion to play and a sense of resistance to formal learning. The dynamic of such a disposition suggests that the resources for capturing children's interest and attention also differ from what inspires adult learners. Young learners need more individualised attention, social guidance, toys, games, props, fantasy, kinaesthetic play and the conditions for exploring the world, which is still fresh to them. With this understanding, Chapter 5, by Dat Bao and Ranran Liu, provides some ideas for the construction of tasks taht will tap into the learners' creative responses. These ideas, which come from a discussion of literature related to both L2 learning and children's creative development, are presented in a framework of references/criteria to assist ELT materials writers in designing English language tasks that simultaneously meet children's learning needs and allow for pleasurable play.

How constraints impede or promote creativity

Although creativity is often defined as freedom from control, Tan Bee Tin in Chapter 6 provokes readers' thinking by restating that creativity can be promoted by decreasing freedom. She argues that when there is less freedom, the constraint will recondition learners' thinking mechanisms, to produce unpredictable outputs. This phenomenon, in my experience, is sometimes known as the psychology of limitation or the energy of despair. According to Wortman (2016), legend has it that Ernest Hemingway wrote the six-word story below, which is an excellent example of how limitation is capable of generating a masterpiece:

For sale: baby shoes, never worn.

Tan Bee Tin also connects autonomy with creativity by arguing that learner autonomy can be promoted through creative tasks. In her observation, some learners faced with excessive freedom might avoid exercising autonomy but tend to rely on external resources, and one way to save them from such dependency is to provide constraints. Here, readers might come up with a counter-argument: in many cases, constraints might serve as guidance, which does not really promote autonomy. For example, when a teacher asks students to write about themselves and they are at a loss, the teacher might recondition the requirement and suggest that students write about what they have done in the past three days that they hated. This task then becomes easy. Would we regard the revised instruction as a constraint or as guidance? One might say it is constraint, which helps students exercise autonomy and write creatively. Another might suggest that it is guidance, which supports students in their writing output but in this case creativity and autonomy are not really involved. These scenarios suggest that constraints might need to be examined more qualitatively to be richly understood.

Materials writers in their task design might like to vary instructions for the same activity by suggesting different constraints and letting coursebook users decide which to try. In a research study on the effect of constraint on creativity, Joyce (2009) manipulated constraints along a continuum from low to high for stimulating learner creativity; moderate constraints tended to be more productive than high or low levels of constraint. The study also concluded that constraints can be either limiting or directing. For instance, when the degree of challenge seems too high, learners may experience a threatening emotion that restricts creativity (Csikszentmihalyi, 1996). In addition, it is believed that both absolute freedom and heavy constraint can be damaging to creative effort (Amabile & Gitomer, 1984). After all, the effect of constraints on creativity is complex, as it is subject to the influences of learner autonomy, personality and motivation, as well as teacher instruction and other conditions in the learning process.

Part 2: Improving ELT Materials Through Specific Resources

Part 2 if the book examines how distinctive resources such as drama, poetry, literature, technological tools and online content can help improve the quality of course materials. In four chapters, the authors present their cases of innovation. Chapter 7 reviews process drama and recommends strategic ways for it to enter into materials. Chapter 8 advocates fiction resources, with rationalisation of how they help enhance the quality of learning. Chapter 9 problematises the current status of ICT in language education and suggests a set of guiding principles to assist the integration of technology in coursebooks. Chapter 10 employs SLA theories as a foundation to connect digital capitals with creative learning. What these discussions have in common is that they look into a number of accessible capitals that have not been exploited to the optimum and find ways to expand their usefulness. In particular, the discussions address four key concerns in the language curriculum:

- Do imaginary worlds have a place in authentic ELT materials?
- What position should literature occupy in the modern-day multi-cultural context?
- To what extent and in what way can technology help writers make materials more effective?
- Can classic SLA theories support creative digital learning?

I shall capture at least one key insight from each author and make some comments, but leave the rest of the conversation for readers to engage with in the chapters themselves.

Attempts to create imaginary worlds in ELT materials

Although scholars in materials development often highlight the need to connect classroom learning to real-world events, an alternative view advocates creative imagination over boring reality as a way to make learning more fantastic. There are multiple methods to make this happen and one of them, as suggested by Hae-ok Park in Chapter 7, is through the use of process drama. Originated from a method of teaching drama, this approach has entered other areas of education (see, for example, Bolton & Heathcote, 1994) for scenario creation or problem-solving skills very much through imagination and unscripted play.

The term 'process drama' was originally used in the 1990s (O'Neill, 1995) to denote the dramatic world co-created by teachers and students. Later, due to its potential in having learners try on different shoes to comprehend the roles or perspectives of others, process drama became a practical tool for students to develop creative language use. Hae-ok Park connects this approach with tasked-based instruction as well as content and language integrated learning and then invites readers to consider ways to integrate it into materials development. The value of creative drama-based pedagogy in tapping into the multiplicity of learner competences has been widely acknowledged in language education discourse. The benefit of drama is that it supports the early stage of L2 development (Elgar, 2002; Heldenbrand, 2003), active involvement (Sam, 1990), emotional response (Whitear, 1998), learning enjoyment (Mordecai, 1985), self-discovery (Maurer, 1987), the freedom to be wrong (Maley & Duff, 1982), multisensory learning (Baldwin & Fleming, 2003), creative thinking (Zafeiriadou, 2009) and improvisation (Hornbrook, 1989).

Nevertheless, one might not wish to assume that drama naturally works for everyone. The potential weaknesses of drama approaches come from their unpredictability and disruption to routine that might take away learners' sense of safety. Some learners resist such pedagogy, as they perceive it to limit their motivation and engagement (Zafeiriadou, 2009) due to their inherent verbal reticence (Dora To *et al.*, 2011). Many teachers also hesitate to employ drama in consideration of time constraints, the lack of training, the requirement of high enthusiasm and self-perceptions of absurdity (Royka, 2002). At some points, coursebook writers might like to consider a reasonable balance between real-world content and imaginary content, to connect with learners in both practical and inventive ways. Again, such decisions cannot be made in a vacuum but need to rely on our knowledge of what the target learner wants from the coursebook.

The role of creative texts in enhancing materials quality

Paul Hullah in Chapter 8 cites one of his former students in Japan speaking of how the use of literature left an impact on his communication facility: 'They don't only know I can speak English. They also know who I am.' This reflection reminds me of how I have learned L2 through literature. I imagine that I would stop learning if curiosity died in me, yet literature offers the linguistic and content substance that keeps me constantly inquisitive. It has been argued that literary works play the role of training the whole person (Clandfield & Duncan, 2004). Literature helps children overcome fear and deal safely with new experiences. Stories of friendship teach one how to love and care about others. Survival stories assist children in dealing with their dark feelings in order to find laughter again in life.

Many language teachers fear literature, and assume that it is complex and difficult for learning, and such apprehension is realistic to some extent. Scholars have recognised that in order to benefit from literary texts, learners need to have achieved a certain level of English proficiency (Hirvela, 2005). The good news, however, is that SLA research has confirmed that literature is closely associated with learners' linguistic gains (Ghosn, 2003) and noticing mechanisms (Johns et al., 2008). Many literature-based writing courses have shown that students develop positive attitudes towards literary resources. It has also been found that students do not need to produce literary works – literature can still serve as a tool for learning writing skills across different genres (Hirvela, 2005).

Language use in literary texts produces an enriching impact on the learning mind in multiple ways. As Paul Hullah contends, literature promotes more complete linguistic competence by tapping into learners' expressive potential with all the language-playing skills that can hardly be achieved through other means. Such skills include register, tone, imagery, irony, metaphor, narrative and symbolism, to name a few. He also implies that literature facilitates critical thinking and creative thinking, which denote both cognitive and affective engagement, and which are advanced ways to reflect, communicate and engage with new knowledge.

Teachers might like to share with learners various ways to select and enjoy online literary resources, such as poetry and novels, and e-literature, such as interactive fiction or blog writing (Unsworth, 2008). This guidance might require a new framework for teachers' pedagogical responses that acknowledges students' range of expertise and experience with multimedia. Such responses are particularly important because learners often feel most motivated to enjoy literature when they are able to relate it to their own identity (Desai, 2006), that is, when their own values are recognised in literary works. In many cases, students resist literature when they feel that literary writings are artefacts originating from a different day and age, detached from today's social media and multiple ways of living their world. It is therefore the responsibility of materials developers to select contemporary themes and cultivate a modern, contextualised way of approaching literature, rather than simply feel upset that the young generation fails to appreciate the beauty of language.

Ways of integrating technology in ELT materials

Discourse in ELT has acknowledged that the 21st century's digital age has contributed tremendously to the adoption of global English (Shyamlee & Phil, 2012). In catching up with modern trends, researchers and course writers are struggling to develop systematic ways to embrace, select, utilise and incorporate the wealth of online resources in education. In the meantime, many classrooms are experimenting with ICT tools. Some teachers overuse multimedia tools in a way that interferes with student learning rather than genuinely improving it. Others continue to use the computer screen in the same way that they would traditionally use a blackboard, adding no new pedagogy to the classroom process.

What the field needs, therefore, is not unplanned, improvised choices but rather a research-informed system that guides course writers in incorporating technology into course materials, to produce the kind of learning effect that could not happen without the help of technology. At the moment, research into the impact of technology on L2 education remains constrained within small-scale ICT projects in the classroom and with focuses on the chat environment, teacher development and entertainment value. This situation leaves a great deal to be desired, especially in the area of teacher participation in ICT research and in the application of ICT research findings in L2 materials development.

Dat Bao and Xiaofang Shang in Chapter 9 present the current challenges facing ICT in materials development and propose a set of principles that might be considered for incorporating technology into ELT materials. For example, the choice of ICT materials should not rely on one's teaching habits or one's excitement with novel technological tools but needs to consider relevancy in learning content, social relationships and learners' cultural values. Occasionally, research attempts have been made to help teachers and learners evaluate online resources and learning websites (Yang & Chan, 2008). Along these lines, Flora Floris, Willy Renandya and Dat Bao in Chapter 10 offer helpful ideas regarding how online resources can be considered as pedagogically effective.

Coursebook writers might like to interact with some suggestions made in Chapters 9 and 10 when employing internet resources, tools and environments. One example of a useful online environment is the guided use of Facebook. Research has acknowledged its usefulness in enhancement of interaction, more opportunities for L2 practice, and an increase in motivation to learn (Bloch, 2008; Godwin-Jones, 2008; Kabilan *et al.*, 2010). A second example of a practical tool is the use of mobile phones. Research conducted by Habbash (2015) demonstrates a certain degree of interest in and support for productive, guided use of mobile phones for vocabulary learning and peer interaction. A third example of students' ICT practice is how web-based listening tasks bring out students' positive learning experiences with online resources (Suarcaya, 2011). These case studies indicate how face-to-face learning can be improved through the use of technology and online resources if teachers develop a clear agenda for what to teach and what tool is needed. It would be exciting to see how materials developers keep track of such research outcomes and utilise these controversial tools to create more innovative technology-based tasks.

Connecting SLA principles with creative use of digital resources

It has been acknowledged that SLA research and theories to some extent have left a positive impact on materials development (Sánchez *et al.*, 2010). In today's digital context, being able to utilise online resources in a pedagogically efficient manner is not an easy task, a situation that requires the development of guiding principles. The more extended the wealth of digital resources becomes, the more challenging it is to decide what is best for a teaching situation. In responding to this need, Flora D. Floris, Willy A. Renandya and Dat Bao in Chapter 10 attempt to connect classic LSA theories with the choice of online materials, which in many cases tends to happen on an arbitrary basis.

Drawing from SLA discourse, the authors argue that if an online resource serves the right level, has a meaningful intended learning value, allows recycled language use, evokes learner response, stimulates interpersonal communication and motivates students to learn, that material has strong potential to facilitate language acquisition and thus can be selected for a coursebook. What especially makes the proposed principles highly applicable is the range of practical examples offered in the chapter to show what websites can be employed for effective learning, as well as how online resources can be selected and optimised.

Many coursebook writers tend to neglect SLA research and make slow progress in writing quality (see, for example, Aski, 2003; Ellis, 2002). Although a number of scholars have summarised SLA research findings in the form of principles to assist coursebook writing (Duran & Ramaut, 2006), practical guidance for developing effective materials remains rare (Tomlinson, 2012). Whether coursebook developers learn from research is a matter of individual effort. For example, Richards (2006), Al-Busaidi and Tindle (2010) and Mishan (2010) have claimed that they have benefited a great deal from research in SLA while developing their materials. In practice, those who are both coursebook writers and researchers will benefit more from research achievements than will those who do not conduct much research in their writing career.

Part 3: Improving ELT Materials Through Teacher and Learner Involvement

Part 3 of the book argues that teachers and learners should have their innovative say in materials design, in this way negotiating the crafting of their classroom materials. Chapter 11 reports an exercise that has been tried out in the construction of English materials in a teacher education programme at a Thai university. Chapter 12 handpicks scholarly insights in visual pedagogy for their creative implications in task construction. Chapter 13 reports a practical case study of coursebook evaluation in the Bangladeshi context, and maps out several creative connections between theory and practice. Not only do the authors share their hands-on experience of course enhancement in authentic settings, but they also offer theorisation from such practice to assist course writers in materials modification. Thus, the chapters in Part 3 focus on the process rather than the product, while also providing examples to show how innovative ideas operate. In doing so, the authors address three questions:

- Are there ways to train teachers in developing materials?
- Why should learners' creative work enter into coursebooks?
- How do teacher perceptions matter in presenting sociocultural values in coursebook content?

I will touch on a few insights from these chapters and interact with them to a small degree, while again leaving the full content for the reader to contemplate later in the book.

Learners as materials co-developers

It has been acknowledged that both teachers and learners should be active participants in coursebook creation (Davies, 2002; Shawer, 2010) so that materials can be more effective, meaningful and well connected with the user. Despite this appeal, it is experienced teachers rather than learners who have been mentioned as inherently and legitimately materials developers, not only because they frequently work with students but also because they have hands-on experience in selecting, adapting and developing tasks. Rajeevnath Ramnath in Chapter 9 provides an insider account of how student teachers during training are guided through a process of creating their own texts or adapting them from reading resources. To focus on texts is to engage with real-life discourse rather than with the sentence level (see, for example, Lin, 2003). This helps teachers practise critical evaluation of texts, build confidence in materials writing, connect resources with the target learner in mind, be motivated to use their own materials and visualise themselves as coursebook writers.

The author resists sacrificing the joy of learning and abandoning learners' sociocultural relevance to attend to assessment grades. He appeals for learners' appreciation of the beauty of the language, for personal engagement and for the pleasure of learning through rich resources. From this ideology, student teachers are guided through a process of creating their own materials, moving away from information texts to learners' own creative writing.

In this constructivist approach to materials development, participants learn to read for writing, evaluation, reflection and revision. They also make personalised efforts, engage in social activities and maintain a positive relationship with a common goal. Besides, flexible materials do not have to come in book form but can be a collection of resources (Candlin *et al.*, 2002) being teacher-driven, process-oriented, computer-mediated, as well as open to situational trials and constant revision. It is also worth exercising caution about the pitfall of genre pedagogy, where learners might perceive language as formulas and conventions (Henry, 2007) rather than internalise the functional diversity of each genre in context.

An additional worthwhile question to raise is: can a coursebook be written with learner involvement in the ongoing process? Research in materials development might like to explore how learners can be organised to select available resources that are attractive and meaningful to them, create visual images and choose favourite genres to represent their voice, and evaluate pre-publication activities with regard to learning usefulness and stimulating cultural values. Arguably, such contributions need to take place at the early stage of a coursebook project rather than at the end, when the printed book is already sitting on the desk and learners are forced to adapt what was not originally written for them.

At the moment, interaction between materials and pedagogy in context remains rare and there should be more action-based evaluation projects for a different way of approaching the field. Although research discourse has not been strong in this, many university programmes with a teacher training component in materials development for a long time have been practising such trials and observations in classroom settings. Unfortunately, the practice often occurs within training rather than research and Rajeevnath Ramnath reports such an experience to demonstrate how materials can be developed in a more proactive manner. In many cases, much of the evaluative research still emphasises post-use reflection (see, for example, Felicia, 2011) while one actually needs to focus more on procedural involvement in ELT materials design (Weltman, 2007). After all, improving an irrelevant textbook after it has been published is not as efficient as creating a relevant or flexible one from the start.

Learner-initiated drawings as a way to personalise ELT materials

Dat Bao in Chapter 12 experiments with the idea of bringing learners' imagination into material creation. He interprets the discourse in pedagogical visuals and highlights the lack of innovative pedagogy in the use of visuals in coursebooks over the past several decades. It is interesting to note that classroom-based research has discovered that learner-generated visuals can serve as methods to create ideas, express meaning, share world view, rehearse problem-solving skills and extend complex thinking ability. The discussion appeals for learners to be social actors who employ their own creative expressive means to take charge of the learning process. One of those tools could be the use of learner-made drawings to demonstrate one's graphical thinking, which could be strategically embedded in L2 materials design. Although drawing has occasionally been practised in the classroom by more creative teachers, this approach is far from conventional in ELT materials development and therefore is worth more than just a passing thought.

How teacher perceptions matter in presenting sociocultural values in materials

Chapter 13, by Mohammod M. Roshi, Md Zulfeqar Haider and Hosne A. Begum, gathers views from teachers on a specific textbook. Their evaluation project taps into teacher perceptions as connected with their experience of having used the book *English for Today* in Bangladesh. The discussion raises interesting, worthwhile issues about who evaluates coursebooks and whom that evaluation serves.

Occasionally, materials writers have carried out trials of their course materials in order to get users' feedback (Hu, 2011). This, however, has not been recorded in a systematic manner. Mohammod M. Roshi, Md Zulfeqar Haider and Hosne A. Begum contribute to this conversation through their study of teachers' views of a particular English textbook in practical use in Bangladesh, which has implications for a broader global context. The chapter also discusses the embedding of learners' sociocultural values in coursebooks, the advocacy of intercultural awareness and the diminution of the dominant native-English-speaking values. It appeals for materials to be sensitive to more humanistic ways of treating issues of gender, race, religion and ethnicity. The discussion recommends selective use of authentic texts that not only reflect various contexts and cultures but also promote intercultural awareness and competence.

Conclusion

By and large, the chapters recommend a range of fresh ideas for making course materials more inspiring, and more likely to encourage students' learning and participation. One special feature of most discussions in the book is that they balance theoretical insights and practical applications, and give concrete examples. Having worked in and conducted research in various international contexts, the authors speak in the role of those who have actually practised what they appeal for and have witnessed some rewarding outcomes from such exercises.

English course materials in today's local and global context need to be more inclusive, so that learners not only share their own experiences and viewpoints but also can interact with diverse voices to become both linguistically proficient and culturally sensitive. Teacher training should focus not only on effective pedagogy but also on teachers' ability to select, adapt and develop materials (McGrath, 2013) in ways that engage learners culturally, intellectually, affectively and aesthetically (Tomlinson, 2011). Coursebook content should be contextualised to reflect the local and global world that teachers and learners live in. In such materials, learners need a balance between the need to find a comfortable space in which to express themselves and a novel space in which to explore the lives of others.

As can be inferred from this book, effective materials should offer pedagogically purposeful creativity rather than aimless creativity for its own sake. Course writers might consider reducing typical activities of low acquisition value, and instead recommend both digital and printed resources, integrating appropriate technology for learning enhancement rather than following ICT trends, refraining from cultural bias, making course content comprise both local personalisation and intercultural interaction, and inviting imagination as a tool for learning enhancement. It should be a constant task to improve upon previous materials by working closely with materials users in action and context.

References

Al-Busaidi, S. and Tindle, K. (2010) Evaluating the impact of in-house materials on language learning. In B. Tomlinson and H. Masuhara (eds) *Research for Materials Development in Language Learning: Evidence for Best Practice* (pp. 137–149). London: Continuum.

Amabile, T.M. and Gitomer, J. (1984) Children's artistic creativity: Effects of choice in task materials. *Personality and Social Psychology Bulletin* 10 (2), 209–215.

Aski, J.M. (2003) Foreign language textbook activities: Keeping pace with second language acquisition research. *Foreign Language Annals* 36 (1), 57–65.

Baldwin, P. and Fleming, K. (2003) *Teaching Literacy Through Drama: Creative Approaches.* New York: Routledge.

Bloch, J. (2008) From the special issue editor. *Language Learning and Technology* 12 (2), 2–6.

Cakir, I. (2006) The use of video as an audio-visual material in foreign language teaching classroom. *TOJET: The Turkish Online Journal of Educational Technology* 5 (4).

Candlin, C.N., Bhatia, V.K. and Jensen, C.H. (2002) Developing legal writing materials for English second language learners: Problems and perspectives. *English for Specific Purposes* 21 (4), 299–320.

Clandfield, L. and Duncan, F. (2004) Teaching materials: using literature in the EFL/ESL classroom. *The Internet TESL Journal* 10 (12). Retrieved from https://scholar.google.com/scholar?q=+Teaching+materials%3A+using+literature+in+the+EFL%2FESL+classroom&btnG=&hl=zh-CN&as_sdt=0%2C5.

Csikszentmihalyi, M. (1996) *Creativity: Flow and the Psychology of Discovery and Invention.* New York: Harper Perennial.

Davies, A. (2002) Using teacher-generated biography as input material. *ELT Journal* 56 (4), 368–379.

Desai, C.M. (2006) National identity in a multicultural society: Malaysian children's literature in English. *Children's Literature in Education* 37 (2), 163–184.

Dora To, L.W., Phoebe Chan, Y.L., Lam, Y.K. and Tsang, S.K.Y. (2011) Reflections on a primary school teacher professional development programme on learning English through Process Drama. *Research in Drama Education: The Journal of Applied Theatre and Performance* 16 (4), 517–539.

Duran, G. and Ramaut, G. (2006) Tasks for absolute beginners and beyond: Developing and sequencing tasks at basic proficiency levels. In K. Van den Branden (ed.) *Task-Based Language Education: From Theory to Practice* (pp. 47—75). Cambridge: Cambridge University Press.

Elgar, A.G. (2002) Student playwriting for language development. *ELT Journal* 56 (1), 22–28.

Ellis, R. (2002) Methodological options in grammar teaching materials. In E. Hinkel and S. Fotos (eds) *New Perspectives on Grammar Teaching in Second Language Classrooms* (pp. 155–180). Mahwah, NJ: Lawrence Erlbaum.

Felicia, P. (ed.) (2011) *Handbook of Research on Improving Learning and Motivation Through Educational Games: Multidisciplinary Approaches*. Hershey, PA: IGI Global.

Ghosn, I.K. (2003) Texts: How some primary school coursebook tasks are realized in the Classroom. In *Developing Materials for Language Teaching* (pp. 275–305). London: Continuum.

Godwin-Jones, R. (2008) Mobile computing technologies: Lighter, faster, smarter. *Language Learning and Technology* 12 (3), 3–9.

Habbash, M. (2015) Learning English vocabulary using mobile phones: Saudi Arabian EFL teachers in focus. *European Scientific Journal* 11 (35), 446–457.

Hall, D. and Hewings, A. (eds) (2001) *Innovation in English Language Teaching: A Reader*. London: Routledge.

Heathcote, D. and Bolton, G. (1994) *Drama for Learning: Dorothy Heathcote's Mantle of the Expert Approach to Education*. Portsmouth, NH: Heinemann.

Heldenbrand, B.R. (2003) Drama techniques in English language learning. *Korea TESOL Journal* 6 (1), 27–37.

Henry, A. (2007) Evaluating language learners' response to web-based, data-driven, genre teaching materials. *English for Specific Purposes* 26 (4), 462–484.

Hirvela, A. (2005) ESL students and the use of literature in composition courses. *Teaching English in the Two-Year College* 33 (1), 70–80.

Hornbrook, D. (1989) *Education and Dramatic Art*. London: Blackwell Education.

Hu, J. (2011) Exploration of a new approach for designing online English language learning materials: A case study in supporting the academic reading of international master's degree students in a British university. In *Computer Science and Education (ICCSE)* (pp. 1041–1046). doi: 10.1109/ICCSE.2011.6028814.

Hutchinson, T. and Torres, E. (1994) The textbook as agent of change. *ELT Journal* 48 (4), 315–328.

Johns, T.F., Hsingchin, L. and Lixun, W. (2008) Integrating corpus-based CALL programs in teaching English through children's literature. *Computer Assisted Language Learning* 21 (5), 483–506.

Joyce, C.K. (2009) The blank page: effects of constraint on creativity. PhD dissertation, University of California, Berkeley. Retrieved from https://papers.ssrn.com/sol3/Papers.cfm?abstract_id=1552835.

Kabilan, M.K., Ahmad, N. and Abidin, M.J.Z. (2010) Facebook: An online environment for learning of English in institutions of higher education? *The Internet and Higher Education* 13 (4), 179–187.

Lin, B. (2003) English in Singapore: An insider's perspective of syllabus renewal through a genre-based approach. *RELC Journal* 34 (2), 223–246.

Maley, A. and Duff, A. (1982) *Drama Techniques in Language Learning*. Cambridge: Cambridge University Press.

Markee, N. (1992) The diffusion of innovation in language teaching. *Annual Review of Applied Linguistics* 13, 229–243.

Maurer, J.K. (1997) Presentation, practice, and production in the EFL class. *The Language Teacher* 21 (9), 42–45.

McGrath, I. (2013) *Teaching Materials and the Roles of EFL/ESL Teachers: Practice and Theory*. London: Bloomsbury.

Mishan, F. (2010) Withstanding washback: Thinking outside the box in materials development. In B. Tomlinson and H. Masuhara (eds) *Research for Materials Development in Language Learning: Evidence for Best Practice* (pp. 353–369). London: Contimuum.

Mordecai, J. (1985) Drama and second language learning. *Spoken English* 18 (2), 12–15.

Ndura, E. (2004) ESL and cultural bias: An analysis of elementary through high school textbooks in the Western United States of America. *Language, Culture and Curriculum* 17 (2), 143–153.

Nicholls, A. (1983) *Managing Educational Innovations*. London: Allen and Unwin.

O'Neill, C. (1995) *Dramaworlds: A Framework for Process Drama*. Portsmouth, NH: Heinemann.

Richards, J. (2006) Materials development and research – making the connection. *RELC Journal* 37 (1), 5–26.

Royka, J.G. (2002) Overcoming the fear of using drama in English language teaching. *The Internet TESL Journal* 8 (6). Retrieved from http://iteslj.org/Articles/Royka-Drama.html.

Sam, W.Y. (1990) Drama in teaching English as a second language: A communicative approach. *The English Teacher* 19 (1), 11. Retrieved from http://otherreferats.allbest.ru/pedagogics/00172674_0.html.

Sánchez, R.C., Pérez, A.S. and Gómez, P.C. (2010) An attempt to elaborate a construct to measure the degree of explicitness and implicitness in ELT materials. *International Journal of English Studies* 10 (1), 103–129.

Schmidhuber, J. (2006) Developmental robotics, optimal artificial curiosity, creativity, music, and the fine arts. *Connection Science* 18 (2), 173–187.

Shawer, S.F. (2010) Classroom-level curriculum development: EFL teachers as curriculum-developers, curriculum-makers and curriculum-transmitters. *Teaching and Teacher Education* 26 (2), 173–184.

Sherlock, Z. (2016) Japan's textbook inequality: How cultural bias affects foreign language acquisition. *Power and Education* 8 (1), 73–87.

Shyamlee, S.D. and Phil, M. (2012) Use of technology in English language teaching and learning: An analysis. Paper presented at the 2012 International Conference on Language, Medias and Culture, Singapore.

Skopinskaja, L. (2003) The role of culture in foreign language teaching materials: An evaluation from an intercultural perspective. In I. Lazar (ed.) *Incorporating Intercultural Communicative Competence in Language Teacher Education* (pp. 39–68). Strasbourg: Council of Europe.

Suarcaya, P. (2011) Web-based audio materials for EFL listening class. *TEFLIN Journal* 22 (1), 1–10.

Timmis, I. (2005) Towards a framework for teaching spoken grammar. *ELT Journal* 59 (2), 117–125.

Tomlinson, B. (2011) Introduction: Principles and procedures of materials development. In B. Tomlinson (ed.) *Materials Development in Language Teaching* (pp. 1–34). Cambridge: Cambridge University Press.

Tomlinson, B. (2012) Materials development for language learning and teaching. *Language Teaching* 45 (2), 143–179.

Unsworth, L. (2008) Multiliteracies, e-literature and English teaching. *Language and Education* 22 (1), 62–75.

Weltman, D. (2007) A comparison of traditional and active learning methods: An empirical investigation utilizing a linear mixed model. PhD Thesis, University of Texas at Arlington.

Whitear, S. (1998) English through drama: A visual/physical approach. *Language Teacher Kyoto – JALT* 22, 31–36.

Wortman, Z. (2016) Ernest Hemingway's six-word sequels. *The New Yorker*. Retrieved from https://www.newyorker.com/humor/daily-shouts/ernest-hemingways-six-word-sequels.

Yang, Y.T.C. and Chan, C.Y. (2008) Comprehensive evaluation criteria for English learning websites using expert validity surveys. *Computers and Education* 51 (1), 403–422.

Zafeiriadou, N. (2009) Drama in language teaching. *Issues* 23, 4–9.

Part 1: Improving ELT Materials Through Creative Pedagogies

2 Making Typical Coursebook Activities More Beneficial for the Learner

Brian Tomlinson

The activities which typically feature in L2 coursebooks have changed very little in the 50 years in which I have been involved in using, writing, evaluating and advising on such coursebooks. This is understandable because such typical activities as matching, true/false, sentence completion and choosing words from a box are relatively easy to write, easy to use, can be readily employed as classroom tests and provide easy practice in doing typical examination-type tasks. Unfortunately, though, most of them seem to be of little value in facilitating language acquisition or in helping learners develop communicative competence (see Tomlinson & Masuhara, 2013; Ellis, 2016). They might be of some additional value to motivated learners with the opportunity and inclination to look out for English outside the classroom (Tomlinson, 2013) but then most users of coursebooks (especially in rural Asia) are not motivated and do not look out for English.

The perpetuation of the typical coursebook activity despite the lack of evidence of positive effect is true of global coursebooks published by British and American publishers for worldwide consumption and is also true of many coursebooks published for use in Asia. Certainly I have not come across many exceptions among the coursebooks I have seen in use in China, Indonesia, Japan, Malaysia, Singapore, South Korea, Thailand or Vietnam in the last 20 years. We tried to focus on more principled activities in *English for Life* (Tomlinson *et al.*, 2000) but the publishers and the Ministry of Education in some of these countries put pressure on us to include more stereotypical activities, as did the publishers of *Success with English for Primary Schools* (Tomlinson *et al.*, 2003) in China. Hitomi Masuhara and I did manage to publish a text-driven coursebook for Japanese university students without many stereotypical activities,

Use Your English (Tomlinson & Masuhara, 1994) but it sold hardly any copies. I tried in vain to steer the publishers away from stereotypical coursebook activities when working as an advisor for the Disney course for China in 2010 and Hitomi Masuhara and I were invited by a Chinese publisher to write a task-based coursebook only for our first drafts to be rejected because they did not contain any grammar drills. The tendency for task-based courses to be commissioned in Asia but then weakened by the publisher or by institutions insisting on the inclusion of stereotypical coursebook activities is reported on and discussed in Tomlinson (2015) with reference to courses in Japan, South Korea and Thailand.

What Are the Typical Types of Coursebook Activity?

I have analysed four coursebooks currently used globally and four coursebooks from Asia (see footnote to Table 2.1). From each book I took unit 4 (a random choice) for detailed analysis. The most common types of activities in these are presented in Table 2.1. The global coursebook units tended to be at least six pages in length, whereas the Asian coursebook units were shorter (and therefore contained fewer activities). It was noticeable, though, that the Asian coursebook activities tended to be longer than those in the global coursebooks.

There were eight instances of activities in the global coursebooks asking learners to choose the correct form of a word and six instances of controlled writing activities. However, choosing correct forms and controlled writing have not been included in the list of the most frequent types of activity because there were no instances of these activity types in any of the Asian coursebooks.

To my surprise, there was only one instance of a multiple-choice activity in the eight books – maybe because it is considered to be a type of activity which is difficult to construct. Altogether, in unit 4 of the eight books, there were 31 types of activity, of which 30 were exercises in which the focus was on getting it right and only one was an activity which encouraged use of English. In total, there were 176 activities, of which 152 were exercises providing practice or knowledge or testing what the learners know. Only 24 of the activities involved producing language and there were no communicative tasks involving the learners communicating within a context to achieve an intended effect.

Are These Types of Activity Likely to Facilitate Language Acquisition?

It is difficult to evaluate types of activity as opposed to actual activities because instances of an activity type can obviously differ in quality and effect when realised in a coursebook. So in evaluating the most frequent types of activity (as listed in Table 2.1) I will try to evaluate their potential

Table 2.1 Numbers of times different types of activity were presented in unit 4 of four global and four Asian coursebooks

Type of activity	Global coursebooks	Asian coursebooks	Total
(1) Closed questions (i.e. only one answer is possible)	23	2	25
(1) Open questions (i.e. more than one answer is possible)	19	6	25
(3) Choosing the correct word from a box to complete a sentence	15	7	22
(3) Controlled conversations (i.e. the learners are told what to talk about and are given phrases to use in their conversation)	17	5	22
(5) Matching exercises (e.g. matching a word with a picture; matching a word with a definition)	11	7	18
(6) Sentence completion (i.e. finishing a given sentence with relevant content and/or correct forms)	3	10	13
(7) True/false questions (i.e. specifying whether a statement is true or false in relation to an accompanying text)	4	5	9
(8) Rearranging sentences (i.e. putting jumbled up parts of a sentence into the correct order)	4	4	8
(9) Listen and repeat (i.e. the learners listen to a sound/word/phrase/sentence and then repeat it)	3	4	7
(10) Correction activities (i.e. the learners are presented with incorrect utterances and asked to correct them)	4	2	6
(11) Dialogue repetition (i.e. the learners are given a transcript of a dialogue to use when repeating it)	3	3	6

The global coursebooks were:
Clandfield, L. (2010) *Global Pre-Intermediate*. Oxford: Macmillan.
Dellar, H. and Walkley, A. (2010) *Intermediate Outcomes*. Andover: Cengage Learning.
Harmer, J. (2012) *Just Right Intermediate* (2nd edn). Andover: Cengage Learning.
Rea, D. and Clementson, T. (2011) *English Unlimited Intermediate*. Cambridge: Cambridge University Press.

The Asian coursebooks were:
Anonymous (2008) *English Grammar for Vietnamese Learners*. Ho Chi Minh: Nha Xuat Ban Giao Duc.
Anonymous (2013) *New College English. Integrated Course*. Shanghai: Shanghai Foreign Language Education Press.
Kay, S. and Jones, V. (2012) *New Inside Out*. Shanghai: Shanghai Foreign Language Education Press.
Tomlinson, B., Barnes, J., Buchanan, H., Islam, C., Masuhara, H. and Timmis, I. (2003) *Success with English for Primary Schools Activity Book*. Guangzhou: Guangzhou Research Bureau.

effect in relation to what I consider to be the five most important criteria for facilitating language acquisition (for justification of these and other criteria see Tomlinson, 2013, 2015). These relate to the extent to which each type of activity is likely to:

(1) expose the learners to a rich, recycled, comprehensible and meaningful input of language in use;
(2) engage the learners affectively (i.e. involve the learners' emotions and or contribute to self-esteem and positive feelings about the learning experience)

(3) engage the learners cognitively (i.e. stimulate the learners to think critically and creatively);
(4) pay attention to form during or after a meaning-focused activity;
(5) provide the learners with opportunities to use the target language for authentic communication.

Evaluation of Activity Types

Closed questions are of three basic types. To use Freeman's (2014) terminology, they can be textually explicit (i.e. the answer can be retrieved verbatim from the text), they can be textually implicit (i.e. the answer can be worked out from understanding different words in the text) or they can involve inferential comprehension (i.e. the answer can be worked out from a holistic understanding of the text). Explicit questions are unlikely to satisfy any of the five criteria because completing the exercise successfully simply involves surface recognition. Implicit questions can satisfy criterion 3 to some extent because the learners have to find synonyms in the text (e.g. 'employed as' when looking for the answer to the question 'What is John's job?). Inferential comprehension questions can satisfy criteria 1 and 3 to some extent because in addition to stimulating learners to look for clues and make connections and inferences they force learners to go back and read large chunks of the text again rather than focus on just one sentence. Unfortunately, most of the closed questions in the eight books analysed were explicit questions, which could be answered by going to an obvious part of a short text, and therefore were unlikely to satisfy any of the five criteria.

Open questions, or 'affect questions', to use Freeman's (2014) term, are of two basic types. Again, to use Freeman's (2014) terminology, they are either personal response questions asking the learners for their response to a text or asking for their views, opinions or ideas; or they are evaluation questions, asking the learners to justify their personal response. Both types can satisfy criterion 1 (if they are being asked about their response to a text), criterion 2 (if the act of responding engages them affectively), criterion 3 (if they have to think rather than just respond automatically) and criterion 5 (especially if they have to articulate their response at length for a communicative purpose such as to persuade somebody to do something). However, evaluation questions are more likely to contribute to eventual acquisition because of the deeper level of processing involved and the likelihood of more mental engagement and of richer and longer acts of communication. Unfortunately, most of the activities in the eight books were personal response questions not involving any deep thinking or justification.

Choosing the correct word is unlikely to satisfy any of the criteria. It might satisfy criterion 3 to some extent if the activity is challenging and just possibly criterion 1 if it involves having to go back and think about an extended text in order to make the right choice. Unfortunately, none of the activities in the eight books did this, as all involved selecting a word from prior knowledge rather than from working it out.

Controlled conversations are unlikely to satisfy any of the five criteria if the constraints lead the learners simply to practise what has been taught rather than to express themselves in authentic conversation. This is what happens when the text situation is repeated and when the learners are given phrases to use in their conversation (as happens with most of the controlled conversations in the eight books). This sort of meaningless rehearsal of given utterances does not expose learners to language in use, does not engage the learners either affectively or cognitively, does not help learners to pay attention to form while engaged in a meaning-focused activity and definitely does not provide opportunities for authentic oral communication (which, by definition, is unplanned, unpredictable and spontaneous).

Matching exercises are unlikely to satisfy any of the five criteria as they do not involve exposure or use, are not typically meaning-focused activities and are unlikely to engage learners affectively (unless they are part of a game) or cognitively (unless they are part of a problem-solving activity or involve a cognitive challenge). Most of the matching activities in the eight books simply involved the learners demonstrating what they already know (or do not know) rather than getting them to think about possible matches, relate the matches to a context or justify the matches they have made.

Sentence completion activities are unlikely to satisfy any of the five criteria as they involve very little exposure (unless the learners have to search an extended authentic text for clues) and no communicative use of language, they are not typically meaning-focused activities and are unlikely to engage learners affectively (unless they are part of a competition) or cognitively (unless they are part of a problem-solving activity or involve a cognitive challenge). However, activities requiring the learners to use their own words to complete a sentence logically and accurately are likely to be of more value than those requiring just the selection and copying of an appropriate utterance.

True/false questions are easy to set, easily usable as tests and very easy to mark. However, they are unlikely to satisfy any of the five criteria unless they require the learners to return to an extended text and to read it holistically, they require implications or inferences to be made, they stimulate personal responses by making provocative statements, they involve learners in justifying their answers or they somehow stimulate communicative use of language (e.g. a group discussion in which two learners are primed to argue for 'yes' and two for 'no').

Rearranging sentences can be cognitively engaging (e.g. if there are apparently many possibilities for rearrangement), can be affectively engaging (e.g. if part of a group race or if the rearranged sentences ultimately combine to tell an engaging story) and can stimulate communication (e.g. if part of a group activity). However, most of these activities in the books analysed were simple and decontextualised and would be unlikely to satisfy any of the five criteria.

Listen-and-repeat activities are typically simple, mechanical, low-level activities aimed at the practice of the recognition and pronunciation of sounds, words or short utterances. They are of some value as aids to decoding and encoding but are unlikely to satisfy any of the five criteria (unless, for example, they require the repetition of an extended oral text such as short story and thus involve inner-voice repetition, visualisation, global understanding and language production).

Correction activities can be engaging (if, for example, they involve correcting lexical items in a story not because they are grammatically wrong but because they are semantically inappropriate in the context of the story) and they can involve communication (if, for example, they require the learners to rewrite a letter which is stylistically inappropriate given its purpose and addressee). However, most of the correction activities in the eight books analysed simply involved recognising and correcting a grammatical error in a decontextualised sentence and were unlikely to satisfy any of the five criteria.

Dialogue repetition can be mechanical and meaningless if the learners simply repeat words. However, if they are asked to act out the dialogue as particular characters in a specific context, the experience can be engaging and could satisfy criteria 2 and 3. It could also satisfy criterion 1 if the original dialogue is authentic and criterion 5 if learners are repeating the dialogue from memory rather than from a script or if they have first of all written the dialogue themselves as a script.

How Can We Make These Activities More Likely to Facilitate Language Acquisition?

The activities discussed above are standard coursebook activities and a coursebook without them would confound expectations and achieve little face validity. However, a coursebook full of these activities in their stereotypical form would be likely to sell well but achieve little. What we need to do is to make alterations to how we use them, both when developing new materials and when adapting existing materials. The most obvious way to improve them is to open them up so that they involve the learners in a deeper and more meaningful experience of the target language in use. We can do this by connecting the activities to authentic texts, by connecting the activities to the lives of the learners, by challenging the learners to discover things for themselves, by stimulating both personal responses and higher-order thinking skills, and by getting the learners to use language for communication rather than just to practise it.

Presented below are some practical suggestions for modifying the typical coursebook activities so that they are more likely to satisfy some (or even all) of the five criteria.

Closed questions

It is relatively easy and quick to modify closed questions and with a little experience this can be done by the teacher in the classroom without prior preparation. Ideally, what is needed is for the question to be re-phrased so that it becomes an open question, permitting more than one acceptable answer, requiring a justification for the answer given (i.e. an evaluative question) and/or adding a supplementary think question. If this is not possible (for example because the teacher is using the questions as a test) then explicit closed questions can be rephrased as implicit closed questions (or, better still, as closed questions involving inferential comprehension) and the students can be asked to justify their answers. Whether the question remains closed or is opened up, the ideal is for answering the rephrased question to engage the learners affectively and cognitively and to involve authentic communication.

An example

In the text it says, 'Bob went to work in his car from Monday to Friday and his wife Mary used the car at weekends'. The explicit closed question asks, 'Who went to work in his car from Monday to Friday?'

The rephrased question could become a series of questions: (1) Who drove to the city five times a week? How do you know? (2) Do you think it's a good idea to drive into the centre of Jakarta? (3) Find somebody with a different answer from you and try to persuade them that you are right.

To answer these questions, the students have to think about what they mean and then search the whole text for an equivalent. They also have to connect it to their own knowledge and views and to communicate their justification persuasively.

Open questions

As stated above, an open question has the potential to satisfy four of the criteria. This is likely to be the case, though, only if the question in its original or rephrased form is evaluative, if it is likely to engage learners affectively and cognitively and if it elicits authentic communication.

An example

Text reports a tourist's amazement at how late at night everybody eats and how discos stay open all night. The open question is, 'Which country do you think this is?'

Rephrased, the exercise could be: 'Tell a partner which country you think this and why. Then discuss with your partner whether or not you would like to live in this country.'

Choosing the correct word

This type of activity can only really satisfy some of the criteria if the selection is from an extended text, if it involves a personal preference for one of a number of correct possibilities, if it involves justifying the choice, if it involves choosing an apparently wrong word and then modifying the utterance so that it becomes 'right', if it involves having to work out meanings from textual clues and/or if the completed utterance is then used for communication.

An example

The students are given five sentences and are asked to fill in the blank in each sentence by selecting the correct word from words in a box. The sentences are not connected and the activity is really just a test of the students' existing knowledge.

The activity could be rephrased as: 'For each sentence choose a word from the box which does not make sense in that sentence. Then add an extra sentence so that your chosen word does make sense. When you have finished, use all your sentences as part of a story. You can add other sentences of your own to make the story interesting.'

Controlled conversations

Controlled conversations can satisfy' some of the criteria only if the control is eventually loosened, if the conversation is encouraged to take an unexpected turn, if each participant knows only what they are supposed to say and/or some of the suggestions for topics/intentions/utterances/ strategies are unexpected.

An example

The following is presented to students:

Role-play a conversation between a tourist and a hotel receptionist.
    Student A: You are a tourist. Ask the receptionist to recommend restaurants for dinner. Use phrases like, 'Could you recommend...', 'Do you know of...?' and 'Is it likely to be...?'
    Student B: You are the hotel receptionist. Suggest some different types of restaurants for the tourist. Use phrases like, 'The best Chinese restaurant is...', 'The nearest good restaurant...' and 'You turn left outside the hotel...'.

This could be rephrased as:

Role-play a conversation between a tourist and a hotel receptionist.
     Student A, look at your instructions on p. 17 for three minutes. Then close your book and act out the conversation.
     Student B, look at your instructions on p. 37 for three minutes. Then close your book and act out the conversation.

On page 17 Student A is told:

You are a tourist. You are attracted to the hotel receptionist and would like to invite her out for dinner. Ask the receptionist to recommend restaurants for dinner. Use phrases like, 'Could you recommend…', 'Do you know of…?' and 'Is it likely to be…?' and at the same time try to be pleasant and interesting. When you've decided on a restaurant, ask the receptionist to go there with you for dinner.

On page 37 Student B is told:

You are the hotel receptionist. Suggest some different types of restaurant for the tourist. Use phrases like, 'The best Chinese restaurant is…', 'The nearest good restaurant…' and 'You turn left outside the hotel…'. Be as pleasant as you can to the guest but try to finish the conversation as soon as you can because in 10 minutes you'll be finishing work and meeting your boyfriend at a restaurant for dinner.

Matching activities

Matching activities are probably the least likely to satisfy any of the criteria unless they are opened up by stimulating the students to be creative and to communicate with each other.

An example

The students are given the instruction: 'Match the verbs in the box to the nouns'. The words do not come from any text and the nouns are only related by all of them having something to do with leisure. All the students have to do is to select the correct word from their prior knowledge and write it in its base form next to the matching nouns (e.g. 'read books/the newspaper').
This could be rephrased as follows:

Use each word in the box with five of the nouns. Write a separate sentence for each noun and phrase the sentence so that the verb makes sense.
e.g. *cook   the gardening*
When I'm doing the gardening I often think about what I'm going to cook for dinner.

Then choose one of your sentences and say it to a partner so that it begins a conversation.
e.g.
'I often cook while I'm talking to people on the phone.'
'Don't you sometimes make mistakes?'
'Well, yes. Last night, for example, I...'

Sentence completion

This type of activity can satisfy some of the criteria if the completions are open ended, if the content and expression are determined by the students rather than by the materials writer and if the sentences become part of a communication activity.

An example

The students are told:

Work in pairs. Look at these sentences from the listening activity you have just done. Try to remember how each sentence ended and write out the sentence in full.

This could be rephrased as:

Look at these sentences from the listening activity you have just done. Can you remember how each sentence finished?
Think of a conversation in which you might use these sentences and decide what your purpose is for using them. Then complete each sentence so that it is a part of your imagined conversation.
Role-play your conversation in your head by using your inner voice. Then use your sentences to have a conversation with a partner.'

True/false questions

Such questions can satisfy any of the criteria only if, for example, the students have to justify their answer, have to persuade other students to accept their answer, have to rewrite the text so that the false answers become true and vice versa or if they are inferential questions requiring a global interpretation of a text.

An example

The students act out a text from the coursebook as the teacher reads it aloud as dramatically as possible. For example, before reading aloud a Korean folk tale about a hard-working but poor farmer and his lazy, greedy and rich brother, the teacher divides the class into two halves and tells one half to act out what the hard-working brother does and the other half to act out what the lazy brother does.

After this dramatisation of the text, the teachers asks the true/false questions from the coursebook as personal questions to the brothers. For instance, instead of saying, 'X was lazy. True or false?', the teacher says to the students representing one of the brothers, 'You were lazy, weren't you? Why?'

Then, in groups, the students rewrite the story so that the true answers become false and vice versa.

Rearranging sentences

This type of activity can be challenging but fun for analytically inclined learners. However, they do not typically involve exposure to language in use, affective engagement, language discovery or language use. For such activities to satisfy the criteria, the rearrangement has to involve an interpretation of a meaningful extended text, discovery of a language feature involved in the rearrangement and use of the rearranged sentence (or an equivalent sentence) in an act of communication.

An example

In the coursebook, the learners are given six jumbled sentences (e.g. 'Most/in/are/interested/women/gadgets/not') and are told to rearrange the given words to make six statements from the article. The six correct responses can be copied mechanically from the article. The learners do not have to understand the article, do not have to think about the meaning of the statements, do not have to make any language discoveries and do not have to use the statements to communicate.

The activity could be rewritten as:

(1) Read the following article about what people really want for their birthday. As you read it, decide which statements in the article you agree with and which you disagree with.
(2) Did you like the article? Why?
(3) Go to A on p. 34.
(4) Without looking back at the article you have just read, write down statements from the article which you agreed with. You can use your own words.
(5) Write down statements from the article which you disagreed with.
(6) Without looking back at the article, rearrange the words below to make six statements from the article.
(7) Look back at the article to see if your rearranged sentences in (6) are right. Correct any which are wrong.
(8) What can you discover from the correct sentences in (6) about how we make statements in English about what we believe is true? How do we usually start the statement? What verb tense do we normally use?
(9) Use your corrected statements in (4) and (5) to write a response to the article in which you state your opinion about what the writer says.

(10) Write an article about 'What students really want to read and write about in English lessons'.

Listen and repeat

Listen-and-repeat activities are typically mechanical and meaningless and rarely satisfy any of the criteria. However, they can be made challenging and engaging if, for example, they frame the repetitions as a character in a context, the repetitions are so lengthy that they have to be re-created rather than memorised, one partner makes the repetitions in a sceptical, questioning way and the other confirms and explains the utterances, or the repetitions are instantaneous translations.

An example

In the coursebook the learners are told, 'Listen and repeat the useful phrases'. They listen to a dialogue and they are given six phrases to listen out for and repeat (e.g. 'I'll try to put you through'). They do not have to understand the dialogue or the phrases. They just need to recognise the phrases and repeat them.

The activity could be rephrased as below:

(1) You are going to listen to a conversation in which somebody telephones a company and asks to speak to the Managing Director. In pairs, write down phrases which you think you might hear in the conversation.
(2) Listen to the conversation to see if your phrases are used.
(3) In your pair, write down phrases which were used in the conversation.
(4) Turn to (2) on p. 66 and look at some of the phrases which are used in the conversation.
(5) Listen to the conversation again.
(6) Act out the conversation with your partner.
(7) Act out another conversation with your partner in which one of you telephones a company and asks to speak to Mr Smith's secretary.

Correction activities

Correction activities typically do not satisfy any of the five criteria; they also run the risk of introducing the learners to mistakes which they might never make. Such activities can be beneficial only if they reflect mistakes that the specific learners do frequently make, if there has been some attempt to help the learners remedy their errors, if the activity makes the learners think, if the learners have to justify their corrections and if the learners have to find further examples of correct/appropriate use.

An example

In the coursebook, the learners are provided with pairs of sentences and are told:

Spot the mistake! Cross out the incorrect sentence.
(a) Did you use to visit the zoo?
(b) Did you used to visit the zoo?

This could be rephrased as:

(1) In each pair of sentences tick the correct sentence.
(2) Rewrite the incorrect sentence so that it is not only correct but it also says something about your life.
(3) Show your sentences to a partner and explain to them the difference(s) between each of your sentences and the other sentence in the pair.
(4) For homework, find other sentences which are similar to the ones you have written.
(5) Use some of the sentences you wrote, some of the correct sentences in the pairs and some of the sentences you found to write a strange story.

Dialogue repetition

Dialogue repetition activities are typically mechanical and meaningless (e.g. 'Work in pairs. Practise reading the conversation, using high and low intonation', from the Dellar and Walkley 2010 coursebook). They can only satisfy any of the criteria if they are made more meaningful and the learners have to think about what they are doing.

An example

To make the activity more valuable, students can be asked to perform dialogues in character. For example, in a dialogue in which A is a salesman in a shoeshop and B is the customer, A is first told that he is the ex-husband of B and has not seen her since the divorce. Or, in a dialogue in which A asks B how to operate her new office computer, B is first told that he is in love with A but she does not know this.

One noticeable feature of my rephrased activities for each of the examples of typical coursebook activities above is that mine are much longer than the originals. This illustrates a problem with many coursebooks. In order to provide as much as possible for the teacher and the students, they cram as many different types of activity as possible into each unit. This creates an attractive illusion of coverage but it rarely creates opportunities for language acquisition. I have long been convinced that if we covered less but did so more extensively, our students would benefit more.

Conclusion

The typical types of coursebook activity discussed above have been around for a long time and they are not going to suddenly disappear. This means that it is our responsibility, as materials developers writing new materials and as teachers using existing materials, to ensure that such activities are made as valuable as possible. As I have stressed above, we can do so by opening them up and aiming to stimulate meaningful mental activity and communication.

References

Ellis, R. (2016) Language teaching materials as work plans: An SLA perspective. In B. Tomlinson (ed.) *Second Language Acquisition Research and Materials Development for Language Learning* (pp. 203–2013). New York: Routledge.

Freeman, D. (2014) Reading comprehension questions: The distribution of different types in global EFL textbooks. In *English Language Teaching Textbooks: Content, Consumption, Production* (pp. 72–110). Basingstoke: Palgrave Macmillan.

Tomlinson, B. (2013) Looking out for English. *Studies in Self-Access Learning* 4 (4), 253–261.

Tomlinson, B. (2015) Challenging teachers to use their coursebook creatively. In B. Tomlinson (ed.) *Creativity in the Language Classroom* (pp. 24–28). London: British Council.

Tomlinson, B. and Masuhara, H. (1994) *Use Your English*. Tokyo: Asahi Press.

Tomlinson, B. and Masuhara, H. (2013) Review of adult ELT textbooks. *ELT Journal* 6 (2), 233–249.

Tomlinson, B., Masuhara, H., Hill, D.A. and Masuhara, H. (2000) *English for Life 1*. Singapore: Marshall Cavendish.

Tomlinson, B., Barnes, J., Buchanan, H., Islam, C., Masuhara, H. and Timmis, I. (2003) *Success with English for Primary Schools Activity Book*. Guangzhou: Guangzhou Research Bureau.

3 Creative Materials: An Oxymoron?

Alan Maley

The word 'creative' is now a currency so overused that it is in danger of devaluation. So when the word 'creative' is combined with the word 'materials' it is surely worth asking a few questions. In what respects can materials be considered creative? Is there a fundamental contradiction embodied in this phrase? Could it be that materials cannot in themselves be creative at all? It is in this spirit that I will try to deconstruct the notion of materials and creativity, and to clarify just what we might mean by 'creative materials'.

So What Might We Mean by 'Creative Materials'?

So why should we be sceptical about claims that materials are in some sense creative?

By definition, materials are put together by one group of people (authors, publishers, ministries, teachers) for use by another group of people (learners, teachers, etc.). This presupposes that those who make the materials already know what will be suitable for those unknown people who will use them. In other words, they already know that input A will lead to outcome B. If this is the case, the result of using the materials is predetermined. So how can it be considered creative? (As we shall see below, a core feature of creativity is innovation and unexpectedness.)

A further presupposition is that the materials will work equally well with class X as with class Y, or with learner C as with learner D. If this is the case, then we are seeking conformity rather than the spontaneity and freshness of unpredictable response, which also characterise creativity.

There is a further key consideration. When we speak of 'creative materials', do we mean that the creativity is somehow inherent in the ingenious way the materials have been devised? That is, does the creativity lie in the input? Or do we mean that the materials somehow produce a creative reaction or response from learners? That is, the materials produce creative outcomes? If the latter, this would imply that we need materials which specifically aim to produce unexpected, unpredictable outcomes.

Before moving to a discussion of how we might approach creativity in materials design, it will be helpful to revisit what we mean by 'creativity' and what we mean by 'materials'.

Defining 'Creativity'

Creativity is a multifaceted quality, and this is one of the reasons it has proved so difficult to define. Amabile (1996) has pointed out that it is unrealistic to identify a clear and sufficiently detailed articulation of the creative process. Yet, even if we cannot define it precisely, we readily recognise creativity when we meet it. For all practical purposes this is enough, and we do not need to spend too much time agonising over a definition. Nonetheless, it is worth examining the cluster of attributes which define creativity.

The core idea of 'making something new' is at the heart of creativity. But novelty is not sufficient on its own for something to be recognised as creative. We could, for example, wear a bikini to class. This would certainly be doing something new and unusual but it would count as creative only if we then did something pedagogically useful with it, like creating a beach scenario, or a fashion show, or using it to spark a discussion about advertising, or different cultural norms.

Creativity also normally exhibits features of unexpectedness, unpredictability, spontaneity, pleasurable surprise and a willingness to consider unusual or unconventional solutions to problems. It can often be provoked by what Koestler (1989) called the 'bisociation' of two conceptual matrices not normally found together. He believed that putting together two (or more) things that do not normally belong together can facilitate a sudden new insight. Below, I shall look at this and some of the other key processes for provoking a creative response. It is also necessary for creative acts to be recognised and accepted within the domain in which they occur. They need to be relevant and practicable – not just novel.

Bisociation was also one of the key principles of the surrealist movement in art, photography, music, film, theatre and literature, which flourished mainly in Paris in the 1920s and 1930s. But in addition, the Surrealists emphasised the importance of the unconscious mind, dreams, memories, playing around and experimenting, and seeing ordinary things from unusual viewpoints. They also explored the creative potential of constraints. Boden (1990: 82), too, draws attention to the importance of constraints in the creative process: 'Far from being the antithesis of creativity, constraints on thinking are what make it possible'.

Csikszentmihalyi (1988) takes a multidimensional view of creativity, as an interaction between individual talent, operating in a particular domain or discipline, and judged by experts in that field. He also has interesting observations about the role of 'flow' in creativity: the state of 'effortless effort' in which everything seems to come together in a flow of seamless creative energy (Csikszentmihalyi, 1990). I shall return to 'flow' states later, as one of the facilitating processes for learning.

Amabile (1996) approaches creativity from a social and environmental viewpoint. Her theory rests on three main factors: domain-relevant skills (i.e. familiarity with a given domain of knowledge); creativity-relevant skills (e.g. the ability to break free of 'performance scripts' – established routines – to see new connections, etc.); and task motivation, based on attitudes, intrinsic motivation, extrinsic constraints and rewards, and so on. The social and environmental factors she discusses include peer influence, the teacher's character and behaviour, the classroom climate, family influence, life stress, the physical environment, degree of choice offered, time, the presence of positive role models, and the scope for play in the environment. These factors clearly have relevance for learning and might be blended into an approach to materials which seeks to promote creativity.

What Do We Mean By 'Materials'?

Materials, like creativity, have also been variously defined. Some would confine materials in this context to coursebooks and their supporting matter – CD-ROMs, DVDs, test packs, listening materials and so on – produced by a commercial publisher. To this can be added resource books for teachers containing classroom activities which teachers can use more flexibly. Others would include materials produced by teachers, alone or in teams, for specific teaching–learning contexts. Tomlinson takes an even broader view of what constitutes materials:

> newspapers, food packages, photographs, live talks by invited native speakers, instructions given by a teacher, tasks written on cards, or discussions between learners. In other words, they can be anything which is deliberately used to increase the learners' knowledge and/or experience of the language. (Tomlinson, 2011: 2)

Elsewhere he says:

> materials can be instructional in that they inform learners about the language, they can be experiential in that they provide exposure to the language in use, they can be elicitative in that they stimulate language use, or they can be exploratory in that they facilitate discoveries about language use. (Tomlinson, 2001: 66)

That is a comprehensive view of what constitutes materials: it seems to include anything we bring to bear on the teaching of language.

Perhaps it will be more helpful to look at materials from the point of view, not so much of what they are, but of what factors in them are likely to lead to successful learning. This would shift the focus from an exclusive concentration on creativity to examining factors in materials which facilitate learning. If good materials can, in some sense, be expected to be creative, we would be entitled to expect some congruence between creativity and effectiveness.

Some Factors Favouring Effective Materials

In one way or another, the following factors would seem to contribute to the pedagogical effectiveness of materials:

Compelling content and engaging processes

Materials which are inherently interesting for their content or appearance have a better chance of attracting and retaining learners' attention. When selecting written texts in particular, those which deal with compelling subject matter which meshes with learners' interests are to be preferred. The same goes for listening, visual and online material. But we need to beware of attractive or sensational appearance for its own sake.

Besides content, processes which intrigue or involve learners are more likely to succeed. This can often be done by creatively adapting familiar procedures, such as dictation, or drilling, or homework, or memorisation (see, for example, Bilbrough, 2011; Davis & Rinvolucri, 1988; Painter, 2003). Alternatively, a set of generative procedures can be applied which give a new slant to the material.

Appropriate level of demand

Materials should be at the right level of challenge. If they are too 'difficult' on the level of language, affective maturity, cognitive demand or cultural specificity, they will usually cause learners to give up. On the other hand, if they are perceived as too easy, too childish or too simplistic or obvious, learners tend to be easily demotivated by them. The judgement on appropriateness of level has to be made by the teachers, as they will have intimate knowledge of their classes. And most teachers are well able to make intuitively sound judgements. Those who prepare materials for publication can only make approximate judgements, at best.

Intensity of engagement and depth of processing

As Craik and Lockhart (1972) demonstrated experimentally, we learn and retain best what engages us most deeply at a cognitive or emotional level. Materials have to have the capacity to fascinate, to engage, to involve and to totally absorb the attention of learners. An example would be when a learner finds herself lost in an engrossing graded reader because the 'cool web of language' (Robert Graves), or the sheer interest of the storyline, winds her in. Or when learners spend hours preparing a presentation of a piece of their creative work. Csikszentmihalyi (1990) terms this 'flow', and it is peculiar to states of intense involvement. Flow states are typically associated with highly personal forms of learning – usually unconscious. With the right kind of materials we can aspire to provoke such flow states.

Variety and diversity

A key element in the success of materials is variety and diversity. It is in learners' best interests to vary the material offered in as many ways as possible: topics and themes, types of input – in terms of text types and of procedures, balance between receptive and productive skills work, between activities requiring conscious effort and those for unconscious acquisition, length and complexity of texts, classroom mode – full class, individual, groups/pairs, and types of evaluation. The more diverse we can make materials, the more chance there is of retaining learners' attention and interest. Learners then come to class in a state of expectancy ('I wonder what interesting stuff we'll do today') rather than in a state of expectation ('Oh no, not unit 10 again...').

Sensory and aesthetic experiences

Learners are clearly not all alike as to their interests and preferred learning modes. Traditionally, materials have been directed to those with a preference for verbal and cognitive modes. This has disadvantaged and often demotivated those with sensory preferences: visual, auditory and tactile in particular. Gardner, with his theory of multiple intelligences (Gardner, 1983, 2011), has been in the forefront of pressure to accommodate all types of intelligence in education. Likewise, there has been growing concern to provide more aesthetic and affective input in language programmes (Arnold, 1999; Grundy *et al.*, 2011; Maley, 2009, 2011). These concerns have produced a greater range of materials with an aesthetic focus, so that music, song, drama, art, creative writing and even dance are beginning to find a place. The effects on motivation and growth of self-esteem cannot be emphasised enough.

Perceived personal relevance

As far as possible, materials should be designed in such a way that they harmonise with learners' interests and are perceived as having relevance. Because all learners are different, so will their interests be, and we cannot assume that, for instance, all teenagers will be interested in pop music, or all boys will be keen football fans. So, topical interest is a deceptive lure. Perhaps, as far as thematic content is concerned, it might be better to focus on universal themes: love, growing up, death, sickness, family relationships, work, belief, culture, history, invention and discovery, what it means to be human – and possible futures for humankind. But even here we need to tread carefully. Ideally, some would argue, we should consult the views of the class before embarking on specific themes or topics. Others would hold that, as teachers (or materials writers), we have a duty not simply to instruct but also to educate. Left to themselves, learners might not be fully aware of the range and depth of possible themes. What is critical, however, is that the materials should not be seen as tedious or trivial. Given the opportunity and the cooperative atmosphere of a close-knit learning community, learners can often surprise us with their ability to engage at a deep level with what might have seemed unlikely themes or ways of working.

Choice and control over processes

One way to render the materials more relevant to learners is to involve them in making choices about the content and the ways they will work with that content. In most institutional settings, opportunities to do this are limited. It is possible to offer a range of choices in extensive reading materials, for example, or in project work. But most work in these settings depends heavily on the use of a coursebook. This is all the more reason, therefore, to design published materials which have choice built into them. This could take any of the following forms: offering several texts in a given unit, from which learners choose the one they prefer to work with; offering texts at different levels of difficulty on the same theme but keeping the task constant; using a single text but offering tasks at different levels of difficulty; offering a range of activities on a given theme and allowing learners to decide which one they will work with…. The scope for choice is wider than we sometimes assume.

Opportunities for genuine interaction

This does not necessarily imply designing activities which simulate 'real-life' situations, though that is one possible approach. But for genuine interaction to occur, we do not need to replicate the situation outside the classroom. What are needed are materials which require learners to interact about something important at the time. For example, in an activity where groups are given a text which they will perform, discussion of who will read which lines, how the lines can be read with greatest effect, how many people will be involved at each point, and many other factors lead to intense discussion, which is highly significant for the learners for that specific moment. This is linked with the discussion of 'Intensity of engagement and depth of processing' above: provided the materials offer opportunities for intense engagement, the interactions will be genuine.

Positive affective climate/atmosphere

Materials do not exist in a vacuum. They are only one part of a complex of factors, including the dynamics of the relationships between the learners in the class, between the teacher and the group, the physical conditions of the classroom, the motivational state of learners, and much more. Much of this can be summed up as 'atmosphere' – yet another term we find it difficult to define with precision, yet can recognise instantly. It is widely agreed that the role of the teacher is a determining factor in the creation of a favourable learning atmosphere (Dörnyei & Murphey, 2003; Hadfield, 1990). Such an 'atmosphere' would be characterised by a high level of attention and energy, along with a relaxed attitude, where learners are at ease with each other and with the teacher, where there is a feeling of trust so that error is not treated as a crime but as a learning opportunity, where the teacher is tuned into the class so that split-second decisions can be taken in order to capitalise on something which may have occurred, or to head off potential blocks or trouble. Most of the time, the classroom is an unpredictable place (Underhill, 2014; Underhill & Maley, 2012), so however well prepared teachers may be, they need additionally to be in a state of preparedness in order to deal with the unpredictability.

Educational impact: Linguistic and developmental

It is surely also legitimate to ask what the payoff is from the materials. They may be attractively presented, have a flair for engaging ideas and provide learners with lots of fun and games, but unless learners actually learn something, they are a waste of time. The kind of outcomes usually referred to are linguistic: have learners acquired new vocabulary, or grammatical structures, or enhanced their skills in speaking, listening, reading and writing? It is often relatively easy to measure this, though the nature of learning as an incremental, recursive and often regressive process, and the individual differences between learners, make even this kind of measurement problematic. Expert opinion is divided about itemised graded objectives, though there is a strong current of opinion which casts doubt on their effectiveness and suggests that we need different forms of evaluation over time to form a realistic idea of a learner's progress.

There are, too, more general educational aims which can potentially be served by the materials. These include developing self-esteem, self-awareness, the ability to work cooperatively, learning to learn, understanding emotional intelligence (Goleman, 1996), becoming more globally aware and responsible, developing critical thinking, personal resilience and independence. These are virtually impossible to measure, yet we can readily appreciate their importance as long-term educational (not just instructional) aims. Can we arrange for the materials, both through their topical and thematic content, and through the quality of the interactions among learners, to go some way to fostering these qualities?

Some Principles for Creative Materials Design

Before moving to some concrete examples of materials, it may be useful to return to the issue of creativity. What principles are available to the materials designer which are likely to favour more creative materials – in the matters of both content and process? The following are no more than suggestions but they have all been successfully applied.

Use heuristics at all levels

A heuristic is a kind of 'rule of thumb'. Rather than applying a formula with a predetermined outcome (an algorithm), heuristics works by trying things to see how they work out – the 'suck it and see' principle. By 'all levels' I mean that many of these heuristics can be used for teacher decisions, for developing materials, for varying classroom routines and for devising student activities. It will be for the teacher to decide exactly how a given heuristic is applied.

Here are some examples of heuristics:

- *Do the opposite*. This has been extensively described by John Fanselow (1987, 2010). Essentially, it involves observing the routines and activities we consciously or unconsciously follow, doing the opposite and then observing what happens. Examples would be: if you always stand up to teach, sit down; if you teach from the front of the class, teach from the back; if you usually talk a lot, try silence.
- *Reverse the order*. Here you would do things backwards. For example: in dictation, instead of giving out the text at the end, you would give it out at the beginning, allow students to read it then take it away, then give the dictation; if you normally read texts from beginning to end, try reading them starting at the end; if you normally set homework after a lesson, try setting it before; if you usually give a grammar rule and then ask students to find examples, try giving examples and asking students to derive the rule.
- *Expand (or reduce) something*. For example, increase (or decrease) the length of a text in various ways; increase (or decrease) the time allotted to a task; increase (or decrease) the number of questions on a text; increase (or decrease) the number of times you do a particular activity. Maley's two volumes of *Short and Sweet* (1994, 1996) suggest 12 different generic procedures, including this one, to develop more interesting activities/materials.

Use the constraints principle

The idea here is to impose tight constraints on whatever activity is involved. For example:

- Limit the number of words students have to write – as in mini-sagas, where a story has to be told in just 50 words.
- Limit the amount of time allowed to complete a task – as when students are given exactly 1 minute to give instructions.
- Limit the quantity of materials – as in a construction task where each group is given just 4 file cards, 10 paper clips and 2 elastic bands with which to build a structure and write instructions on how to construct it.

Use the random principle

This is essentially using bisociation – putting two or more things together that do not belong together and finding connections. For example;

- Students work in pairs – all the 'A's write 10 adjectives each on slips of paper, all the 'B's write 10 nouns. The slips are put in two boxes. Students take turns to draw a slip from each box, making an unusual combination (e.g. broken birthday). When they have 10 new phrases they combine them into a text.
- Students are given pictures of five people taken at random from magazines. They then have to write a story involving all five characters.

Use the association principle

This involves using evocative stimuli for students to react to. For example:

- Students listen to a sequence of sounds, then describe their feelings or tell a story suggested by the sounds.
- Students are given a set of character descriptions and a set of fragments of dialogue. They then match the characters with what they might have said.
- Students are all given a natural object (a stone, a leaf, etc.). They then write a text as if they had become their object.
- Drawing on their own experience, students choose a taste, a smell or a sound which brings back particular memories.

Use the withholding-information principle

This involves offering only part of the information needed to complete a task. Jigsaw listening/reading are examples of this. Other examples would be:

- A text is cut up into short fragments. Each student has one fragment. They have to reconstitute the text without showing their fragments to others. (The same can be done with a picture.)

- A picture is flashed on the screen for just a second. Students must try to recall it.

Use the divergent-thinking principle

The core idea here is to find as many different uses for a particular thing or ways of carrying out a task. For example:

- Teachers find alternative ways to do some of their routine tasks – set homework (Painter, 2003), take the register, give instructions, arrange the seating, do dictations (Davis & Rinvolucri, 1988) and so on.
- Students find as many uses for a common object (e.g. a comb) as possible.
- Students have to find as many different ways of spending a given sum of money as possible.

Some Examples of Creative Materials

For each example, I will first describe the material and then suggest what might be happening in the learner's mind. I will then examine how closely they fit the criteria listed in the previous section (pp. 42–44). To what extent can we consider them to be creative – and effective in terms of the inputs, processes, outcomes? How might they be extended or adapted?

Word arrays

In this example, learners are given the following set of words. Their first task is to write as many sentences as they can using only these words, and no others. They are set a time limit. They then compare their sentences with others'. Together, they add more sentences. Groups then pool their sentences and select some of them to compose a short text. At the end, they share by reading out what they have written. Finally, they are given the original text from which the words were taken. Here is the original text:

> He never sent me flowers. He never wrote me letters. He never took me to restaurants. He never spoke of love. We met in parks. I cannot remember what he said but I remember how he said it. Most of it was silence anyway. (Leszek Szkutnik)

he	in	me
sent	I	most
parks	anyway	was
of	never	flowers
silence	took	wrote
it	said	what

letters	restaurants	how
to	cannot	love
spoke	we	remember
met	but	

What is going on in the learners' minds as they do this task? There is intense concentration on the array of words as they try to piece together sentences from their repertoire of sentence types. This often involves lots of backtracking and false starts. Vague ideas are beginning to form about the meanings linking the words – flowers, restaurants, love and so on. When they start to work together there is scope for discussion, and the meanings begin to coalesce as possible associations are forged between words. Gradually, various narratives begin to surface.

How well does this piece of material match the criteria above? The content is interesting, partly because it involves universal human feelings – love, relationships and so on. It is at a relatively low level, though, interestingly, it can be done at higher levels: if students have greater syntactic resources, they can make longer sentences. The process involves deep processing of both language and content, and in terms of both cognitive and affective engagement. There is scope for varying the input as we shall see below, with extension and adaptation. Most learners find personal relevance in the texts they construct and in the original text. And this is an aesthetic experience, in that they are constructing a piece of narrative or even poetry of their own. Their only choice at this stage is in the sentences they construct and the story they develop. Genuine interaction takes place because group members really want to arrive at an agreed and effective text. This generally fosters a positive affective climate both at the stage of devising their texts and when sharing them. Groups are genuinely interested in hearing what others have done. The students may not learn any new vocabulary but they get plenty of practice in using and manipulating what they know. And they are often made aware of new grammatical structures as they share each other's sentences. They certainly learn how to cooperate, and develop rapport, while gaining in self-confidence and self-esteem. Note also that the material uses the association and the constraints principles.

There would be a number of options for extending this idea, which would give more control and choice to the learners. These would include: asking different groups to choose one from among a number of short texts, and then to prepare their own word arrays, to be processed by a different group. At an advanced level, they could be asked to find other suitable texts or to write some very short texts, and base word arrays on them. (In order to prepare a word array, they first make a list of all the words in the text and then arrange them as above. If words are used more than once in the text, they appear only once in the array.)

Metaphor poems

Learners are asked to create three metaphors by combining any word from a first column with any phrase in a second column, joining them with 'is'. Below is an example of the two columns for this task:

Hope	a vacuum cleaner
Life	a knife
Marriage	an egg
Love	a brush
Anger	a window
Disappointment	a mirror
Work	a banana
Happiness	a rope
Time	a bus
Hate	a cup
Fear	an alarm clock

(Adapted from Spiro, 2004)

From this, learners might produce:

Marriage is a window

Disappointment is a brush

Anger is a vacuum cleaner

They share their metaphors with other class members. They then choose one metaphor to work with. The task is to write one or two more lines to make a short poem (it does not need to rhyme). The lines should put the metaphor in context so that we understand why X is Y. For example:

Disappointment is a brush:
It sweeps away all our hopes
And throws them in the rubbish bin.

Learners share their poems with their partners, then with the whole class. For homework, they write out their poems and illustrate them. In the next class, they make a wall display of their work.

The material is based on the random, bisociative principle. What is happening in the learners' heads this time? The activity does not require any thinking about the language initially: any item from the first column will go with any from the second. It is purely automatic, though many learners make a conscious choice even though they are told not to! It is natural. But the moment they have put the two words together in this way, their minds begin to look for connections. Why is love a rope? Or happiness an alarm clock? Or fear a banana? The human mind is hard-wired to seek closure, meaning or pattern, even when there is none, so there is intense mental activity as they do this. Their minds are buzzing with ideas to justify the metaphors they have created. They then have to find a verbal formulation for their thoughts, having in mind that they are writing a poem, not an essay. There is again intense mental activity in formulating the lines they will use, calling on all the vocabulary and grammatical structures at their disposal.

How well does this piece of material meet the criteria discussed above? There is something compelling about metaphors, especially when some of the words in the columns evoke strong emotions: knife, fear, love, marriage. The task's level of demand is low initially, as all they have to do is randomly connect items. It increases when they have to contextualise their metaphors. But this can be done at an elementary or a more advanced level both in terms of language and conceptually. For example:

Elementary
Anger is a knife:
It hurts people.

More advanced
Anger is a knife;
but it cuts both ways.
Be careful you don't cut yourself!
Keep your anger in its sheath.

Learners tend to engage intensely with this activity as they relate the metaphors to themselves – they cannot do otherwise. So there is keen personal relevance. There is genuine depth of processing as learners search for ways to contextualise their metaphors. The material can easily be adapted by changing the vocabulary items, and learners themselves can be asked to do this, thus offering greater choice and control. The material offers scope for aesthetic choices in the writing, and in the way the wall display is arranged. Interaction with others in the sharing of the poems is always intense and helps sustain a positive affective climate. Learners are genuinely interested in displaying their own work and in hearing what others have done. Again, this material serves to reinforce and activate language the learners already know, though some peripheral learning, especially of vocabulary, often takes place. It certainly helps develop qualities such as self-esteem, cooperation and critical thinking.

Backwards writing

Prepare a few sentences in which the words are written back to front. For example:

yrevE tixe si na yrtne erehwemos esle. moT drappotS

kooL erofeb uoy pael.

emiT stiaw rof on nam.

eW evah on aedi fo woh eht retaw fo eht lacisyhp niarb si denrut otni eht eniw fo ssensuoicsnoc.… niloC nniGcM

Give learners five minutes to choose one of the sentences and write it out the right way round. For example:

kooL erofeb uoy pael.
Look before you leap.

Ask the learners how they felt about doing this. For homework, ask each of them to bring in one short sentence – perhaps a quotation, or a proverb or saying – written in this way.

What goes on in learners' heads as they do this? There is the urgency of the time limit, so a degree of pressure. By presenting something familiar in an unfamiliar way, they have an extra layer of processing to do. As they flip each word, they have a small eureka moment – ah, so 'era' is 'are'. Their whole language network is on high alert. As they become more familiar with the reversal, and as more words are revealed, they will gradually start to make predictions about how the sentence will go on.

In terms of the criteria, the process is clearly compelling, given the time pressure to find a solution. There is also the opportunity to make the content compelling too, by choosing memorable quotes and proverbs. The level can be adjusted to learners' competence through the choice of sentences. It involves deep processing, as they have to process the words twice in order to make sense of them. There are opportunities for diversifying the activity through choice of sentences. It can also be made more demanding by reversing not only the letters in the words but the order of words in the sentence, which adds an extra layer of processing. For example,

pael. uoy erofeb kooL

There is an opportunity to inject an aesthetic element through the choice of sentences. And by asking learners to bring in their own sentences to a later class, they are given a degree of control over the materials. There is always a lively discussion after the activity, which generates genuine interaction and helps maintain a positive atmosphere among the group.

Conclusion

There has been much recent interest in developing more creative ways of teaching and learning foreign languages (Maley & Cirocki, 2014; Maley & Peachey, 2015; Pugliese, 2010), including the formation of the

C Group (Creativity for Change in Language Education) in 2013 (http://thecreativitygroup.weebly.com). This has inevitably affected the way we think about materials.

In this chapter, I have attempted to shed some light on what we mean by 'creative materials' by questioning whether, or in what sense, materials might be considered creative. I conclude that there are some principles and some processes which are more likely to encourage effective learning than others. These principles and processes can also be considered to facilitate creative responses. I have tried to demonstrate how this might work with some concrete examples.

However, as I have tried to make clear, it is not the materials themselves which are creative, so much as those who use them. The teacher has a central role in bringing about an atmosphere conducive to creative outcomes. Even the best, most creative-looking materials can turn to dust in the hands of an insensitive or unsympathetic teacher. And even the least creative-looking materials can turn to gold in the hands of an inspired teacher. And we should never forget that it is the learners who are ultimately the arbiters of the materials.

References

Amabile, M.T. (1996) *Creativity in Context*. Boulder, CO: Westfield Press.
Arnold, J. (ed.) (1999) *Affective Language Teaching*. Cambridge: Cambridge University Press.
Bilbrough, N. (2011) *Memory Activities for Language Learning*. Cambridge: Cambridge University Press.
Boden, M. (1990) *The Creative Mind*. London: Abacus.
Craik, F.I.M. and Lockhart, R.S. (1972) Levels of processing: A framework for memory research. *Journal of Verbal Learning and Verbal Behaviour* 11 (6), 671–684.
Csikszentimihalyi, M. (1988) Society, culture and person: A systems view of creativity. In L.J. Sternberg (ed.) *The Nature of Creativity: Contemporary Psychological Perspectives* (pp. 325–339). New York: Cambridge University Press.
Csikszentmihalyi, M. (1990) *Flow: The Psychology of Optimal Experience*. New York: Harper and Row.
Csikszentmihalyi, M. (1997) *Creativity: Flow and the Psychology of Discovery and Invention*. New York: Harper Perennial.
Davis, P. and Rinvolucri, M. (1988) *Dictation*. Cambridge: Cambridge University Press.
Dörnyei, Z. and Murphey, T. (2003) *Group Dynamics in the Language Classroom*. Cambridge: Cambridge University Press.
Fanselow, J. (1987) *Breaking Rules*. London: Longman.
Fanselow, J. (2010) *Try the Opposite*. Charleston, SC: Booksurge.
Gardner, H. (1983) *Frames of Mind: The Theory of Multiple Intelligences*. London: Paladin/Granada.
Gardner, H. (2011) *The Unschooled Mind*. New York: Basic Books.
Goleman, D. (1996) *Emotional Intelligence*. London: Bloomsbury.
Grundy, P., Bociek, H. and Parker, K. (2011) *English Through Art*. London: Helbling Languages.
Hadfield, J. (1990) *Classroom Dynamics*. Oxford: Oxford University Press.
Koestler, A. (1989) *The Act of Creation*. London: Arkana/Penguin.

Maley, A. (1994, 1996) *Short and Sweet, vols 1 and 2*. London: Penguin.

Maley, A. (2009) Towards an aesthetics of ELT. Part 1. *Folio* 13 (2), December.

Maley, A. (2010) Towards an aesthetics of ELT. Part 2. *Folio* 14 (1), September.

Maley, A. and Cirocki, A. (eds) (2014) TESOL teacher education and development. *European Journal of Applied Linguistics and TEFL* 3 (2).

Maley, A. and Peachey, N. (eds) (2015) *Creativity in the Language Classroom*. London: British Council.

Painter, L. (2003) *Homework*. Oxford: Oxford University Press.

Pugliese, C. (2010) *Being Creative: The Challenge of Change in the Classroom*. London: Delta.

Spiro, J. (2004) *Creative Poetry Writing*. Oxford: Oxford University Press.

Tomlinson, B. (2001) Materials development. In R. Carter and D. Nunan (eds) *The Cambridge Guide to Teaching English to Speakers of Other Languages* (pp. 66–71). Cambridge: Cambridge University Press.

Tomlinson, B. (ed.) (2011) *Materials Development in Language Teaching*. Cambridge: Cambridge University Press.

Underhill, A. (2014) Training for the unpredictable. *European Journal of Applied Linguistics and TEFL* 3 (2), 59–69.

Underhill, A. and Maley, A. (2012) Expect the unexpected. *English Teaching Professional* 82, 4–7.

4 Materials for Creativity: A Constructivist Perspective

Dat Bao

Understanding Teachers' Frustration with ELT Materials

Language teaching materials sometimes cause frustration to the user. This very much depends on two factors: how self-reliantly the teacher approaches textbooks and how flexible the textbook is. In 1981, when Allwright wrote his scathing article about the coursebook, he believed that language learning materials could only 'embody decisions, but they cannot themselves undertake action' (p. 9). Being simply a lifeless object, the textbook has been viewed as the tyrant within the classroom (Williams, 1983), demanding that teachers and learners conform to it with no room for deviation or personalisation on either's part. O'Neill (1982) offers an expanded view by stating that despite the broadness or narrowness of it, the essential language components present in a coursebook should allow for applicability in most situations with most students. The main purposes of materials, arguably, are: to maintain quality of education and to standardise instruction (Richards, 2001); to keep 'order within potential chaos' (Hutchinson & Torres, 1994: 327) by providing structure; and to reassure students that structure is present (Harmer, 1998; O'Neill, 1982).

Critics have pointed out that commercially viable coursebooks tend to aim for a gainful target market. Serving a profit-making industry, they eventually become a 'compromise between the financial and the pedagogical' (Sheldon, 1987, 1988). While trying to appeal to everyone everywhere in every language-learning situation (Cunningsworth, 1984; McGrath, 2002), the textbook ends up being too broad to be interesting and relevant. As Dat (2006) elaborates, 'since coursebooks reflect the writer's knowledge and view of the world, when they are transferred and used by people whom the writer knows little about, irrelevance of content and subject matters are likely to result' (p. 52). Other scholars who touched on such irrelevance in materials (Edge & Wharton, 1998; Hutchinson, 1987; Jolly & Bolitho, 1998; Murray, 2003) have noted that although coursebook writers may not be consciously aware of their own beliefs, these individual views still permeate the book in both content and organisation of activities.

A coursebook, therefore, has potential to be subjective, and whether it proves to be effective depends on how well it anticipates the multiple ways of being relevant to the users and how effectively it supports their teaching and learning as a result of such imagined potentiality. To reduce subjectivity requires course writers to stop controlling and leave the task of interpreting and implementing materials more open to course users. As Canniveng and Martinez (2003) emphasise, dealing with the limitation of second language materials requires teachers to be consciously proactive in bridging the gap. This stance needs to be spelled out concretely, the range of resources needs to be expanded, and suggestions for use need to be pedagogically strategic. Such actions will help generate space for teacher and learner creativity.

Why Creativity Matters

The term 'creativity' reminds us of new ways of seeing, generating novel ideas and demonstrating divergent thoughts, all of which help us escape mundane or typical ways of addressing an issue or answering a question. Although this understanding seems straightforward, scholarly efforts to define creativity often encounter a complicated challenge, as evidenced by the extended range of definitions of this construct which, according to Torrance (2003), are all far from accurate. Indeed, ways of describing this process seem too diverse to be consistent. For instance, researchers who look into this construct have collected as many as 112 definitions (Trerffinger, 2000) of and 1400 terms (Aldrich, 2001) related to creativity. Among these, significant concepts that stand out include mental and social process, cognitive thinking, affective responses and a form of intelligence. Perhaps the closest word to 'creativity' is 'imagination', which refers to the ability to see the invisible. In an ideal situation, creativity turns that fancy into a concrete idea and innovation continues to expand it further, into actual practice.

This conceptualisation, however, might not be agreeable to everyone. Instead, creativity from an applied point of view has been widely misunderstood by both educators and other members of society. Some assume that it is a dimension of abstract thinking that operates in a small number of disciplines, such as the sciences and the arts, rather than something to be practised throughout all aspects of schooling. Others feel that it works more for individuals with special talents rather than for everyone. Some perceive creativity as a final product, that is, being materially accomplished, rather than a continual process in the mind to be mentally nurtured. Others regard it more as an inborn aptitude than as a competency that can be established via coaching effort. Despite such misperceptions, scholars involved in teaching and promoting creativity know very well that this is a versatile facility that, if one desires, can pervade all levels of education (Robinson, 2011).

With the above awareness in mind, educators in an increased global movement are making efforts to incorporate creativity in curriculum reform (Gariboldi & Catellani, 2013; Shaheen, 2010) as a way to enable deeper engagement among students and help them reach their full potential. This is due to the wide acknowledgement that creative abilities play a powerful role in academic achievement (Bano *et al.*, 2014; Chamorro-Premuzic, 2006; Hansenne & Legrand, 2012; Molaei & Abasi, 2014; Powers & Kaufman, 2004). As a matter of fact, empirical research conducted into creative programmes in many school curricula has yielded evidence of their benefit for learning outcomes. There are at least five main reasons why creative education has developed into a highly significant obligation. Those reasons concern how creativity is connected to: skills development; multiple possibilities; societal benefit; enhanced affect; and learnability. Each of these is explained below.

Skills development

Achieving creative problem-solving ability involves building a wide collection of skills (Haler, 2016). Examples of such skills include sensitivity to problems, hypothesis formulation, diverse guessing, novel association, resistance to routine, thinking fluency, original interpretation, attentiveness to imagination and the courage to explore.

Multiple possibilities

Creativity encourages the thinking of endless possibilities (Amabile, 1983; Kohn, 1987) whereby the learner explores various sets of attributes within an issue of concern and combines them in ways that make novel sense. Possibility thinking also represents a form of intelligence that would be useful in any aspect of life (Carlo, 2009; Craft, 2002) as it enables the mind to perceive the world in a renewed fashion.

Societal benefit

The practice of creativity has the potential not only to produce competitive advantage for individuals but also to bring collective benefit to humans on various global and societal levels (Kader, 2008). This is because creativity is not something that grows solely from inside the mind but tends to arise as the mind interacts with the thoughts of others in a specific sociocultural context (Csikszentmihalyi, 2013).

Enhanced affect

Creativity triggers the emotional channel in learners so that they become frequently curious about the surrounding social environment. Such curiosity stimulates them to intuitively recognise what seems missing, to adopt a risk-taking attitude towards one's self-expression, and to willingly stretch their potential responses. With this experimental mindset, learners would enjoy moving from fantasy thinking to consequential action.

Learnability

Creativity is learnable and achievable, which is why creative practices have been introduced into the classroom in many education programmes. The extensive amount of research being conducted on interactive pedagogies for creativity have proven that thoughtful stimulation of learners' enthusiastic participation has the power to improve learning outcomes (Besancon & Lubart, 2008; Gariboldi & Catellani, 2013; Honig, 2000; Kader, 2008; Woods, 1990).

Materials for Creativity

I would like to draw a helpful distinction between the term *creative materials*, which refers to originality in course design, including content and pedagogy, and *materials for creativity*, which refers to resources that help their users become creative in teaching and learning. Arguably, there is a logical connection between the two: the latter require the former, as it would be impossible for boring, conventional materials to turn teachers and learners into resourceful discussants of exciting ideas. On the contrary, if participants experience a great deal of innovative moments while working with materials, their learning mechanism will get inspired and their creative behaviour is likely to be fostered. On the basis of research evidence, scholars argue that curriculum development plays an essential role in the development of creativity among students, which can be oriented towards particular subject areas (see, for example, Blamires & Peterson, 2014).

Inside the language classroom, one can observe evidence that teachers and learners are exhibiting creative behaviour. For instance, participants engage with a large repertoire of strategies to teach and learn. They become playful with both language and content. They perform a wide range of both cognitive and affective processing in their discussion. They recycle previous knowledge and skills in new, personalised ways that break away from common, tedious routine.

A Constructivist Approach to Creative Materials Design

This section argues for a constructivist stance towards materials development, with an open-minded view of learning as a continuing, adaptable process. A major concept that lays the foundation for constructivism, as highlighted by Spiro *et al.* (1991), is flexibility, a factor that has been recognised as a significant facilitator of creativity (Bao, 2015). A closer look at the tenets of constructivism reveals a number of features with rich potential to support creative effort, such as an emphasis on:

- the need for original adaptation (Wanniarachchi, 2016);
- support for customised learning needs and experiences (Yildirim, 2005);
- encouragement of situated learning in real-life contexts (Driscoll, 2007);
- open-mindedness towards accepting multiple perspectives (Staits & Wilke, 2007).

Constructivist-based pedagogy as inspired by the work of Dewey (1929), Piaget (1954) and Vygotsky (1978) – as well as other cognitive, social and practical constructivists – advocates practices that make use of learners' individuality, applicability and social context. In Vygotsky's educational philosophy, learning happens on two levels: intra-psychologically (i.e. within everyone) and inter-psychologically (i.e. among social members) (Wink & Putney, 2002). To make this possible, education needs to provide the duality of conditions under which learners not only pursue their independent thinking but also interact with the thinking of others. With this consideration, teaching materials, which situate the learner in its centre, should be designed in a way that responds to individual priority, social concern and real-world practicality.

The approach has strong potential to be applied to materials design, in the sense that materials will no longer be predetermined throughout but always have an open space for further challenge, participation and decision. In a constructivist coursebook, although some texts are given, there are also provisions for students to select what to read. Some questions are asked by the textbook but learners are also invited to initiate their own questions. Many tasks are open-ended and process-based, to encourage different ways of obtaining the answer. Assessment does not always have the answer key but might accept a variety of responses. When a comparison task is included, criteria are provided but students can also add their own criteria. Vocabulary on a topic may be given but that list may be incomplete, to be additionally elicited by the teacher and contributed by the learner. These are only some examples to show how constructivism as a tool can reshape the internal structure of materials. More systematically, the next section presents a set of principles for materials to make the creative mode of learning happen.

Five Key Principles Underlying Materials for Creativity

Materials need to invite teachers and learners to navigate their ways around available resources with a proactive attitude rather than as submissive visitors. The coursebook can encourage this stance by organising for the following dimensions to be activated, namely curiosity, response, experience, challenge and negotiation.

Stimulating curiosity in teachers and learners

A coursebook for creativity should be able to instil in its users some degree of inquisitiveness, so that they enjoy interacting with course content to discover and generate more meaning from it. This requires a diverse selection of amusing texts, topics for debate, attention-grabbing task design and functioning visuals, among other innovative resources that are not usually found in the typical textbook.

Inspiring unconventional responses

Materials for creativity should organise for learners to play out their innovative aptitude, performing actions such as creating, inventing, discovering, imagining, supposing and predicting. These actions will generate original ideas and diverse ways of self-expression. Of course, helpful conventional coursebooks have asked students to rehearse language in many ways, such as to review, apply, use, repeat, recycle, produce, speak out, which activates their practical ability; or have invited learners to analyse, criticise, judge, compare, evaluate, which strengthens their critical thinking. In reality, though, we rarely see materials that actively inspire such a wide range of responses or stimulate students' artistic talents in the learning process, which is something that materials for creativity should do.

Promoting open-ended learning experiences

The meaning generated from a discussion may not be the same for all learners, due to differences in individuals' world-views, interests and personalities. To utilise such diversity, materials could suggest a series of elements (such as multiple conditions for solving a problem, different views about an issue, various places to be compared, or a set of items for associating and constructing meaning), from which teachers and learners are able to decide which elements to use and how to combine them.

Here is an example. The proposed activity is writing a play script, and the class is provided with a set of characters. First of all, learners in small groups are invited to pick out any two characters from the given list and to develop a conflict situation between them. Secondly, learners are to choose another character or a pair or group of other characters to either make the conflict more complex or to find a solution to the problem. Thirdly, each group can decide on a setting or context for the story. What makes the activity unique each time it is conducted in a new class is that although everyone has the same set of characters, all the scenarios they develop are likely to end up being very different from one another in their plots, titles, genres, mood, actions and moral lessons. Learners can also draw an illustration and present it together with the story for the class to interact with.

Creating emotional and intellectual challenge

For content to be integrated into learners' affect and intellectuality, materials should bring together different background knowledge, experiences and interests into the learning situation, whereby students are encouraged to provide their personal responses. Without much divergence and conflict, it is hard to produce anything challenging and unpredicted that would make learning exciting. One example would be to build into an activity multiple degrees of challenge so that mixed-level learners can find their own reactions; another example is a task that touches on various senses and emotions so that learners can utilise more than one channel of responding to the same issue.

Facilitating teacher and learner negotiation with materials

The extent to which a coursebook can simultaneously meet the contentment of the writer, be appropriate to users and meet the ambition for commercial sales is often minimal and tends to require a great deal of negotiation. Materials for creativity need to allow flexible conditions for different teachers and students to implement course content not only to meet their own preferred ways but also to make the learning process highly entertaining. With such support, teachers are making changes towards more relevance to learners' needs, levels and learning styles. With such support, students are also given the pleasure of experiencing some degree of novelty in learning.

Proposed Strategies for Materials to Support Creative Negotiation

Adaptability

The idea of course adaptation as a way to avoid the use of irrelevant materials has been promoted since the 1990s by scholars such as Maley (1998) and Hodder (1994). For this to happen, coursebooks can invite some degree of teachers' and learners' creative manipulation through activities with multiple options for teachers and learners to acclimatise them. Based on this, teachers can exercise more control of materials by excluding what learners do not enjoy, expanding a discussion with learners' self-reflection or comparative views, diminishing monotonous content with minimal response capacity, improving insufficient language through more vocabulary supplement for learners to discuss a topic, rewriting texts that are not linguistically or culturally appropriate, recycling language that learners need to use with more frequency, discarding or replacing irrelevant elements, modifying an argument that does not follow learners' logic, dividing a difficult task into more manageable steps, and combining sub-tasks to increase challenge.

Sequence change

Materials can provide suggestions for teachers to alter the sequence of a task, a lesson or even the entire coursebook so as to suit learners' preferred system of internalising language. The need for flexibility in teaching and learning procedures has been advocated for decades in materials development (Bell & Gower, 1998; Mares, 2003). This could mean being able to exploit the same text in different processing procedures (Maley, 1998) or the re-sequencing of units and tasks within a textbook (Mares, 2003) based on what teachers and learners feel most comfortable with.

Re-timing

Creative time management requires teachers' ability to lengthen or shorten the duration of tasks and lessons. As Pilbeam (1987) indicates, not every class will go through the same task within the same amount of time but duration might vary for various reasons. Creative materials therefore can provide suggestions for teachers and learners to decide how much time they would like to spend rehearsing certain skills. To make this possible, a task might include multiple steps and a lesson might comprise multiple optional activities for selection. On this basis, learning duration can stretch or shrink depending on time availability, learner proficiency and learning interest.

Contextualisation

Contextualisation means being able to localise content to suit the learning environment and any given situation (Masuhara et al., 2008; McDonough & Shaw, 1993; Tomlinson, 2001; Widdowson, 2000). One method to make this happen is to provide multiple ways of stimulating responses so that learners of various backgrounds can participate with resources drawn from their own lives, views, feelings, knowledge and experiences. In addition, knowledge, skills and strategies developed by learners need to be regularly recycled for sustainability. To enable this, materials can suggest a range of circumstances for learners to apply language and, hopefully, as Crawford (2002) indicates, learners' flexibility in coping with contextualised language use will play a significant role in skills development.

Pedagogical and learning selection

Students become more productive if they are able to select what to learn and how to learn it (O'Neill, 1982; Saraceni, 2003). To allow this happen, materials can offer rich communication activities to ensure opportunities for both formal learning and informal acquisition. They need to provide multiple options of the same task or diverse ways of developing the same skill. Teachers with different teaching styles and abilities also need a coursebook that allows them to choose their favourite way of teaching as well as to obtain the kind of support they need to conduct a difficult lesson successfully. As Saraceni (2003: 76) suggests that good materials 'should provide learners with the possibility of choosing different activities, tasks, projects and approaches, and therefore of adapting the materials to their own preferred learning needs'. This understanding suggests that classroom decisions should be shared by both students and teachers, so that students are exposed to a variety of different ways of learning.

Variety

To encourage students' persistence in language learning, monotony needs to be removed from the coursebook. Boring teachers, poor pedagogies, irrelevant cultural content, inflexible materials and a dull classroom atmosphere are factors that put students off learning. To prevent this from happening, materials should feature variety, an element advocated by scholars such as Hutchison and Waters (1987)and Howard and Major (2005). In particular, materials need to offer supplementary resources, such as optional appendixes, and variations of tasks in terms of both method and content. Diverse texts should be included, both factual and fiction, to facilitate both practical knowledge and novel imagination.

Supporting various cultures of learning

Since students have the right to choose not only what to learn but also how to learn it (O'Neill, 1982; Saraceni, 2003), the coursebook has to cater for different learning styles and preferences (Breen & Candlin, 1987; Masuhara et al., 2008). This requires authors to care about individualisation, that is, taking into account the fact that students in the same classroom may vary in age, abilities, interests, personalities, seating, formality, cultural and learning backgrounds (Doff & Jones, 2007).

Once the coursebook provides these options, teachers can easily adapt learning content to suit students' personalities and performance styles, taking into account analytical learners, who focus their attention on discrete learning points, kinaesthetic learners, who prefer physical movement, experiential learners, who enjoy a discovery approach, and so on. Pedagogically, a creative coursebook should incorporate not only the Western-style communicative approach but also a wide range of strengths from other teaching traditions, such as the use of translation as a way to support second language learning (which is strong in the reading approach), intensive use of pictures and actions for visual and kinaesthetic learners (as found in the direct approach), memorisation as connected with the development of linguistic automaticity (as advocated by audio-lingualism), opportunity for sequential and individualised consultation (as advised by community language learning educators), and so on.

Opportunity for localisation

Localisation means making the coursebook suited to students' learning environments (Masuhara *et al.*, 2008; McDonough & Shaw, 1993; Tomlinson, 2001) and allowing students to ease their engagement with a syllabus or curriculum (McDonough & Shaw, 1993). To do so, course materials should avoid subjective views that might disturb learners' beliefs and values unless there is a chance for learners to argue with those views.

Open-ended participation

Open-ended activities can be provided so that different students can tailor the task to their own level of proficiency and ability to participate. In this way, both weaker and stronger students will have opportunities to feel they learn something during the lesson. Discussion content, such as famous quotes, visuals, poems and stories, can also be open to reinventing, interpretation and creation of the conclusion.

Conditions for building intercultural skills

Course materials can nurture intercultural competence by equipping learners with linguistic and cultural behaviour that welcomes positive interpretation of various cultures. The English that students learn needs to help them communicate successfully beyond the native-speaker model. For example, instructional materials might involve both local and international contexts that are familiar and relevant to diverse cultural lives. Activities should have suitable discourse samples pertaining to interactions between native and non-native speakers, as well as interactions among non-natives. Discourse exclusively between non-native speakers should be kept to a minimum.

It is through the use of models from both native and non-native speakers that students can develop strategies to understand various accents and ways to behave cross-culturally. Adaptation skills need to be part of such content and the language should contain more than just common English vocabulary but also foreign words that are frequently borrowed in everyday conversation in English. Learners need to be made aware that a diverse range of interactional patterns exists and thus they need to be flexible in recognising different cultural forms of politeness rather than forcing the whole world to behave in one unrealistically consistent way.

An Example of Flexible Task Design

To demonstrate how ELT materials can be made more flexible to maximise learning, in this section I show how a task taken from a real coursebook can be changed to make it more flexible.

In *English File Intermediate Student's Book* (Oxenden & Latham-Koenig, 1999: 92), one activity asks learners to make sentences to state where people come from. The accompanying illustration displays a collection of funny-looking characters in some typical appearance that obviously shows their nationality, and learners are supposed to decide which country each person comes from: an overweight American wears a Hawaiian shirt and a cowboy hat and is using a pair of binoculars in a manner which suggests that he is a nosey person; a young European lady looks slim, wears fashionable clothes and walks elegantly to suggest that she is Italian; a mean-looking man wearing sunglasses and smoking a pipe, dressed in a flamboyant, flashy suit to demonstrate a well-off mafia figure is South American. In a word, members of various cultures are reduced to cliché in an attempt to make the characters recognisable to serve a predetermined pattern of language practice.

Not only does the visual illustration decrease representation of various cultures to conventional, narrow formulations but it also provides misleading icons of what would occur in the real world: all people coming from the same country must share a similar image and give the same simplified impression about their origin. One way to take learners out of this stereotypical construction would be to invite them to select one (or more) of the following options.

- Each student finds pictures of at least three people who they know come from three different countries and asks either a classmate or the whole class to guess their origins. They can be celebrities or ordinary people that the students know.
- Each student imagines he/she is from a country other than his/hers. Without saying what their names are and without mentioning any famous landmarks, they show pictures to the class and ask them to guess where the characters come from. If the class cannot guess, the student then provides some clues, such as 'this country is in East Asia', 'there is snow in winter' or 'the country is known for its manufacture of mobile phones'.
- Students work in groups of three to select a country and look for a set of pictures representing various people from it. They then show the pictures to the class and ask everyone to guess the country.

- Classmates work in pairs to create a drawing with two or three images representing three actions or activities that people normally do if they live in that country (such as taking the bullet train, sleeping on the floor and eating sushi). Other students are then invited to guess where that pair of classmates come from.
- If learners are in a multicultural class, everyone gets up from their seats to walk around and ask one another where they are from. Students can chat with those they do not know the origin of and participants can even make guesses if they like.
- Students write down the name of a country on pieces of paper, which are then put in a box. The teacher then shuffles and redistributes those names to the whole class. Each student now has to imagine he/she comes from the named country. Individually, students stand up to say a few key words related to that country, for the class to guess which it is.

These optional sub-tasks allow learners to use their own resources not only to assist the teacher in his/her teaching but also to create meaning for themselves. Although the eventual output is simply to say someone is from a particular country, the process of participating makes learners become open-minded to multicultural information. The approach makes it easier to develop 'noticing' as a tool in learning new words and structures, to encourage resistance to fixed ideas about the world being imposed on learners, to build rich information into the learning content, to encourage students to interpret how people fit in their living environment, to make lesson content less conservative, and to create fun in the learning process. These creative options also help teachers move away from over-simplification of reality and share new information about other cultures, and to enrich learners' experience and expand their cultural awareness.

Conventional images and stereotypical information in coursebooks reflect flawed thinking about people and cultures, provide an inaccurate picture of the real world and cause damage to learners' thinking. As Hinton (2000) points out, if a wide range of people hold the wrong view it becomes easy for more people to stick with it. Such conveniences become harmful as 'much of our knowledge of other people does not come from personal contact with them but through other sources' (Hinton, 2000: 25–26) and for this reason many EFL learners may never have a chance to find out the truth about other cultures. As Cunningsworth (1995) indicates, language is a cultural phenomenon. Learners while studying language also subconsciously take in cultural elements and it is the writer who has the power to affect that view in many positive ways.

Implications of Creativity for Teacher Development

A creative coursebook can serve as a toolbox, with resources open to any new arrangement of teaching and learning in context. It is not right for materials to be created with inherent irrelevance to learners' context and leave the task of modification to the teacher. To avoid excessive repairing of existing problems, the coursebook should contain rich, diverse resources with systematic guidance for teachers and learners to organise new combinations for their own situations. When such conditions are provided, there is no longer the need to evaluate the whole coursebook, which might be a waste of time, but only the relevance of each tool to meet what the everyday classroom requires. Only when such conditions are provided will teachers and learners be able to make the classroom process effective. Such flexibility plays an important role in creating a vibrant learning impact which includes outcomes such as negotiation, experience, collaboration, inspiration, enhancement and empowerment:

- *Negotiation.* Course materials can provide a valuable negotiation space for teachers to interact with course content and allow further negotiation to happen between the teacher's ability and learners' need, between the teacher's decision-making skills and the everyday classroom setting.
- *Experience.* Course materials can equip teachers with more experience in adaptation and enable them to evaluate and reconstruct pedagogical resources in context, which in the end makes a contribution to teacher development in terms of both knowledge and competence.
- *Collaboration.* Different teachers using the same coursebook may end up teaching differently, depending on their choices, strengths, personality, pedagogical skills and classroom situations. Such practice may be worth sharing among teachers.
- *Inspiration.* Course materials can offer creative substance that inspires teachers rather than bores them with the same routine when using textbooks. Good materials should alert teachers to the fact that there is never a single logical way to teach a lesson but there can be multiple ways and opportunities for the same lesson to be taught successfully. Such processes not only increase the range of action but also open the mind.
- *Enhancement.* Course materials can allow the teacher to play with possibilities, try out options, reflect on practice, evaluate tasks and revise the materials for increased learning opportunities. Such a process also encourages a stronger sense of classroom experiment and enhances creativity in teachers.
- *Empowerment.* Course materials should respect and empower teachers to be the owner of the materials, to treat coursebooks as tools, not authority. By reducing the control of materials over the teacher and by liberating teachers from being reliant on the written text, this position expands options in lesson planning and allows teachers to share responsibility with textbook writers.

The role of materials is to help teachers develop creative insights into pedagogies and into the principles of materials design, based on knowledge about learners and teaching context. It is difficult to see how adaptation can take place without such a foundation. According to Tomlinson (2003) to the impromptu intuitions of teachers are under pressure of time and institutional constraints.

The moment a coursebook has been written, it already contains a set of inherent restraints, simply because the writer was not in a position to see who would eventually use the material or in what particular setting the book would be used. To address this difficulty, it is important to recognise and act upon the shared obligation of course writers and teachers. Instead of blaming the author for the failure of a textbook, it would be better for the material to be developed with negotiation opportunities incorporated in it so that the product represents a shared process with the teacher. It is the teacher who will then implement the material, based on profound knowledge of pedagogy, a clear understanding of learners' profiles and effective management skills. For decades, empirical research publications have reported hundreds of coursebook evaluation projects with far more dissatisfaction than contentment with course materials. Arguably, it is not really useful for researchers to keep conducting coursebook evaluations with a target learner group in mind whom the book was never written for in the first place.

Conclusion

Teaching is all about making choices (Dougill, 1987; Graves, 2001) and flexible materials can promote this process. Since flexibility is closely connected with creativity (Edge & Wharton, 1998), coursebooks can serve as an 'ideas bank' which stimulates teachers' creative potential (Cunningsworth, 1984: 65). As Graves (2001: 188) elaborates, 'textbooks are tools that can be figuratively cut up into component pieces and then rearranged to suit the needs, abilities, and interests of the students in the course'. It is through the teacher's resourceful dialogue with the textbook (Islam & Mares, 2003) and non-predetermined incidents in the classroom (O'Neill, 1982) that relevant, meaningful learning can happen. It is important to perceive coursebooks not as decision-makers but as tools 'which only have life and meaning when there is a teacher present' (Bell & Gower, 1998: 118).

Learning is a self-discovery process. The role of course materials is to help learners construct authentic experiences for themselves beyond what is contrived in the book. This can happen through constructivist education, which cares about learners' adaptation and multiple realities (Wanniarachchi, 2016), social context and self-directed learning (Driscoll, 2005; Staits & Wilke, 2007), personal reflection and collaborative work (Gazi, 2009), as well as learners' self-determination of their own learning needs (Yildirim, 2005). Materials writers are in a unique position to construct a negotiable playground for teachers and learners to explore their creativity. In that playground, the toys are optional components, task variations, multicultural texts, experimental ideas, supplementary resources, suggestions for re-sequencing, multiple answers to questions, incomplete texts and ways of contextualising course content.

Once the above conditions are met, course materials can liberate teachers rather than control them. The triumph or disaster of materials implementation, instead of being the liability solely of the writer, should become a shared responsibility with the teacher. Coursebooks are no longer fixed or imposing but are appropriated every time the book is opened. In this shared responsibility, teachers are textbook co-designers who participate with their practical knowledge. Teacher knowledge, which is largely drawn from teaching experience, is perceived by Calderhead (1988) as the substance that prompts action. A good coursebook, therefore, empowers teachers by positioning them as co-creators of materials and by engaging them in a dialogic approach to pedagogy. With creative support from course materials, every class will be novel and exciting as the teaching and learning progression are frequently customised.

References

Aldrich, G.S. (2001) Developing a dictionary of creativity terms and definitions. Master of Science thesis, State University of New York, College at Buffalo, International Center of Studies in Creativity, USA.

Allwright, R.I. (1981) What do we want teaching materials for? *ELT Journal* 36 (1), 5–18.

Amabile, T. (1983) *The Social Psychology of Creativity*. New York: Springer.

Bano, A., Naseer, N. and Bibi, Z. (2014) Creativity and academic performance of primary school children. *Pakistan Journal of Social Sciences* 34 (2), 597–606.

Bao, D. (2015) Flexibility in second language materials. *European Journal of Applied Linguistics and TEFL* 4 (2), 37–52.

Bell, J. and Gower, R. (1998) Writing course materials for the world: A great compromise. In B. Tomlinson (ed.) *Materials Development in Language Teaching* (pp. 116–129). Cambridge: Cambridge University Press.

Besancon, M. and Lubart, T. (2008) Differences in the development of creative competencies in children schooled in diverse learning environment. *Learning and Individual Differences* 18, 381–389.

Blamires, M. and Peterson, A. (2014) Can creativity be assessed? Towards an evidence-informed framework for assessing and planning progress in creativity. *Cambridge Journal of Education* 44 (2), 147–162.

Breen, M.P. and Candlin, C.N. (1987) Which materials? A consumer's and designer's guide. In L. Sheldon (ed.) *ELT Textbooks and Materials: Problems in Evaluation and Development* (pp. 13–28). Oxford: Modern English Publications.

Calderhead, J. (1988) The development of knowledge structures in learning to teach. In J. Calderhead (ed.) *Teachers' Professional Learning* (pp. 51–64). London: Falmer.

Canniveng, C. and Martinez, M. (2003) Materials development and teacher training. In B. Tomlinson (ed.) *Developing Materials for Language Teaching* (pp. 479–489). London: Continuum.

Carlo, M. (2009) Explaining the creative mind. *International Journal of Research and Review* 3, 10–19.

Chamorro-Premuzic, T. (2006) Creativity versus conscientiousness: Which is a better predictor of student performance? *Applied Cognitive Psychology* 20 (4), 521–531.

Craft, A. (2002) *Creativity and Early Years Education: A Lifewide Foundation*. London: Continuum.

Crawford, J. (2002) The role of materials in the language classroom: Finding the balance. In J.C. Richards and W.A. Renandya (eds) *Methodology in Language Teaching: An Anthology of Current Practice* (pp. 80–91). Melbourne: Cambridge University Press.

Csikszentmihalyi, M. (2013) *Creativity: The Psychology of Discovery and Invention*. New York: Harper Perennial Modern Classics.

Cunningsworth, A. (1984) *Evaluating and Selecting EFL Teaching Materials*. London: Heinemann Educational Books.

Cunningsworth, A. (1995) *Choosing Your Coursebook*. Oxford: Heinemann.

Dat, B. (2006) Developing EFL materials for local markets: Issues and considerations. In J. Mukundan (ed.) *Focus on ELT Materials* (pp. 52–76). Petaling Jaya: Pearson Malaysia.

Dewey, J. (1929) *The Sources of a Science of Education*. New York: Horace Liveright.

Doff, A. and Jones, C. (2007) *Language in Use: Pre-Intermediate*. Cambridge: Cambridge University Press.

Dougill, J. (1987) Not so obvious. In L. Sheldon (ed.) *ELT Textbooks and Materials: Problems in Evaluation and Development* (pp. 29–36). Oxford: Modern English Publications.

Driscoll, M.P. (2005) *Psychology of Learning for Instruction* (3rd edn). Boston, MA: Pearson.

Driscoll, M.P. (2007) Psychological foundations of instructional design. In R.A. Reiser and J.V. Dempsey (eds) *Trends and Issues in Instructional Design and Technology* (pp. 36–44). Upper Saddle River, NJ: Pearson Education.

Edge, J. and Wharton, S. (1998) Autonomy and development: Living in the materials world. In B. Tomlinson (ed.) *Materials Development in Language Teaching* (pp. 295–310). Cambridge: Cambridge University Press.

Gariboldi, A. and Catellani, N. (eds) (2013) *Creativity in Pre-school Education*. Bologna: Lifelong Learning Programme, European Commission.

Gazi, Z.A. (2009) Implementing constructivist approach into online course designs in Distance Education Institute at Eastern Mediterranean University. *Turkish Online Journal of Educational Technology* 8 (2), 68–81.

Graves, K. (2001) A framework of course development processes. In D.A. Hall and A. Hewings (eds) *Innovation in English Language Teaching: A Reader* (pp. 178–196). New York: Routledge.

Haler, G. (2016) 21st century skills. In *Salem Press Encyclopedia*. Database: Research Starters.

Hansenne, M. and Legrand, J. (2012) Creativity, emotional intelligence, and school performance in children. *International Journal of Educational Research* 53, 264–268.

Harmer, J. (1998) *How to Teach English*. Basildon: Addison Wesley Longman.

Hinton, P.R. (2000) *Stereotypes, Cognition and Culture*. Hove: Psychology Press.

Hodder, I. (1994) *The Interpretation of Documents and Material Culture*. In N.K. Denzin and Y.S. Lincoln (eds) *Handbook of Qualitative Research* (pp. 393–402). London: Sage.

Honig, A.S. (2000) Promoting creativity in young children. Paper presented at the Annual Meeting of the Board of Advisors for Scholastic, Inc., New York.

Howard, J. and Major, J. (2005). Guidelines for Designing Effective English Language Teaching. Paper presented at the 9th Conference of the Pan-Pacific Association of Applied Linguistics, Tokyo.

Hutchinson, T. (1987) What's underneath? An interactive view of materials evaluation. In L. Sheldon (ed.) *ELT Textbooks and Materials: Problems in Evaluation and Development* (pp. 37–44). Oxford: Modern English Publications.

Hutchinson, T. and Torres, E. (1994) The textbook as agent of change. *ELT Journal* 48 (4), 315–328.

Hutchinson, T. and Waters, A. (1987) *English for Specific Purposes: A Learner-Centred Approach*. Cambridge: Cambridge University Press.

Islam, C. and Mares, C. (2003) Adapting classroom materials. In B. Tomlinson (ed.) *Developing Materials for Language Teaching* (pp. 86–100). London: Continuum.

Jolly, D. and Bolitho, R. (1998) A framework for materials writing. In B. Tomlinson (ed.) *Materials Development in Language Teaching* (pp. 90–115). Cambridge: Cambridge University Press.

Kader, S.A. (2008) Enhancing creative behavioural expressions in school systems: The need for educational reform and a centre for creativity. PhD Dissertation, Pennsylvania States University, USA.

Kohn, A. (1987) Art for art's sake. *Psychology Today* 21 (9), 52–58.

Maley, A. (1998) Squaring the circle – reconciling materials as constraint with materials as empowerment. In B. Tomlinson (ed.) *Materials Development in Language Teaching* (pp. 279–294). Cambridge: Cambridge University Press.

Mares, C. (2003) Writing a coursebook. In B. Tomlinson (ed.) *Developing Materials for Language Teaching* (pp. 130–140). London: Continuum.

Masuhara, H., Hann, N., Yi, Y. and Tomlinson, B. (2008) Adult EFL courses. *ELT Journal* 62 (3), 294–312.

McDonough, J. and Shaw, C. (1993) *Materials and Methods in ELT: A Teacher's Guide*. Oxford: Blackwell.

McGrath, I. (2002) *Materials Evaluation and Design for Language Teaching*. Edinburgh: Edinburgh University Press.

Molaei, R. and Abasi, M. (2014) Relationship between preschool on academic achievement and creativity of elementary students. *Advances in Environmental Biology* 8 (6), 1739–1744.

Murray, D.E. (2003) Materials for new technologies: Learning from research and practice. In W.A. Renandya (ed.) *Methodology and Materials Design in Language Teaching* (pp. 30–43). Singapore: SEAMEO Regional Language Centre.

O'Neill, R. (1982) Why use textbooks? *ELT Journal* 36 (2), 104–111.

Oxenden, C. and Latham-Koenig, C. (1999) *English File Intermediate Student's Book*. Oxford: Oxford University Press.

Piaget, J. (1954) *The Construction of Reality in the Child*. New York: Basic Books.

Pilbeam, A. (1987) Can published materials be widely used for ESP courses? In L. Sheldon (ed.) *ELT Textbooks and Materials: Problems in Evaluation and Development* (pp. 119–123). Oxford: Modern English Publications.

Powers, D.E. and Kaufman, J.C. (2004) Do standardized tests penalize deep-thinking, creative, or conscientious students? Some personality correlates of graduate record examination test scores. *Intelligence* 32 (2), 145–153.

Richards, J.C. (2001) *Curriculum Development in Language Teaching*. Melbourne: Cambridge University Press.

Robinson, K. (2011) *Out of Our Minds: Learning To Be Creative*. London: Capstone Publishing.

Saraceni, C. (2003) Adapting courses: A critical view. In B. Tomlinson (ed.) *Developing Materials for Language Teaching* (pp. 72–85). London: Continuum.

Shaheen, R. (2010) Creativity and education. *Creative Education* 1 (3), 166–169.

Sheldon, L. (1987) Introduction. In L. Sheldon (ed.) *ELT Textbooks and Materials: Problems in Evaluation and Development* (pp. 1–10). Oxford: Modern English Publications.

Sheldon, L. (1988) Evaluating ELT textbooks and materials. *ELT Journal* 42 (4), 237–246.

Spiro, R.J., Feltovich, M., Jacobson, J. and Coulson, R.L. (1991) Cognitive flexibility, constructivism, and hypertext: Random access instruction for advanced knowledge acquisition in ill-structured domains. *Educational Technology* 31 (5), 24–33.

Straits, W. and Wilke, R. (2007) How constructivist are we? Representations of transmission and participatory models of instruction in the *Journal of College Science Teaching*. *Journal of College Science Teaching* 36 (7), 58–61.

Tomlinson, B. (2001) Materials development. In R. Carter and D. Nunan (eds) *The Cambridge Guide to Teaching English to Speakers of Other Languages* (pp. 66–71). Cambridge: Cambridge University Press.

Tomlinson, B. (2003) Comments on Part A. In B. Tomlinson (ed.) *Developing Materials for Language Teaching* (pp. 101–103). London: Continuum.

Torrance, E.P. (2003) The millennium: A time for looking forward and looking back. *Journal of Secondary Gifted Education* 15 (1), 6–12.

Treffinger, D.J. (2000) *Creativity, Creative Thinking, and Critical Thinking: In Search of Definitions*. Ellisville, MO: Center for Creative Learning, Inc.

Vygotsky, L. (1978) *Mind in Society: The Development of Higher Psychological Processes*. Cambridge, MA: Harvard University Press.

Wanniarachchi, N. (2016) Using a constructivist approach to develop self-learning materials and promote learner engagement for out-of-school children in Sri Lanka. *Oasis. Commonwealth of Learning* online journal. Retrieved from http://oasis.col.org/handle/11599/2559.

Widdowson, H.G. (2000) Object language and the language subject: On the mediating role of applied linguistics. *Annual Review of Applied Linguistics* 20, 21–33.

Williams, D. (1983) Developing criteria for textbook evaluation. *ELT Journal* 37 (3), 251–255.

Wink, J. and Putney, L.G. (2002) *A Vision of Vygotsky*. Boston, MA: Allyn and Bacon.

Woods, P. (1990) *Teacher Skills and Strategies*. London: Falmer Press.

Yildirim, Z. (2005) Hypermedia as a cognitive tool: Student teachers' experiences in learning by doing. *Educational Technology and Society* 8 (2), 107–117.

5 Incorporating Creativity in Primary English Coursebooks

Dat Bao and Ranran Liu

This chapter discusses ways to instil creativity in coursebook tasks by proposing a set of principles for ELT course writers to employ as references. It is important, first of all, to clarify that we are not looking for ways to *measure* creativity. In fact, such efforts among scholars have failed, as have efforts to formally teach children how to become creative (see, for example, Chen *et al.*, 2006; Kim, 2011). Instead, we argue that one of the most natural and supportive ways to help children develop their innovative minds is to play with them. If English coursebooks allow the dynamics of play to enter into the learning process, they can be considered to have taken one step towards creativity. With this ideology in mind, the chapter provides a brief overview of the discourse related to children's creativity in education. Based on that foundation, it suggests a theoretical framework not only to help coursebook users evaluate the creative extent of a task but also to assist materials writers in making tasks more conducive to creative learning. The discussion then shares some examples of creative tasks taken from an English coursebook to demonstrate part of the aforementioned framework.

The Need to Nurture Children's Creativity

Children brought up in the digital age need not only to be equipped with the ability to cope with rapid advances of technology in society but also to develop a problem-solving mind from their early years. All areas of human knowledge are constantly changing. Because of this, it is hard for individuals to succeed in any field by holding on to a fixed body of knowledge without the competence to use it in innovative ways. Across many disciplines, evidence of human achievements and successes has been linked to one's creative capabilities (Powers & Kaufman, 2004).

Unfortunately, many classrooms are unable to provide conducive conditions to promote creative learners. Some schooling systems even cause damage to students' creative inclination. While creativity operates not only on individual and societal levels but also transfers its impact on a global level (de Bono, 1986; Kader, 2008; Torrance, 1962), there is dissatisfaction all over the world with the current educational limitations in responding to rapid global changes and challenges (Bertram, 2014; Shaheen, 2010).

In many cases, the decline in creativity among students comes with their gradual decrease in interest in reading. In Australia, for example, it is observed that many children love reading books until they get to fourth grade, when some start to complain that books are boring, a phenomenon known as literacy slump, which negatively affects children's creative growth (Darvishi & Pakdaman, 2012; Smith & Carlsson, 1983). Scholars have attempted to rationalise this situation. Some assume it is due to the education setting, especially when children internalise formal school experiences such as poor pedagogy, strict rules and fixed daily schedules. Others are concerned that creativity might not be well fostered in the home, where parents do not know how to cultivate the family's connection with the child's performance in school.

The Connections Between Creativity and Play

Creativity among children needs conditions to develop, one of which is the freedom to play. Play in education is conceptualised mainly through imagined experience, which can be fostered through simulation, role-play and make-believe situations in a safe, stress-free environment. Some concrete examples of these elements are acting in the role of animals, using props, toys and miming. When children share these experiences with peers in interactive contexts, reality from their inner world gets connected with various kinds of social and educational meaning.

Since children enjoy playing in whatever they learn, ELT materials need to construct a world that makes such participation possible. Some educators believe that play should be purposeful, that is, children must acquire something new. Others argue that play sometimes does not have to produce immediate learning benefit but can be voluntary, pleasurable involvement for its own sake (Burghardt, 2011). A balance of these views can be helpful. On the one hand, children need to feel that their learning environment brings pleasure,such that they want to be there. On the other hand, a set of pedagogical objectives can be incorporated into that process so that fun time can also be educationally rewarding.

Besides linguistic need, children must also develop psychologically, emotionally and socioculturally. ELT course writers might consider providing: sensory motor exercises whereby young learners repeat words in context to build memorisation and automaticity; freedom for children to perform symbolic actions for shared imagination; and a chance to imitate something they observe as a practice of creative efforts. Language tasks can allow children to use language in context (such as developing vocabulary about cooking), to adapt socially (such as imagining being parents) and to understand the many rules of the world (such as to avoid particular things or activities), and so on. These examples show that coursebooks can offer more than just teaching the language.

In addition to the above, there is a range of methods for materials writers to consider in constructing a play world for children to enjoy not only learning but also creative freedom. According cultural-historical theories, play can occur in a variety of forms: narratives, such as role-play, telling stores, dramatisation (Bredikyte, 2010); abstract meaning-making, such as imaginary situations (Vygotsky, 2004), expressing emotions according to situations, and giving new meaning to objects (Fleer, 2011); cultural expression, such as enacting one's social world (Göncü & Gaskin, 2011); child–adult collaboration, such as through discussion and role-play with the teacher (Lindqvist, 1995); I-image play, that is, taking on a new position different from who one is in reality, such as pretending to be an animal or a waiter in a restaurant (Kratsov & Kratsova, 2010); and modelling, that is, manual creation, such as drawing, painting, collage or making a mask (Davydov, 2008). It is essential for course developers to be well informed with such theoretical resources before outlining a set of materials that would support play and nurture creativity.

The Gap in Research on Children's Creativity

An overview of scholarly publications in education over the past six decades reveals three important insights related to creativity among children:

- first, there is undisputed agreement that nurturing creativity must begin at a young age for individuals to blossom into creative adults (Lowenfeld, 1987; Starko, 2010; Torrance, 1963);
- second, to serve the holistic development of individuals, creativity needs operate across many cognitive, affective, social and physical domains (Runco, 2004; Saracho, 2012; Saracho & Spodek, 1995);
- third, creativity plays a facilitating role in academic achievement (Bano et al., 2014; Chamorro-Premuzic, 2006; Hansenne & Legrand, 2012; Molaei & Abasi, 2014; Powers & Kaufman, 2004).

Decades of research into the influences of creativity on achievement in school-aged children have shown that creativity programmes across curricula produce a highly rewarding impact on students' outcomes. In Australia, for example, educational research has supported the conviction that, in literacy, the influence of creativity ranks second highest, after repeated reading and vocabulary programmes. In turn, an increase in educational achievements (a better-educated workforce) benefits any nation economically (Craft, 2005; Jeffrey, 2006).

Despite the discourse above, empirical studies pertaining to young children's creative development in formal early-learning settings remain fairly limited, as more attention is paid to teaching than learning. For example, research by Leggett (2015) investigated teachers' intentional strategies in helping young children with creative thought processes. A study by Liska (2013) introduced an innovative pedagogy with small steps that takes children through a process of acting as individuals, taking risks, making choices, feeling curious and becoming flexible. The limitation of many projects is that they hardly provide rich information regarding learners' responsive processes and do not show how creative thinking abilities develop in young children. Besides, the connection between creativity and learning quality has not been analysed in depth or been made explicit (Reed & Canning, 2012); and hardly any research actually follows up on children's performance long enough to document the evidence on the sustainability of outcomes.

In the meantime, there have been appeals for creativity to stretch beyond artistic skills (Craft, 1997, 2002; Saracho, 2012; Torrance, 1963). This is because the large majority of studies on children's creativity mainly have targeted the arts, dance and music education (Garvis & Pendergast, 2012; Garvis et al., 2011; Lambert, 2006; Niland, 2007; Nyland et al., 2013; Reynolds, 2002). While the arts undoubtedly provide opportunities for promoting creativity in young children, in many cases they mislead teachers to a focus on the judgement of the products and their creative yields (Saracho, 2012).

Although there is a need for creativity to spread across all disciplines and be integrated into the curriculum (Craft, 1997, 2002; Saracho, 2012), international research that connects curricular areas and creativity is scarce (Davies et al., 2013; Saracho, 2012). It is not known to what extent creativity is integrated and implemented as a whole-school curriculum. The question of how educators might support the progression of students' creative potential has not been satisfactorily answered (Beghetto & Kaufman, 2014). Studies have concentrated on the teacher and contexts of teaching (Chan & Yuen, 2012; Davies et al., 2013; Honig, 2000; Horng et al., 2005; Kader, 2008; Soydan & Erbay, 2013; Woods, 1990) and hardly any investigation has been done of learners' responsiveness to pedagogy and the role of materials development in promoting creativity. Besides, although extensive studies have reported on teacher–child interactions through broad interactional domains (Mashburn et al., 2008; Pianta et al., 2008), few have examined the relationship between interaction and creativity (Saracho, 2003, 2012).

Some Considerations for Creative Task Design

It seems unrealistic to find creativity principles that apply to all contexts, subjects and disciplines. Every particular subject area needs a set of exclusive strategies oriented towards that particular subject, and a helpful curriculum should consider supporting such practice (see, for example, Blamires & Peterson, 2014). By the same token, ELT materials for young learners need to specify conditions for children's imagination and creativity to grow in relation to both their linguistic and their social skills. If creativity is not cultivated in young children, the opportunity may be lost as children get older. Creative potential might be suppressed by a society that encourages intellectual conformity and by the influence by curriculum accountability in many schools.

It is uncommon to find ELT discourse that examines ways of connecting children's creativity with second language learning. This is true of a wide range of academic books devoted primarily to children's L1 and L2 education theories, such as the works of Moon (2005), Pinter (2011), Rixon (1999) and Kirsch (2008). A notable exception is a recent book by Copping (2016) that deals with creative case studies. While many scholars highlight the need to nurture children's creativity, few principles and approaches are offered to provide such support. In the meantime, the discourse related to teacher training mentions a number of qualities that enable someone to effectively teach English to children. The qualities include knowledge of children's holistic development, cultural understanding, age-appropriate pedagogy, scaffolding skills and effective communication (Moon, 2005) without much discussion on teacher strategies to bring out children's creative potential.

Based on a combination of the literature on children's creativity and some insights into L2 learning among children, we would like to recommend the following five conditions that task designers might need to consider as elements to promote children's creative learning.

Activate rich imagination

Children with good imagination have more inner space than others. They tend to be resourceful, observant, adaptable and capable of coping with challenging situations. Coursebook tasks need to inspire in children the passion to see the world through their own lenses. An example of such a task would be one that invites learners to invent or complete a story, which allows imagination as connected with the child's experience and personality (see, for example, Wood, 2016). Besides, tasks should activate learners' intrinsic motivation, so that children want to engage with an activity, out of interest, enjoyment and willingness to take on the challenge. Amabile (1996) believes that children vary in how they develop creative behaviour. Some are born with a creative disposition while others depend more on learning experience and interaction with the social environment. Because of these differences, some learners might need more stimulus than others.

Create the desire for sharing

As children have different dispositions, preferences and behavioural styles, their responses to events can be highly diverse. Possibility thinking is fundamental to creativity (Craft, 2002), which can be manifested through both self-creation and self-expression. When being encouraged to find their way around a problem, children are likely to activate their resourcefulness in determining what their options are. Once a child produces an exciting idea or a lovable item, he or she might wish to make it known to peers. Csikszentmihalyi (2013) contends that creativity does not happen inside one's head, but through interactions between a person's mind and the sociocultural context. Course materials need to build the social space for such interaction to happen and tap into individuals' original efforts.

In addition, activities can be designed in ways that allow teachers to interact positively with children. As Saracho (2012) indicates, creative thinking, which is connected to enquiry and problem solving, should be encouraged through teacher support. Classroom interaction can either nurture or repress creative development (Runco, 1990; Torrance, 1962, 1965). For example, negative verbal interactions can make young children feel inadequate, confused and frustrated (Clark, 2008; Torrance, 1963, 1965). Conversely, children feel capable, enlightened and encouraged when verbal interactions are positive (Rusch et al., 1965, 1967). According to Nikolov (1999), it is important that during their early years of L2 learning, children like their teacher, as this means they will be more likely to enjoy learning the language and willing to participate in classroom activities.

Combine thinking with feeling

Many educators and theorists conceive creativity as a cognitive and socio-affective process (Carlo, 2009; Cohen, 2011; Feldhusen, 2001; Guilford, 1984; Isenberg & Jalongo, 2014; Russ, 2011; Sternberg, 2006). They believe that creativity encompasses both rational and emotional dimensions. The rational dimension refers to creativity as thinking practice, such as to guess or pursue an idea; to come up with relevant ideas around issue; to seek unusual or clever alternatives; to combine things into a novel form. The emotional dimension internalises creativity as a feeling process, which includes curiosity about a topic, manifested in wondering and asking questions; a tendency to play with ideas and follow intuition to see what happens; the courage to expose oneself; and a willingness to share ideas with others, as well as to take risks or accept challenges. Some of the above elements have been widely discussed in the discourse which contends that creativity involves divergent thinking (Guilford, 1959), self-determination (Amabile, 1996; Burnard et al., 2006; Torrance, 1977), curiosity (Craft, 2005; Sternberg, 2006), imagination (Craft, 2008; Vygotsky, 1930), flexibility (Claxton et al., 2006; Craft, 2008), risk-taking

(Amabile, 1996; Cohen, 2011; Craft, 2008), immersion (Claxton *et al.*, 2006; Craft, 2008), innovation (Craft, 2008) and collaboration (Lucas *et al.*, 2013).

Evoke a risk-taking, playful nature

Being playful refers to the inclination to be humorous, the desire to give an unusual response and the willingness to accept risk or ambiguity. The unprejudiced tendency to explore the world is in the nature of many children, and when such behaviour occurs an extensive range of alternatives might result. Divergent thinking is a process well recognised in young children in particular (Albert & Runco, 1988; Baer & Kaufman, 2005; Isenberg & Jalongo, 2001; Runco, 2003; Runco *et al.*, 2010; Sarocho, 2012; Torrance, 1977, 1981; Zachopoulou *et al.*, 2009). Rich thinking proves to be active across different types of play which stimulate young children's creativity (Saracho, 2012). Materials need to allow alternatives to occur through open-ended, problem-solving and imaginative resources (e.g. puzzles, play-dough, blocks, sand) that can be employed in multiple ways. Of course, divergent thinking alone is not equal to creativity, simply because divergence does not capture the entire description of creativity (Treffinger *et al.*, 1971); instead, such thinking needs to interact with a range of other factors, some of which have been mentioned in this chapter.

Bring out individual personality

Children's creativity is often demonstrated in an original, unplanned and self-expressive manner (Saracho & Spodek, 2013; Torrance, 1963). A number of features make children's L2 learning processes quite distinctive from adults' L2 learning. For example, children's concentration tends to be shorter than adults'; young learners easily lose interest in activities that are predictable (Clark, 1990); children tend to focus more on meaning than form (Moon, 2005); they resist formal teaching and prefer to learn experientially and acquire language incidentally.

It is important to note the above inclinations among young children in order to provide age-appropriate support. Sometimes, to encourage young learners' expressive disposition, educators might like to focus more on the creative process itself rather than worry about the excellence of their creations (Saracho, 2012). Children may not yet have the expertise and skills to ensure high quality in the output (Craft, 2003; Tegano *et al.*, 1991). It is also necessary to realise that the creative ability of each child is linked to his/her stage of development (Malaguzzi, 1994) and is unique to that child in relation to others in the same class or age group (Runco, 2014). Besides, the knowledge and skills that children employ for their creative expression are not confined to second language learning but may be transferred from their first language and culture (Cummins, 2000).

A Framework for Incorporating Creativity in Tasks

Table 5.1 opposite presents a list of questions, processed from the principles discussed above, which can serve as an instrument for course writers to consider for supporting creative activities. These criteria can also be used to detect the innovative nature of second language tasks, that is, to recognise the extent to which a task brings out learners' creative potential. Concrete examples are provided to clarify what each question means. In recommending these dimensions of creative effort, we do not mean to divide and place creativity into convenient compartments. Instead, these features of creativity are likely to be overlapping.

Examples of Creative Tasks from an English Coursebook

This section presents a number of samples to show how creative tasks reflect some of the criteria proposed in Table 5.1. The tasks are taken from a coursebook entitled *Success with English*, which was the main text for primary schools in Guangzhou City and much of Guangdong Province in China between 2003 and 2006. The material contributed to the English education reform in China in recent decades, which aimed to make English teaching and learning more communicative, contextualised, inspiring and connected to learner needs.

Success with English by Guangzhou Education Bureau (2003–2006) was first published in 2003 in Beijing. Each year, a volume might be reprinted to meet the need from student numbers in that year. Because of this, please note that in this chapter sometimes the year of reprint will be mentioned in the citation instead of the original year of publication. *Success with English* is based on the national English curriculum standard set by China's Ministry of Education in consideration of continuity with the middle-school English curriculum. The title comprises eight volumes, ranging from grade 3 to grade 6. Each grade covers two volumes and each volume covers one semester of teaching and learning. The set comes with a *Teachers' Manual* for pedagogical support and additional resources such as instructions, listening texts, flash cards, videos and so on. The coursebook was developed by a team of writers from Leeds Metropolitan University (LMU) in the UK, working together with Guangzhou Education Bureau in China. The LMU team included Brian Tomlinson, Hitomi Masuhara, Carlos Islam, Heather Buchanan and Dat Bao; and the Guangzhou team involved Zonggan Lu, Zicheng Huang, Liyan Huang, Shuhong Zhao and Guoling Cao (鲁宗干, 黄子成, 黄丽燕, 赵淑红, 曹国玲). The project was based on empirical research by the LMU team, who collected data on local teachers' perceptions and local students' interest. Participants were from a number of primary schools in Guangzhou City.

Promoting creativity in children's learning is part of the ideology of the coursebook in response to the reform. The national Ministry of Education in China created an education reform policy known as *Jian Fu*

Table 5.1 A framework for creativity

Criteria for creative activities	Examples of activities
Imagination	
1. Do tasks stimulate learners' observation and adaptive responses?	Choosing what to wear for different types of party; painting with unconventional tools (i.e. not a brush)
2. Do learners have a chance to visualise something hidden, or incomplete, or non-existent?	Seeing through a closed door; imagining a missing part; walking through a jungle
3. Do tasks encourage multiple ways of seeing?	Reinventing a new function for object items; noticing something one never saw before; drawing a green sky and blue grass
4. Is there a chance to tie objects or events together in an uncommon way?	Imagining how the wind makes friends with a tree; building a character with peculiar features
Social sharing	
5. Do tasks build a social space for children to enjoy interaction?	Making up a story together
6. Are learners asked to brainstorm ideas?	In groups, guessing what happens next
7. Can learners share personal thoughts?	Making new rules for classroom conduct
8. Are learners encouraged to be resourceful?	Finding ways to save a cat that fell into a pond
Thinking/feeling	
9. Do tasks arouse learners' curiosity as well as pursue it?	Guessing, asking, observing, finding, comparing, describing, explaining, drawing, etc.
10. Are there stories for learners to say what they think and how they feel?	Expressing ideas and feelings about characters, events and problems
11. Do activities allow learners to explore a range of emotions?	Helping or comforting a less fortunate person; reading to children and asking them to share feelings
12. Are learners invited to take risks and challenges?	Discussing how to build a tree house or how to wash a gorilla
Playful	
13. Do tasks make learners sometimes laugh? Do they encourage learners to become flexible thinkers? Do they tease out learners' unusual responses?	Removing constraints from reality; changing the proportions of things; pretending one can fly; giving human features to animals
14. Do tasks collect new ways of seeing, acting and saying things?	Becoming someone else or slipping into the role of non-humans; making characters out of sticks and leaves; giving new names or new functions to items
15. Do tasks allow for different types of play?	Miming, decorating a cake, travelling through space, singing a song, finding as surprise gift for a close friend
16. Do tasks meet learning purposes through clever, unusual content or structures or sequences?	Showing an alien around; shuffling words to make up new texts; answering questions before reading the story
Self-expression/personality	
17. Do tasks respect learners' differences by allowing choices and preferences?	Designing a dream bedroom; making a floor-plan of one's favourite school
18. Is there a chance for self-expression or personality-based responses?	Creating a new dish; designing an ideal television programme
19. Do tasks sometimes focus on the creative process itself rather than judgement of the outcome?	Drawing an alien; designing a robot; collectively developing a cute monster
20. Are tasks suited to the child's own stage of development (without too much emphasis on adults' judgement and social knowledge)?	Designing a bird nest, creating a bird family, making paper planes, miming an animal's walk

('to reduce the burden'), whereby primary- and secondary-school students are given more time and less work in the study schedule so that they can utilise more space for practising creativity (Woronov, 2008). The pressure of formal learning was reduced dramatically by removing examinations and extracurricular activities. The whole idea of this reform is for students to become more socially engaged and to develop innovative skills.

Curriculum reform with a focus on creativity, in fact, has been in progress across the globe for several decades (Shaheen, 2010). For example, in the UK, the National Advisory Committee on Creative and Cultural Education (1999) has outlined a core role for creativity in learning and pedagogy and the School Curriculum and Assessment Authority (1997) has identified creative development as a desirable early-years learning outcome. In Australia, the education system emphasises that in the new work order, young generations need excellent operational skills, including digital literacy, critical thinking, creativity, flexibility and the ability to collaborate in coping with a radically altered economy. Many education reformers highlight the need for a reassuring environment that allows errors in a non-judgemental atmosphere to stimulate creativity. One example of that would be a model of 'possibility thinking', which comprises four features, namely posing questions, play, immersion and making connections (Cremin et al., 2006). Despite all this, empirical research has revealed a decline in students' creativity. Although IQ scores among students have risen for the last 20 years, creative thinking scores have decreased significantly in many parts of the world since 1990. This is most significant between kindergarten and grade 3 (Kim, 2011). Among the reasons for this are standardised testing (Lingard, 2010; Sawyer et al., 2003), the rigidities of learning schedules and the nature of classroom activities (Robinson, 2011). Because of this, it is essential to incorporate elements of creativity in course materials, especially at the earlier stages of learners' development, wherever possible.

This section presents five types of task, each of which facilitates one main dimension of the child's creative mind. The first task type explores play in kinesthetic, social and emotional responses. The second type supports effort towards innovative design. The third set of tasks activates imagination to optimise both linguistic development and content creativity. The fourth type inspires learning through creative contextualisation and the last stimulates personal responses.

Kinaesthetic and personal responses

A number of activities in the book ask students to mime animal behaviour or imitate actions of characters in films or plays. In participating in these tasks, learners share rich imagination, act silly, use the target language, explore new experiences and enjoy a chance to laugh. Such tasks play with learners' imagination, choice, imitation and dramatisation.

Figure 5.1 Miming animal walk (p. 18, Vol. 2 of *Success with English*, Guangzhou Education Bureau, 2005b)

Figure 5.2 Making animal masks (p. 27, Vol. 2 of *Success with English*, Guangzhou Education Bureau, 2005b)

They activate linguistic, emotional and kinaesthetic domains in children's learning repertoire (see, for example, p. 18 and p. 27, Vol. 2; p. 48, Vol. 4; p. 62, Vol. 4).

In the examples here, learners are asked to pretend they are animals by miming (Figure 5.1) and wearing animal masks (Figure 5.2). This type of activity is known as creative drama (Heinig, 1981), a form of process-centred enactment which enables children to take risks, explore new experiences and express themselves. Research has shown that creative drama facilitates spontaneity, improvisation and social awareness (Heinig, 1981) and assists creative thinking among children (Karioth, 1967; Prokes, 1971).

Supporting innovative effort through design

Learners are exposed to a wide range of creative thinking not only through reading about items and being involved in verbal discussion but

Figure 5.3 Designing a puppet (p. 48, Vol. 1, *Success with English*, Guangzhou Education Bureau, 2005a)

also by manually doing things by themselves. For example, many activities involve students drawing their own uniforms, handkerchiefs and birthday cakes as well as hand-making stamps and models of their bedroom. Such tasks offer children a chance to play and use language to talk about what they are creating but are also connected to an educational purpose, such as nature conservation. In unit 12 in Vol. 2 for grade 6, learners are asked to design a cover of a story book, write an imagined title for the book on it and develop a few words about the story. In unit 15 of Vol. 1 for grade 5, learners are asked to design a poster and write a sentence based on a target structure using 'Don't do something'. To assist this process, the task provides three example three posters, each of which depicts an animal, namely a tiger, a panda and a buffalo, which all exclaim: 'Don't kill us'.

Activities that tap into learners' creativity are spread out through the eight volumes in a fairly consistent manner. Learners are asked to reinvent various everyday items in their own personalised way. They include making uniforms (p. 89, Vol. 1); puppets (p. 48, Vol. 1; Figure 5.3); handkerchiefs (p. 48, Vol. 1); stamps (p. 41, Vol. 2, p. 34, Vol. 2); the floor-plan of a school (p. 83, Vol. 2; Figure 5.5); the floor-plan of their home (p. 69, Vol. 2); a model of their bedroom (p. 55, Vol. 2; Figure 5.4); a mask depicting their favourite animal (p. 27, Vol. 2); birthday cakes (p. 11, Vol. 4); gardens (p. 39, Vol. 4); tickets (p. 55, Vol. 4); posters (p. 69, Vol. 5, p. 41, Vol. 7, p. 41, Vol. 8); maps (p. 76, Vol. 4); fruit baskets (p. 20, Vol. 6); invitation cards (p. 38, Vol. 7); Christmas cards (p. 76, Vol. 7); questionnaires (p. 81, Vol. 7); a picture made from leaves and flowers (p. 27, Vol. 8); and creative stories (p. 53, Vol. 8).

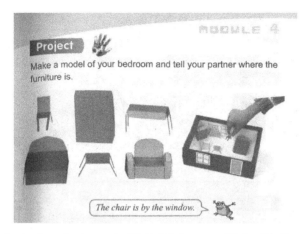

Figure 5.4 Designing a bedroom (p. 55, Vol. 2, *Success with English*, Guangzhou Education Bureau, 2005b)

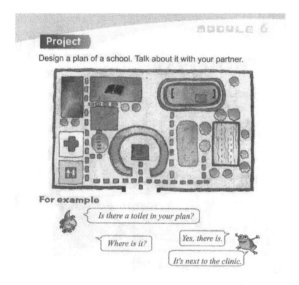

Figure 5.5 Designing a school (p. 83, Vol. 2, *Success with English*, Guangzhou Education Bureau, 2005b)

Using imagination to create new content

One way to inspire learner creativity is to provide opportunities for personalising output, whereby learners share their own thinking, experiences and imagination, without being judged as right or wrong. Telling one's own story is a helpful way not only to personalise learning but also to enhance confidence in using vocabulary, practising pronunciation, communicating ideas and improving fluency (Heathfield, 2015; Sciamarelli,

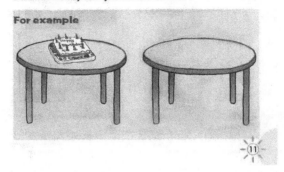

Figure 5.6 Drawing a birthday cake (p. 11, Vol. 2 *Success with English*, Guangzhou Education Bureau, 2005b)

Figure 5.7 Robot story (p. 40, Vol. 3 *Success with English*, Guangzhou Education Bureau, 2006a)

Figure 5.8 A strange dream (p. 67, Vol. 8 *Success with English*, Guangzhou Education Bureau, 2006c)

2015). A number of activities in the coursebook encourage children to talk about their own families, experiences and things they love. For example, unit 15 of Vol. 2 asks learners to draw a picture about their favourite meal, to include the colour and shape of the food as well as different ingredients.

In a number of tasks, learners are invited to utilise their own imagination to invent or reinvent a story, a dialogue or a drawing. In most cases, learners are both inspired and supported to perform the task. They are provided with a stimulus, such as a picture, a song or a story. These stimuli set the tone for the learners' creative effort, model how the activity works and construct language through guided narrative or description. One occasional method used in these sections is to ask for groups of learners to co-construct a plot. According to Hadfield and Hadfield (2015), guiding questions can be provided to help the students exploit the stimulus.

Based on such processes, learners are asked to create a new story or to write the second half of an ongoing story by drawing pictures (p. 50, Vol. 3). They are also invited to complete an ongoing dialogue or make a new dialogue (p.5 9, Vol. 3; p. 53, p. 77, p. 87, p. 89, Vol. 4; p. 36, Vol. 7). Unit 15, Vol. 2, for grade 5, introduces vocabulary on the topic of home and has learners sketch a plan of their home to describe it to peers. This activity encourages students to create their own model of home and practice English words at the same time. Similar activities are also found elsewhere in the coursebook in which learners draw and share ideas with the class (p. 34, p. 69, p. 81, Vol. 6; p. 20, Vol. 8). Specific examples ask learners to draw a cake (Figure 5.6), complete a story (Figure 5.7) and personalise their response to a scenario (Figure 5.8).

In the robot story below (Figure 5.7), learners are given a story to read. Comprehension is then stimulated through engagement and visualisation. Children are provided with the background of the main character, in this case a robot, through illustrations and are encouraged to talk about the robot in their own way. The subsequent activity (Figure 5.8) follows the same concept as the robot story but also offers the element of choice. With the provided input (which is the plot in Figure 5.7 and characters in Figure 5.8), learners then create an image of what happens next. Not only does the task encourage children to find out things for themselves but it also allows them to make things happen. Such combination between contextualised comprehension and spontaneous visualisation is well supported in the literature as a way to support creative engagement with reading among children (see, for example, Copping, 2016; Cowley, 2005).

Creative contextualisation

The activity shown in Figure 5.9 is a variation on two of the scenarios discussed above, whereby the input is not long a text or a set of characters, but is a fictional scenario only in pictures. Learners this time use their observation and imagination to talk about what they see, and then role-play what they think the aliens are saying. The alien character is a creative idea of the course writers to provide context and even excitement. Several aliens come into the coursebook. They do not simply appear at one time but actually live through part of the book to socialise with children, have conversations, learn new hobbies and observe life on earth.

The alien acts as a stimulus for learners to live through imagination. Seeing things through the eyes of aliens, children learn to ask about object items and express emotions such as curiosity, amusement and surprise. They also exchange information for a reason. One anecdote involves learning names of vehicles, including a car, a bicycle, a motorbike, a bus and a spaceship. In another incident, a group of humans who spotted an alien getting off a spaceship discuss how he looked. The alien then joins a conversation with Billy's family about clothing. Other units contain more

Figure 5.9 Aliens play (p. 21, Vol. 4 of *Success with English*, Guangzhou Education Bureau, 2006b)

episodes, such as a boy sharing a photo album with an alien and introducing places of interest. They also discuss food and time of day. At some point, learners are asked to continue the story, imagining they meet an alien and have to teach him or her about the human world.

In many coursebooks, the topic of everyday habits are presented as routine and are humdrum, simply because learners are not helped to see any exciting reason for talking about ordinary life. In *Success with English*, however, the presence of alien friends makes everyday topics amusing. As evident in Figure 5.9, aliens learn to perform activities with humans and also show humans the similar and dissimilar things the aliens do, which includes competing in games, playing musical instruments, fishing and painting. In the end, learners have a chance to design their own stories which depict how Aki, an alien character, learns about things on earth that are new to him.

Stimulating personal responses

It is important to trust children's ability to learn and figure out things for themselves, and then to find the space for that to happen. McConaghy (1990) believes that children have the inclination to explore, initiate events, solve problems and express viewpoints through play. Such abilities in young learners need to be encouraged rather than doubted. The tasks presented here create the conditions for some of those capabilities to occur. The activity shown in Figure 5.10 presents a scenario in which a cat gets stranded on a rooftop and encourages learners to come up with a way to save the poor animal. Learners interact in groups to come up with a solution, which they then depict in the form of visuals and share with the class. In this way, learning is co-constructed through imagination, divergent thinking and personalised knowledge. It is acknowledged that children enjoy observing and making sense of the world around them (Kenner, 2000; Kirsch, 2008) and that they tend to remember things better if they learn them through creative, interactive and active engagement (Clipson-Boyles, 2012; Desailly, 2012). In other examples, learners are invited to personalise the learning process by expressing how they would participate in a festival (Figure 5.11), what would be an ideal television programme (Figure 5.12), and how to draw images by comparing details (Figure 5.13).

Figure 5.10 Saving a cat (pp. 49–50, Vol. 3 of *Success with English*, Guangzhou Education Bureau, 2006a)

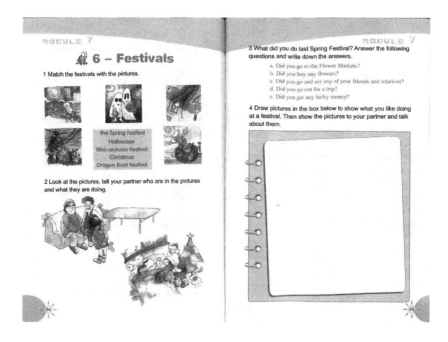

Figure 5.11 Halloween (pp. 94–95, Vol. 6 of *Success with English*, Guangzhou Education Bureau, 2005c)

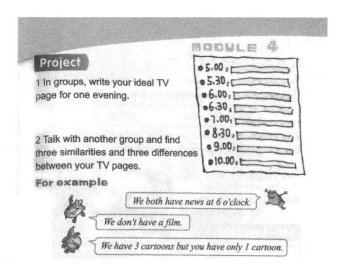

Figure 5.12 Ideal television programme (p. 55, Vol. 4 of *Success with English*, Guangzhou Education Bureau, 2006b)

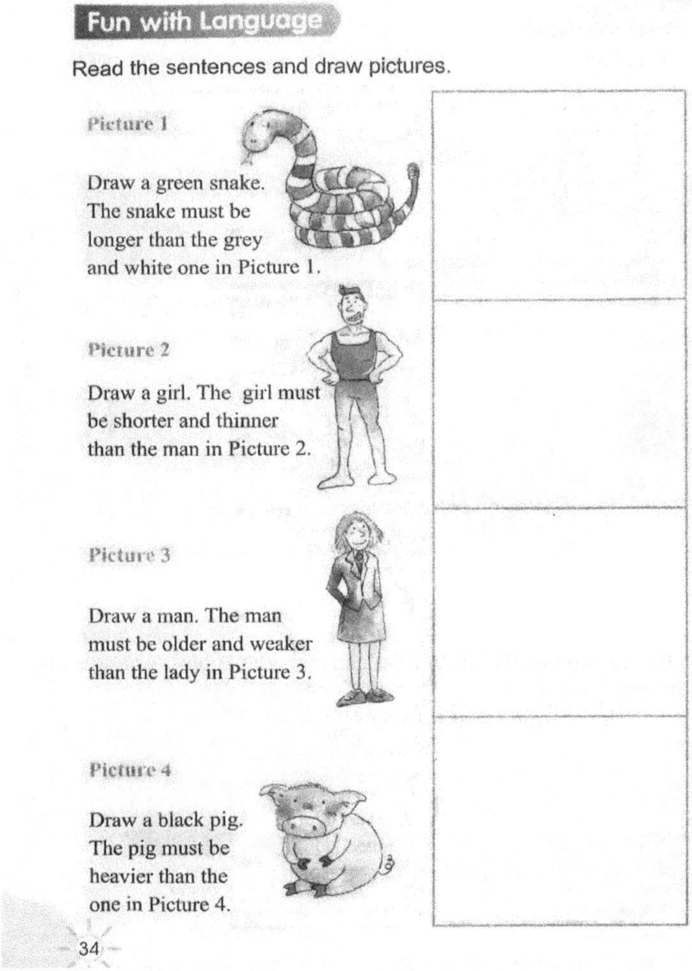

Fun with Language

Read the sentences and draw pictures.

Picture 1

Draw a green snake.
The snake must be
longer than the grey
and white one in Picture 1.

Picture 2

Draw a girl. The girl must
be shorter and thinner
than the man in Picture 2.

Picture 3

Draw a man. The man
must be older and weaker
than the lady in Picture 3.

Picture 4

Draw a black pig.
The pig must be
heavier than the
one in Picture 4.

34

Figure 5.13 Drawing through observation (p. 34, Vol. 3 of *Success with English*, Guangzhou Education Bureau, 2006a)

Conclusion

In a study by Fredriksson and Olsson (2006), an English teacher being interviewed believes that she might not need to use the coursebook much if her class is a very creative one. This comment seems to suggest that materials and the learning process may be two mutually independent entities: regardless whether the coursebook is a mundane or creative one, a creative class will go on being creative anyway. Although the scenario may be true in some cases, this perception downplays the value of course materials. What if the class is an uncreative one and the coursebook is boring? This combination might make it hard for the lesson to become exciting. What if the class is a not creative one but the coursebook contains a range of creativity-facilitating activities? Perhaps there is more chance for learners to become motivated and learn better. Arguably, it might be helpful to provide inspiring resources, which means that course writers still need to play an active role in nurturing children's creative learning.

Fostering creativity is important in helping learners achieve the affective and cognitive engagement vital for language acquisition (Tomlinson, 2015). Coursebooks should fulfil their role as a stimulus for communication rather than simply as an organisational tool for the teacher (Garinger, 2002). ELT materials play a role in stimulating learners' interest, developing creativity and supporting interactive learning (Fenner & Newby, 2000). Both course writers and learners can share the same space as co-creative storytellers, so that creative thinking can arise from the emotional quality of mutual engagement. Such collaboration will build the flow of creativity that enhances both motivation and learning outcomes (Csikszentmihalyi, 1996; Read, 2015).

Creativity does not work as an independent construct but needs to be combined with our knowledge of how children acquire language. For example, besides freedom, stimulus and a flexible space for creativity, understanding individual learners' personal styles and abilities is another important endeavour to keep in mind. This is because each child would require a specific kind of attention. Some children prefer to watch and learn, while others are more willing to be involved in hands-on experiment; some prefer to speak for themselves, while others enjoy participating in group responses. There are also children who to tend maintain complete silence until they feel comfortable with their surroundings (Ashworth & Wakefield, 1994). Other factors to be taken into consideration to assist second language acquisition among children include imaginary play, love and attention, praise and encouragement (Ashworth & Wakefield, 1994), simplified language input, the opportunity to name things, as well as positive peer socialisation and collaboration (Pinter, 2011). Such knowledge and understanding are fundamental to children's language development and need to be considered together with the elements of creative task design discussed in this chapter.

References

Albert, R.S. and Runco, M.A. (1988) Independence and the creative potential of gifted and exceptionally gifted boys. *Journal of Youth and Adolescence* 18 (3), 221–230.

Amabile, T. (1996) *Creativity in Context: Update to 'The Social Psychology of Creativity'*. Boulder, CO: Westview Press.

Ashworth, M. and Wakefield, H.P. (1994) *Teaching the World's Children: ESL for Ages Three to Seven*. Markham: Pippin Publishing Corporation.

Baer, J. and Kaufman, J.C. (2005) Theoretical and interdisciplinary perspectives. Bridging generality and specificity: The Amusement Park Theoretical (APT) model of creativity. *Roeper Review* 27 (3), 158–164.

Bano, A., Naseer, N. and Zainab (2014) Creativity and academic performance of primary school children. *Pakistan Journal of Social Sciences* 34 (2), 597–606.

Beghetto, R.A. and Kaufman, J.C. (2014) Classroom contexts for creativity. *High Ability Studies* 25 (1), 53–69.

Bertram, V. (2014) We have to get serious about creativity and problem solving. *Huffington Post* (US edn), 7 July. Retrieved from http://www.huffingtonpost.com.

Blamires, M. and Peterson, A. (2014) Can creativity be assessed? Towards an evidence-informed framework for assessing and planning progress in creativity. *Cambridge Journal of Education* 44 (2), 147–162.

Bredikyte, M. (2010) Psychological tools and the development of play. *Cultural–Historical Psychology* 4, 11–18.

Burghardt, G.M. (2011) Defining and recognizing play. In A.D. Pellegrini (ed.) *The Oxford Handbook of Development of Play* (pp. 9–18). Oxford: Oxford University Press.

Burnard, P., Craft, A., Cremin, T., Duffy, B., Hanson, R., Keene, J., Haynes, L. and Burns, D. (2006) Document 'possibility thinking': A journey of collaborative enquiry. *International Journal of Early Years Education* 14 (3), 243–262.

Carlo, M. (2009) Explaining the creative mind. *International Journal of Research and Review* 3, 10–19.

Chamorro-Premuzic, T. (2006) Creativity versus conscientiousness: Which is a better predictor of student performance? *Applied Cognitive Psychology* 20 (4), 521–531.

Chan, S. and Yuen, M. (2015) Teachers' beliefs and practices for nurturing creativity in students: Perspectives from teachers of gifted students in Hong Kong. *Gifted Education International* 31 (3), 200–213.

Chen, C., Himsel, A., Kasof, J., Greenberger, E. and Dmitrieva, J. (2006) Boundless creativity: Evidence for the domain generality of individual differences in creativity. *Journal of Creative Behaviour*, 40(3), 179–199.

Clark, B. (2008) *Growing-up Gifted: Developing the Potential of Children at Home and at School* (7th edn). Columbus, OH: Merill.

Clark, J. (1990) Teaching children: Is it different. *JET* 1 (1), 6–7.

Claxton, G., Edwards, L. and Scale-Constantinou, V. (2006) Cultivating creative mentalities: A framework for education. *Thinking Skills and Creativity* 1 (1), 57–61.

Clipson-Boyles, S. (2013) *Teaching Primary English Through Drama: A Practical and Creative Approach*. New York: Routledge.

Cohen, A.J. (2011) Creativity in singing: Universality and sensitive developmental periods? In D.M. Hargreaves and R. Macdonald (eds) *Musical Imaginations: Multidisciplinary Perspectives on Creativity, Performance and Perception* (pp. 173–188). New York: Oxford University Press.

Copping, A. (2016) *Being Creative in Primary English*. London: Sage.

Cowley, S. (2005) *Letting the Buggers Be Creative*. London: Continuum.

Craft, A. (1997) *Can You Teach Creativity?* Nottingham: Education Now Publishing Co-operative.

Craft, A. (2002) *Creativity and Early Years Education: A Lifewide Foundation*. London: Continuum.

Craft, A. (2003) Creative thinking in the early years education. *Early Years* 23 (2), 143–154.

Craft, A. (2005) *Creativity in Schools: Tensions and Dilemmas*. New York: Routledge.

Craft, A. (2008) Creativity. In *The Routledge International Encyclopaedia of Education* (pp. 138–139). New York: Routledge.

Cremin, T., Burnard, P. and Craft, A. (2006) Pedagogy and possibility thinking in the early years. *Thinking Skills and Creativity* 1 (2), 108–119.

Csikszentmihalyi, M. (1996) *Creativity: Flow and the Psychology of Discovery and Invention*. London: Harper Collins.

Csikszentmihalyi, M. (2013) *Creativity: The Psychology of Discovery and Invention*. New York: Harper Perennial Modern Classics.

Cummins, J. (2000) *Language, Power and Pedagogy: Bilingual Children in the Crossfire*. Clevedon: Multilingual Matters.

Darvishi, Z. and Pakdaman, S. (2012) 'Fourth grade slump in creativity': Development of creativity in primary school children. *GSTF Journal of Law and Social Sciences* 1 (2), 40–48.

Davies, D., Jindal-Snape, D., Collier, C., Digby, R., Hay, P. and Howe, A. (2013) Creative learning environments in education – a systematic literature review. *Thinking Skills and Creativity* 8, 80–91.

Davydov, V.V. (2008) *Problems of Developmental Instruction: A Theoretical and Experimental Psychological Study*. New York: Nova Science.

De Bono, E. (1986) *Six Thinking Hats*. New York: Viking.

Desailly, J. (2012) *Creativity in the Primary Classroom*. London: Sage.

Feldhusen, J.F. (2001) Multiple options as a model for teaching the creatively gifted child. In M.D. Lynch and C.R. Harris (eds) *Fostering Creativity in Children, K-8* (pp. 3–13). Needham Heights, MA: Allyn and Bacon.

Fenner, A.B. and Newby, D. (2000) *Approaches to Materials Design in European Textbooks: Implementing Principles of Authenticity, Learner Autonomy, Cultural Awareness*. Strasbourg: Council of Europe.

Fleer, M. (2011) Conceptual play: Foregrounding imagination and cognition during concept formation in early years' education. *Contemporary Issues in Early Childhood* 12 (3), 224–240.

Fredriksson, C. and Olsson, R. (2006) English textbook evaluation. An investigation into criteria for selecting English textbooks. MA dissertation, Malmö högskola, Sweden.

Garinger, D. (2002) Textbook selection for the ESL classroom. Retrieved from https://scholar.google.com.au/scholar?hl=en&q=Textbook+selection+for+the+ESL+classroom&btnG=&as_sdt=1%2C5&as_sdtp=.

Garvis, S. and Pendergast, D. (2012) Storying music and the arts education: The generalist teacher voice. *British Journal of Music Education* 29 (1), 107–123.

Garvis, S., Twigg, D. and Pendergast, D. (2011) Breaking the negative cycle: The formation of self-efficacy beliefs in the arts. A focus professional experience in pre-service teacher education. *Australasian Journal of Early Childhood* 36 (2), 36–41.

Göncü, A. and Gaskins, S. (2011) Comparing and extending Piaget's and Vygotsky's understandings of play: Symbolic play as individual, sociocultural, and educational interpretation. In A.D. Pellegrini (ed.) *The Oxford Handbook of the Development of Play* (pp. 48–57). Oxford: Oxford University Press.

Guangzhou Education Bureau (2004) *Success with English (Volume 5)*. Beijing: Life, Reading, New Knowledge Joint Publishing Co. (生活 读书 新知 三联出版社).

Guangzhou Education Bureau (2005a) *Success with English (Volume 1)*. Beijing: Life, Reading, New Knowledge Joint Publishing Co. (生活 读书 新知 三联出版社).

Guangzhou Education Bureau (2005b) *Success with English (Volume 2)*. Beijing: Life, Reading, New Knowledge Joint Publishing Co. (生活 读书 新知 三联出版社).

Guangzhou Education Bureau (2005c) *Success with English (Volume 6)*. Beijing: Life, Reading, New Knowledge Joint Publishing Co. (生活 读书 新知 三联出版社).

Guangzhou Education Bureau (2005d) *Success with English (Volume 7)*. Beijing: Life, Reading, New Knowledge Joint Publishing Co. (生活 读书 新知 三联出版社).

Guangzhou Education Bureau (2006a) *Success with English (Volume 3)*. Beijing: Life, Reading, New Knowledge Joint Publishing Co. (生活 读书 新知 三联出版社).

Guangzhou Education Bureau (2006b) *Success with English (Volume 4)*. Beijing: Life, Reading, New Knowledge Joint Publishing Co. (生活 读书 新知 三联出版社).

Guangzhou Education Bureau (2006c) *Success with English (Volume 8)*. Beijing: Life, Reading, New Knowledge Joint Publishing Co. (生活 读书 新知 三联出版社).

Guilford, J.P. (1959) Traits of creativity. In H.H. Anderson (ed.) *Creativity and Its Cultivation* (pp. 142– 161). New York: Harper.

Guilford, J.P. (1984) Varieties of divergent production. *Journal of Creative Behaviour* 18, 1–10.

Hadfield, J. and Hadfield, C. (2015) Teaching grammar creatively. In N. Peachey and A. Maley (eds) *Creativity in the English Language Classroom* (pp. 51–63). London: British Council.

Hansenne, M. and Legrand, J. (2012) Creativity, emotional intelligence, and school performance in children. *International Journal of Educational Research* 53, 264–268.

Heathfield, D. (2015) Personal and creative storytelling: Telling our stories. In N. Peachey and A. Maley (eds) *Creativity in the English Language Classroom* (pp. 44–50). London: British Council.

Heinig, R.B. (1981) *Creative Drama for the Classroom Teacher*. Englewood Cliffs, NJ: Prentice Hall.

Honig, A.S. (2000) Promoting creativity in young children. Paper presented at the Annual Meeting of the Board of Advisors for Scholastic, Inc., New York, 19 May.

Horng, J-S., Hong, J-C., ChanLin, L-J., Chang, S-H. and Chu, H-C. (2005) Creative teachers and creative teaching strategies. *International Journal of Consumer Studies* 29 (4), 352–358.

Isenberg, J.P. and Jalongo, M.R. (2001) *Creative Expression and Play in Early Childhood* (3rd edn). Upper Saddle River, NJ: Merill Co.

Isenberg, J.P. and Jalongo, M.R. (2014) *Creative Thinking and Arts-Based Learning: Preschool Through Fourth Grade* (6th edn). New York: Pearson Education.

Jeffrey, B. (2006) Creative teaching and learning: Towards a common discourse and practice. *Cambridge Journal of Education* 36 (3), 399–414.

Kader, S.A. (2008) Enhancing creative behavioural expressions in school systems: The need for educational reform and a centre for creativity. PhD dissertation, Pennsylvania State University.

Karioth, E. (1967) Creative dramatics as an aid to developing creative thinking abilities. Doctoral dissertation, University of Minnesota, Minnesota.

Kennr, C. (2000) Children writing in a multilingual nursery. In M. Martin-Jones and K. Jones (eds) *Multilingual Literacies* (pp. 127–144). Amsterdam: John Benjamins.

Kim, K.H. (2011) Proven reliability and validity of the Torrance test of creative thinking (TTCT). *Psychology of Aesthetics, Creativity and the Arts* 5 (4), 314–315.

Kirsch, C. (2008) *Teaching Foreign Languages in the Primary School*. London: Continuum.

Kratsov, G.G. and Kratsova, E.E. (2010) Play in L.S. Vygotsky's nonclassical psychology. *Journal of Russian and East European Psychology* 48 (4), 25–41.

Lambert, E.B. (2006) Can drawing facilitate problem-solving? An exploratory study. *Australian Journal of Early Childhood* 31 (2), 42–47.

Leggett, N. (2015) Intentional teaching practices of educators and the development of creative thought processes of young children within Australian early childhood centres. PhD Thesis, University of Newcastle, Faculty of Education and Arts, School of Education, New South Wales, Australia.

Lindqvist, G. (1995) The aesthetics of play: A didactic study of play and culture in preschools. Doctoral dissertation. Retrieved from http://files.eric.ed.gov/fulltext/ED396824.pdf.

Lingard, B. (2010) Policy borrowing, policy learning: Testing times in Australian schooling. *Critical Studies in Education* 51 (2), 129–147.

Liska, I.H. (2013) A pedagogic analysis: Middle years of schooling and the role of creative practice. Masters thesis, Victoria University, Melbourne, Australia.

Lowenfeld, V. (1987) *Creative and Mental Growth* (8th edn). London: Collier Macmillan.

Lucas, B., Claxton, G. and Spencer, E. (2013) *Progression in Student Creativity in School: First Steps Towards New Forms of Formative Assessments*. OECD Working Papers 86. Paris: OECD Publishing.

Malaguzzi, L. (1994) Your image of the child: Where teaching begins. *Child Care Information Exchange* 96, 52–56.

Mashburn, A.J., Pianta, R.C., Hamre, B.K., Downer, J.T., Barbarin, O.A., Bryant, D., Burchinal, M., Early, D.M. and Howes, C. (2008) Measures of classroom quality in prekindergarten and children's development of academic, language and social skills. *Child Development* 79 (3), 732–749.

McConaghy, J. (1990) *Children Learning Through Literature: A Teacher Researcher Study.* Portsmouth, NH: Heinemann.

Molaei, R. and Abasi, M. (2014) Relationship between preschool on academic achievement and creativity of elementary students. *Advances in Environmental Biology* 8 (6), 1739–1744.

Moon, J. (2005) *Children Learning ENGLISH.* London: Macmillan.

National Advisory Committee on Creative and Cultural Education (NACCCE) (1999) *All Our Futures: Creativity, Culture and Education.* A Report for the Secretary of State for Education and Employment and for the Secretary of State for Culture, Media and Sport. London: NACCCE.

Nikolov, M. (1999) 'Why do you learn English?' 'Because the teacher is short.' A study of Hungarian children's foreign language learning motivation. *Language Teaching Research* 3 (1), 33–56.

Niland, A. (2007) Musical stories. *Australian Journal of Early Childhood* 32 (4), 7–11.

Nyland, B., Acker, A., Ferris, J. and Deans, J. (2013) How do you make a bear look like a butterfly? Exploring the Metropolitan Opera's production of Mozart's *Magic Flute* with a group of preschool children. *Australasian Journal of Early Childhood* 38 (1), 29–34.

Pianta, R.C., La Paro, K.M. and Hamre, B.K. (2008) *Classroom Assessment Scoring System Manual for Pre-K.* Baltimore, MD: Paul H. Brookes.

Pinter, A. (2011) *Children Learning Second Languages.* New York: Springer.

Powers, D.E. and Kaufman, J.C. (2004) Do standardized tests penalize deep-thinking, creative, or conscientious students? Some personality correlates of graduate record examination test scores. *Intelligence* 32 (2), 145–153.

Prokes, S.D. (1971) Exploring the relationship between participation in creative dramatics and development of the imagination capacities of gifted junior high school students. Doctoral dissertation, State University of New York, New York, USA.

Read, C. (2015) Seven pillars of creativity in primary ELT. In N. Peachey and A. Maley (eds) *Creativity in the English Language Classroom* (pp. 29–36). London: British Council.

Reed, M. and Canning, N. (eds) (2012) *Implementing Quality Improvement and Change in the Early Years.* London: Sage.

Reynolds, N. (2002) Computers, creativity, and composition in the primary school: An analysis of two compositions. *Australian Journal of Music Education* 1, 16–26.

Rixon, S. (ed.) (1999) *Young Learners of English: Some Research Perspectives.* Basildon: Longman.

Robinson, K. (2011) *Out of Our Minds: Learning To Be Creative.* Hoboken, NJ: John Wiley & Sons.

Runco, M.A. (1990) The divergent thinking of young children: Implications of the research. *Gifted Child Today (GCT)* 13 (4), 37–39.

Runco, M.A. (2003) Idea evaluation, divergent thinking and creativity. In M.A. Runco (ed.) *Critical Creative Processes* (pp. 69–94). Cresskill, NJ: Hampton Press.

Runco, M.A. (2004) Creativity. *Annual Review of Psychology* 55, 657–687.

Runco, M.A. (2005) Motivation, competence, and creativity. In A. Elliott and C. Dweck (eds) *Handbook of Competence and Motivation* (pp. 609–623). New York: Guilford Press.

Runco, M.A. (2014) *Creativity: Theories and Themes: Research Development and Practice.* New York: Elsevier Academic.

Runco, M.A., Millar, G., Acar, S. and Cramond, B. (2010) Torrance test of creative thinking as predictors of personal and public achievement: A fifty-year follow-up. *Creativity Research Journal* 22 (4), 361–368.

Rusch, R.R., Denny, D.A. and Ives, S. (1965) Fostering creativity in sixth grade. *Elementary School Journal* 65 (5), 262–268.

Rusch, R.R., Denny, D.A. and Ives, S. (1967) Fostering creativity in the sixth grade and its effect on achievement. *Journal of Experimental Education* 36 (1), 80–86.

Russ, S.W. (2011) Emotion/affect. In M.A. Runco and S.R. Pritzer (eds) *Encyclopedia of Creativity* (2nd edn) (pp. 449–455). New York: Elsevier.

Saracho, O.N. (2003) Teachers cognitive styles and their instructional implications. In O.N. Saracho and B. Spodek (eds) *Studying Teachers in Early Childhood Settings, Vol. IV* (pp. 161–179). Greenwich, CT: Information Age Publishing.

Saracho, O.N. (2012) *Contemporary Perspectives on Research in Creativity in Early Childhood Education*. Greenwich, CT: Information Age Publishing.

Saracho, O.N. and Spodek, B. (1995) Children's play and early childhood education: Insights from history and theory. *Journal of Education* 177 (3), 129–148.

Saracho, O.N. and Spodek, B. (2013) *Handbook of Research on the Education of Young Children* (3rd edn). London: Routledge.

Sawyer, R.K., John-Steiner, V., Moran, S., Sternberg, R.J., Feldman, D.H., Nakamura, J. and Csikszentmihalyi, M. (2003) *Creativity and Development*. New York: Oxford University Press.

School Curriculum and Assessment Authority (SCAA) (1997) *Looking at Children's Learning: Desirable Outcomes for Children's Learning on Entering Compulsory Education*. London: SCAA.

Sciamarelli, M. (2015) Teaching children with mascot-inspired projects. In N. Peachey and A. Maley (eds) *Creativity in the English language classroom* (pp. 104–114). London: British Council.

Shaheen, R. (2010) Creativity and education. *Creative Education* 1 (3), 166–169.

Smith, G.J.W. and Carlsson, I. (1983) Creativity in early and middle school years. *International Journal of Behavioral Development* 6 (2), 167–195.

Soydan, B. and Erbay, S.F. (2013) The methods applied by pre-school teachers to raise the curiosity of children and their views. *Educational Research and Reviews* 8 (13), 997–1008.

Starko, A.J. (2010) *Creativity in the Classroom: Schools of Curious Delight* (4th edn). New York: Routledge.

Sternberg, R.J. (2006) The nature of creativity. *Creativity Research Journal* 18 (1), 87–98.

Tegano, D.W., Morgan, J.D. and Sawyers, J.K. (1991) *Creativity in Early Childhood Classrooms* (NEA Early Childhood Education Series). West Haven, CT: National Education Association.

Tomlinson, B. (2015) Challenging teachers to use their coursebook creatively. In N. Peachey and A. Maley (eds) *Creativity in the English Language Classroom* (pp. 24–28). London: British Council.

Torrance, E.P. (1962) *Guiding Creative Talent*. New Jersey, NJ: Prentice-Hall.

Torrance, E.P. (1963) *Education and the Creative Potential*. Minneapolis, MN: University of Minnesota Press.

Torrance, E.P. (1965) Guidelines for creative teaching. *High School Journal* 48 (8), 459–464.

Torrance, E.P. (1977) *Creativity in the Classroom: What Research Says to the Teacher*. Research Report. Washington, DC: National Education Association.

Torrance, E.P. (1981) *Thinking Creatively in Action and Movement*. Bensenville, IL: Scholastic Testing Service.

Treffinger, D.J., Renzulli, J.S. and Feldhusen, J.F. (1971) Problems in the assessment of creative thinking. *Journal of Creative Behaviour* 5 (2), 104–112.

Vygotsky, L. (1930) *Mind in Society: The Development of Higher Psychological Process* (eds

M. Cole, V. John-Steiner, S. Scribner, and E. Souberman). Cambridge, MA: Harvard University Press (1978).

Vygotsky, L.S. (2004) Imagination and creativity in childhood. *Journal of Russian and East European Psychology* 42 (1), 7–97.

Wood, J.D. (2016) Using stories to help children learn a foreign language. Research paper from University of Granada. Retrieved from http://digibug.ugr.es/bitstream/10481/46235/1/WOOD_TFGLearnLanguage.pdf.

Woods, P. (1990) *Teacher Skills and Strategies*. London: Falmer Press.

Woronov, T.E. (2008) Raising quality, fostering 'creativity': Ideologies and practices of education reform in Beijing. *Anthropology and Education Quarterly* 39 (4), 401–422.

Zachopoulou, E., Makri, A. and Pollatou, E. (2009) Evaluation of children's creativity: Psychometric properties of Torrance's 'Thinking Creatively in Action and Movement' Test. *Early Child Development and Care* 179 (3), 317–328.

6 Promoting Autonomy Through Creative Tasks: Broadening Possibilities Within Constraints

Tan Bee Tin

'Autonomy', desirable for language learning, can be exercised at various levels. At a macro level, autonomy refers to learners' ability and willingness to make decisions and choices about language learning objectives and materials. At a micro level, autonomy involves learners taking responsibility, exploring alternatives and choosing both language patterns and the meaning they want to express during language-learning tasks. In this chapter, I propose 'creativity' as a form of learners exercising autonomy as a communicator at a micro level during language-learning tasks. Exploring alternatives and making creative choices during language learning depends on initial task conditions. Giving learners freedom does not necessarily lead to autonomous creative behaviour. Too much freedom can restrict possibilities for learners to explore and broaden their language repertoire as learners may retrieve safe options and make familiar choices. This chapter discusses how disciplined use of constraints in creative tasks can provide opportunities for learners to act and think creatively and independently, and for their language to grow in complexity.

'Autonomy' as a Universal Human Potential

The term 'autonomy' has been widely discussed and various definitions have been offered. One common definition describes autonomy as the ability and willingness to take charge of one's own learning (e.g. Dickinson, 1995; Littlewood, 1996). Alternatives have included 'taking responsibility for', 'taking control over' one's own learning individually and collectively (e.g. Benson, 2006) and 'making informed choices' about what we want to learn and how we want to learn it (Nunan, 1996).

Various types of autonomy have also been proposed in the literature. For example, Littlewood (1996) proposes three types: 'autonomy as a communicator', 'autonomy as a learner' and 'autonomy as a person'. 'Autonomy as a communicator' is associated with linguistic creativity – a person's ability and willingness to use language creatively, to make creative choices with language to express personal meaning in specific situations or tasks. 'Autonomy as a learner' refers to the ability and willingness to engage in self-directed learning, making decisions about learning at a more general, macro level. 'Autonomy as a person' is the ability and willingness to express personal meanings and involves creating personal learning contexts and learning opportunities at a macro level. In this view, autonomy refers not only to making decisions and choices at a higher, macro level but also at a lower, micro level. Autonomy can refer to taking charge of and making choices not only about one's own learning but also about one's own language use in specific situations or tasks.

Benson (1997, 2006) proposes the term 'versions of autonomy' and categorises various studies of autonomy in terms of three versions, 'psychological', 'technical' and 'political'. The psychological version focuses on cognitive processes and views autonomy as the human capacity and potential to take charge of one's own learning. The technical version focuses on learning management and is concerned with equipping learners with technical skills and techniques which enable them to learn language independently. The political version focuses on learners' control over the content and process of their own learning and is concerned with empowering learners by helping them to adopt a critical stance to issues of autonomy, power and authority.

The version of autonomy adopted in this chapter is a 'psychological' version which views 'autonomy' as a universal human potential which can be demonstrated in various forms. As Benson (2006) notes, studies on autonomy have shown a wide range of autonomous, creative activities engaged in by students, especially in situations where opportunities for out-of-class learning appear to be limited. In Table 6.1, accounts given by students about their out-of-class learning behaviour are examples of students demonstrating autonomy as a learner and autonomy as a person in various creative forms.

The accounts in Table 6.1 show how autonomy as a form of universal human potential can be exercised in various forms, even in unfavourable circumstances with limited opportunities for learning. However, all those various forms of autonomy are forms of 'autonomy as a learner' and 'autonomy as a person', which take place outside the class, initiated by students and triggered by personal circumstances. In these examples, students take responsibility for and take control over their own learning by creating various language-learning opportunities outside the class.

Following Littlewood's (1996) proposal, this chapter adopts the view that autonomy refers not only to exercising 'autonomy as a learner or

Table 6.1 Students demonstrating autonomy in various forms

Student	Student's account of language learning
A student from Thailand (Tan Bee Tin, 2013a) talked about how a surprising failure experienced outside the class triggered his interest in studying English and made him willing to exercise his autonomy. Although previously he did not have much desire to study English despite his father's push, his failure to understand an English customer during his internship experience at a hotel made him want to exercise his autonomy. This extract indicates various forms of self-initiated autonomy to improve his English.	'But before that [incident], I was lazy. I was waiting for my dad to push me into [an] English environment. But when I had the inspiration to study English, then I didn't wait for any command. I knew what I had to do. When I wake up, I turn on the English radio. I tried to spend my time in the English environment, even thinking. I don't have anyone speaking English with me too. I speak Thai one sentence [...]. I think in English to practise my brain speaking English because I think that when I'm in the real situation, I can use it straight away, immediately, without thinking so much because my brain has practised it all the time.'
A student from Nepal (Tan Bee Tin, 2014a) talked about how he exercised autonomy in various forms in a highly constrained learning/teaching environment. He continued to seek learning opportunities in his home environment, using family members, siblings and others in his community	'Whatever experience I have in the classroom and in this college, I express it in front of my parents when we are having dinner. I usually tell the joke [the teacher tells us in class] when we are having dinner and they laugh. They congratulate me.' 'I usually look at the dictionary. Actually, I don't have a dictionary but I borrow it from my friends and I look at the dictionary. If I get any difficult words, I take the help of the dictionary and I also have my teachers and my guiders in my locality and they also help me to make my English good.' 'There are so many strong English words in the textbook. I just try to use them in my writing that my teacher gives me. I include those words so that the memory of those words will be kept in my mind and I will never forget it.' 'If there is any mistake that I write, you know I try to read it once again. If I get any mistake there I correct it.' 'My sister encourages me to write about something. She often gives me some topics to write and I write. I write whatever I know. I write and she checks and she reads and if it is good she congratulates me. If it's not good she suggests to me to make it good.'
A student from Myanmar (Burma) (Tan Bee Tin, 2014b) talked about how she created opportunities, using Bibles in three languages – Myanmar, Karen (her mother tongues), English – the only resources freely available to her at home. Despite unfavourable circumstances at home, lack of family support and her busy schedule at the restaurant where she worked, she showed creative autonomous behaviour.	'I usually read the Bible in all three languages, Burmese, Karen, English, and work out the meaning in the English text by comparing it with the other two[...]. I choose some quotes and lines from the Bibles and write them in all three languages on the notice-board of my restaurant, for example, 'Like food we eat to survive, there is spiritual food to give strength' [...]. I write it in three languages. One day, a foreigner who was a regular customer saw those lines and gave me other quotes from the Bible (in English) to write on the board for six months. I became friendly with him and had a chance to speak with him in English.'

as a person' but also to exercising autonomy as 'a communicator' or as a 'language maker'. It involves not only making decisions and choices about language learning at a higher, macro level but also making choices about language one uses at a lower, micro linguistic level during specific language-learning tasks. Autonomy can refer to taking charge of and making choices not only about one's own learning but also about one's own language use in specific situations.

Although autonomy is a form of universal human potential, like any form of human knowledge and potential it is 'deeply contextual' (Snowden, 2002: 102) and is triggered by certain circumstances. For example, students may look 'passive' and 'non-autonomous' inside the class due to various circumstances such as teacher-dominated talk, the types of task used and the teaching approaches adopted. But the same students, other certain circumstances, may activate their autonomous potential, making various creative choices and taking control over their learning and language use.

One circumstance under which linguistic autonomy can prosper involves the design of language-learning tasks. This chapter proposes creativity and creative tasks as a circumstance which can help to trigger autonomous potential in learners at a micro linguistic level. It proposes features of creative tasks which can be generated by the teacher to help students exercise linguistic autonomy as a communicator, making creative choices with their language. I will first define what creativity means and why it is important for linguistic autonomy and language learning.

Creativity in Language Use as a Form of Linguistic Autonomy

'Creativity' has been widely researched in various disciplines such as education, psychology, linguistics, business and arts. Various approaches have been used to study and define creativity. Two particular approaches will be referred to here: a product approach and a process approach.

First, in a product approach, creativity is defined as the ability to produce new, surprising yet intelligible and valuable ideas (e.g. Boden, 2001). Such an ability is widely valued in various disciplines. In the field of linguistics, creativity in language use, or language creativity, is a novel, surprising, valuable way of talking about the world and is a ubiquitous feature of everyday language use (Carter, 2004). Creative language use can empower students to become 'language makers' and not just 'language users' (Carter, 2004). It enables students to exercise a form of linguistic autonomy by making creative choices with, taking control over and transforming their language. Language creativity can thus be seen as a way of exercising autonomy at a micro linguistic level, a form of exercising 'autonomy as a communicator' (Littlewood, 1996), using language in a novel, appropriate way to construct new, valuable ideas.

Second, researchers working in a process approach to creativity have identified various processes and thinking types involved in producing new, valuable ideas. Boden (2001), for example, proposes three types of thinking: exploratory, combinational and transformational creativity. Exploratory creativity is the ability to generate new ideas by exploring all the possibilities within the current conceptual space, using the existing set of rules and patterns. Combinational creativity is the ability to produce new valuable ideas by combining existing familiar ideas in an unfamiliar, unusual way. Transformational creativity, on the other hand, is the manipulation, transformation or the changing of some existing rules of the current conceptual space so as to produce new, valuable ideas. In terms of language use, these types of creative thinking can be applied to help language learners to 'make language' – to demonstrate new ways of talking about the world.

Creativity, that is, producing new ideas through exercising various types of creative thinking, plays an important role in promoting autonomy as a communicator and in language learning. On the one hand, it creates opportunities for learners to take control over and transform their language. On the other hand, the cognitive processes they need to go through in producing new valuable ideas and language contribute to the development of complex language (Tan Bee Tin, 2011). According to the complex dynamic theory of language, the need to say something new leads us to stretch and explore our language, which in turn leads to the development of complex grammar and complex language (e.g. Lakkaraju *et al.*, 2008). The new experience we encounter gives us a desire to explore and transform our language. Such a creative view of language as a tool for creating new meanings needs to be reflected in the design of language-learning tasks to promote linguistic autonomy and to facilitate the development of complex language among second language learners.

Promoting Linguistic Autonomy and Language Learning Through Creative Tasks

Many language-learning tasks promote the use of language to talk about 'known' meaning (i.e. known to oneself) rather than unknown meaning. Students are often required to use language to talk about familiar, known topics. Information to be communicated is often pre-given, in either the verbal or the non-verbal mode (e.g. pictures). This kind of condition, often found in popular information-gap tasks, could lead to what researchers call a 'signal redundancy' – the information to be communicated is already known, pre-given, or knowable in advance. This may make the desire to explore and stretch one's language redundant. Even when the meaning to be communicated is not pre-given and even when students are encouraged to use their imagination, in role-play tasks for instance, signal redundancy can occur due to two features: too much freedom given to learners, and the generally well defined nature of such tasks, when students are informed of the outcome they are expected to achieve. In such circumstances (i.e. situations with focus on known meaning, the presence of too much freedom and well defined goals), learners often avoid exercising their linguistic autonomy. They may avoid the exploration of new language utterances in the process of maturing and instead resort to the use of known, safer, familiar utterances to convey the familiar meaning. This avoidance is reflected in statements such as the following made by students and teachers:

> We think students will come up with imaginative ideas and language but they finish the task very quickly without much use of imaginative language and information. [Teacher]

> As we know the topic in advance, we arrange our language and use known words and sentences to complete the task. [Student]

> … we tried to use what we knew; didn't want to risk ourselves. [Student]

When faced with an unknown situation or problem, we tend to retrieve the known to solve the unknown if we have too much freedom. In cognitive psychology, this phenomenon is known as the 'cognitive fixation tendency'. Too much freedom can disable rather than enable student's autonomy and creative choices with language. So, how might we pull our students and language users out of such a 'cognitive fixation tendency'? How might we help them to make creative choices: to explore and transform language, to broaden possibilities with their language and meaning, and to test their linguistic boundaries and conceptual space, to exercise both linguistic and conceptual autonomy, to demonstrate autonomy as a communicator and as a person?

As creativity researchers have noted, it is 'constraint' rather than 'freedom' that facilitates creativity (e.g. Joyce, 2009). In cognitive psychology, constraint is twofold: one part restricts the search to a known area, while the other part encourages searching in the unknown area (Stokes, 2006). An imaginative and disciplined use of constraint is required for creativity and linguistic autonomy. Previous studies (Tan Bee Tin, 2011, 2015) indicated the role of constraints in facilitating students' linguistic autonomy and creativity in language use. For example, in one study (Tan Bee Tin, 2015), the same pair of students were assigned two tasks with different design features. While Task 1 had a high level of constraint, Task 2 had a high level of freedom. It was discovered that the students had more opportunities and desire to explore and transform their language and to exercise linguistic autonomy while working on Task 1 than on Task 2. The findings of the study are summarised in Table 6.2.

In Task 1, the meaning to be communicated is not knowable in advance due to the formal constraint (the need to start each line with the letter of the word) and this creates a desire for the pair to engage in exploring and transforming their language as they search for the new meaning. Their language (a complex sentence structure) emerges along with the meaning (the new meaning of 'time'). On the other hand, in Task 2, students are free to retrieve known meaning from previous experience. The pair fall into a cognitive fixation tendency, retrieving both familiar ideas and language as the task gives them freedom to choose any reasons. Too much background

Table 6.2 Summary of an exploratory study on task constraint, with a pair of students, N and S

Task 1 (high constraint)	Task 2 (high freedom)
Write an acrostic on 'TIME'.	Write a simile on 'Hope is like parking spaces'. Give two reasons.

Task features

1. Every line must start with the letter of the word 'TIME' (formal constraint)	1. Students have high freedom to choose any two reasons to support the simile given.
2. The whole poem must be related to the concept of 'TIME' (semantic constraint)	

Outcomes produced by the students

The one thing that Inhibits Marriage to last Eternally	Hope is like parking spaces Because it is hard to get and People steal each other's parking spaces Like destroying their hope.

Summary of the process the students go through during the tasks (for details of the full transcripts and comments, see Tan Bee Tin, 2015)

Idea generation (generating ideas and words randomly without knowing what they will be used for; examples of words the pair generated randomly were gold, money, marriage, patience, life, pressure, age, study, universe, belief, forever)	Retrieving existing experiences (N had much background knowledge/experience about parking and came up with the ideas for the simile right from the beginning)
Idea exploration within task constraints (the pair explored the words generated earlier within task constraints and gradually transformed them into a sentence and also engaged in exploring words, for example transforming 'prevents' into 'inhibits', 'go' into 'hold', 'sustain', 'last').	Less opportunity for negotiating meaning, exploring and transforming their language and meaning. Not much desire to transform their language as the ideas for the simile were already formed.

Examples from the transcripts (in both tasks, N and S used Chinese (L1) and English (L2): the translation of their discussion in Chinese is in italics, while the English words that they used are in roman).

Example of syntactic exploration using words generated by N (e.g. 'marriage', 'eternal', 'the one'); S transforms them into a sentence: S: 'time may cause marriage to...prevent marriage from going ...... eternally' S: 'The one thing that prevents marriage going eternally'... *'cause time has limits...* Example of lexical exploration: S: Or 'the one that...inhibit'...? Uh inhibit *is like* 'prevent', right? S: *Is there better word than* 'go'? S: To...hold? N: To...sustain? N: Last! S: To last. Yes yes to last! *That'll do.*	Example of lack of desire to explore and transform language and use of a familiar structure: N: 'And 'people steal ... people steal each other's' ... 'each other's ... parking spaces ... like ... hmmm ... destroying their hope'... yeah.' S (reads the sentence written): *Should we split the sentence?* N: *What do you mean?* S: *Like writing a poem we have to have ... different lines...* N: *Oh ... we can add the thing in the middle ... the ... slash?* S: Yeah yeah ... *so do we need the* 'and'? N: *These two sentences are already connected by* 'and'. *So full stop and then next one.*

Data originally collected by Tzu Ning Huang (2013) reanalysed by the author (Tan Bee Tin, 2015).

knowledge and known experience about the topic (about parking spaces) coupled with freedom leads to a lack of desire to explore and transform their language. The pair fail to explore other possibilities and fall into the cognitive fixation tendency. The known idea is retrieved to solve the problem and there is a lack of desire to transform their language further.

This exploratory study shows that constraint can broaden possibilities – both linguistic and conceptual possibilities and boundaries. Imaginative and disciplined use of constraints can help students to test their linguistic as well as conceptual boundaries, to exercise creative autonomy with their language and ideas. Constraint can lead to unpredictable novel outcomes and creative autonomy.

In order to facilitate linguistic autonomy and creativity for language learning, I propose the following task features:

- focus on unknown/new meaning rather than on known meaning;
- focus on partially defined goals rather than on well defined goals;
- disciplined and imaginative use of constraints rather than freedom to broaden possibilities.

These features can be implemented in 'creative tasks' through the following procedure (also see Tan Bee Tin, 2012, 2013b):

(1) *Idea generation phase.* This phase involves generating ideas and forms without knowing what they will be used for. The goal of the task is ill-defined so as to prevent students from deliberately arranging their vocabulary and sentences to achieve the outcome (i.e. to prevent them from the cognitive fixation tendency).

(2) *Idea exploration phase.* This phase involves exploring ideas generated in the idea generation phase within the constraints imposed. Constraints (formal rules and semantic rules) are revealed or discovered and students are required to make sense of the words and ideas generated earlier by exercising various types of creative thinking. This encourages students to use exploratory, combinational and transformational creativity (combining ideas and words generated earlier in an unfamiliar way, transforming their linguistic and conceptual space in the process of doing so, making creative choices with language and ideas).

With this imaginative, disciplined use of constraints, we can transform a language-learning task into a creative task, from a focus on known meaning to a focus on unknown meaning, from a focus on a well defined goal to a partially defined goal. Table 6.3 gives an example of how we can transform a free task into a creative task. In Example 1, as in Task 2 (the simile task), students are given freedom to choose any idea for the pre-given topic, 'What they would do if they were a millionaire?' The task is well defined: students know in advance what the topic is about (to write about things they would do if they were a millionaire). This can lead students to

Table 6.3 Transformation of a free task into a creative task

Task with high degree of freedom	Creative task (focus on unknown meaning, partially defined goal and imaginative use of constraints)
What would you do if you were a millionaire?	*1. Idea generation* Students generate words without knowing what they will be used for. i. On a piece of paper, write: 'Names of objects' (e.g. mobile phone, watch, window, car); 'Natural elements' (e.g. storm, sun, flower); 'Names of animals' (e.g. kangaroo). *2. Idea exploration with constraints* Students are given formal and semantic constraints and are asked to explore ideas and words generated in the earlier phase within the constraints revealed. ii. Go back to the list of words generated earlier and use them in the following sentence structure: 'If I were a/an ... (I/noun) would ...' (formal constraint) to express your emotion to someone you love (semantic constraint). Example: If I were a window, I would find every crack to get inside your heart. If I were a car, our mileage of love would continue even after the fuel of desire had run out.

retrieve known familiar utterances and ideas (e.g. 'I would travel around the world', 'I would buy a house'), often resulting in a lack of exploration and transformation of their language and ideas. In Example 2, as in Task 1 (the acrostic task), the task is ill-defined and students are encouraged to produce random words without knowing what they will be used for. The constraints revealed after the idea generation phase would reduce the possibility of retrieving known ideas and linguistic utterances to talk about love. The task would encourage students to combine familiar ideas (words generated in step 1 and the topic of 'love') in an unfamiliar way to construct new meaning. The meaning to be communicated is unknown in advance. This in turn is more likely to lead to more exploration and transformation of their language, exercising linguistic autonomy and creative language use.

Conclusion

'Autonomy', desirable for language learning, can be exercised at various levels – at a macro level, as an autonomous language learner or an autonomous person in general, as well as at a micro level, as an autonomous creative language maker or an autonomous communicator in specific language-learning tasks. This chapter views autonomy as a universal human potential which can be triggered by various circumstances. Creativity and creativity tasks are proposed as one type of circumstance for triggering linguistic autonomy, that is, learners' desire to exercise autonomy as a communicator, making creative choices with their language to construct new ideas and meaning.

Certain features of creative tasks can encourage students to make creative choices and broaden their linguistic and conceptual boundaries. Three features of creative tasks are proposed: focusing on the need to construct unknown meaning or the need to say something new, setting up an only partially defined goal, and the disciplined and imaginative use of constraints. These features can be integrated in the design of creative tasks in terms of two procedures: an idea generation phase and an idea exploration phase.

In short, learning is about providing space for new meaning to emerge: space in which old meaning is transformed and new meaning emerges. Imaginative and disciplined use of constraints can help students to test their linguistic as well as conceptual boundaries, to exercise creative autonomy with their language and ideas. Constraints can lead to unpredictable novel outcomes and creative autonomy. Teachers could find ways of using constraints in various imaginative and disciplined ways. Different degrees of constraints that suit the levels and ages of students can be experimented with in language-learning tasks. A better understanding of the processes learners encounter and the language they produce in different creative tasks will help teachers to design more effective creative tasks which enable learners to exercise linguistic autonomy. More research is needed to understand the nature of the affordances offered by various creative tasks.

Acknowledgements

An earlier version of this chapter, titled 'Creativity as a form of autonomy: Broadening "possibilities" within constraints', was presented at the Doing Research in Applied Linguistics 2/Independent Learning Association Conference 2014 (DRAL 2/ILA 2014), King Mongkut's University of Technology Thonburi, Bangkok, Thailand, 12–14 June 2014.

References

Benson, P. (1997) The philosophy and politics of learner autonomy. In P. Benson and P. Voller (eds) *Autonomy and Independence in Language Learning* (pp. 18–34). London: Longman.

Benson, P. (2006) Autonomy in language teaching and learning. *Language Teaching* 40 (1), 21–40.

Boden, M.A. (2001) Creativity and knowledge. In A. Craft, B. Jeffrey and M. Leibling (eds) *Creativity in Education* (pp. 95–102). London: Continuum.

Carter, R. (2004) *Language and Creativity: The Art of Common Talk*. London: Routledge.

Dickinson, L. (1995) Autonomy and motivation: A literature review. *System* 23 (2), 165–174.

Joyce, C.K. (2009) The blank page: Effects of constraint on creativity. PhD dissertation, University of California, Berkeley, California, USA.

Lakkaraju, K., Gasser, L. and Swarup, S. (2008) Language scaffolding as a condition for growth in linguistic complexity. In A.D.M. Smith and K. Smith (eds) *The Evolution of Language: Proceedings of the 7th International Conference*. Hackensack, NJ: World Scientific Publishing.

Littlewood, W. (1996) Autonomy: An anatomy and a framework. *System* 24 (4), 427–435.

Nunan, D. (1996) Towards autonomous learning: Some theoretical, empirical and practical issues. In R. Pemberton, S.L. Edward, W.W.F. Or and H.D. Pierson (eds) *Taking Control: Autonomy in Language Learning* (pp. 13–26). Hong Kong: Hong Kong University Press.

Snowden, D. (2002) Complex acts of knowing: Paradox and descriptive self-awareness. *Journal of Knowledge Management* 6 (2), 100–111.

Stokes, P.D. (2006) *Creativity from Constraints: The Psychology of Breakthrough*. New York, NY: Springer.

Tan Bee Tin (2011) Language creativity and co-emergence of form and meaning in creative writing tasks. *Applied Linguistics* 32 (2), 215–235.

Tan Bee Tin (2012) Freedom, constraints and creativity in language learning tasks: New task features. *Journal of Innovation in Language Learning and Teaching* 6 (2), 177–186.

Tan Bee Tin (2013a) Exploring the development of 'interest' in learning English as a foreign/second language. *RELC Journal* 44 (2), 129–146.

Tan Bee Tin (2013b) Towards creativity in ELT: The need to say something new. *ELT Journal* 67 (4), 385–397.

Tan Bee Tin (2014a) A look into the local pedagogy of an English language classroom in Nepal. *Language Teaching Research* 18 (3), 397–417.

Tan Bee Tin (2014b) Learning English in the periphery: A view from Myanmar (Burma). *Language Teaching Research* 18 (1), 95–117.

Tan Bee Tin (2015) Creativity in second-language learning. In R.H. Jones (ed.) *The Routledge Handbook of Language and Creativity* (pp. 433–451). London: Routledge.

Tzu Ning Huang (2013) A small-scale study: Creative tasks and second/foreign language learning. Unpublished coursework, University of Auckland, New Zealand.

Part 2: Improving ELT Materials Through Specific Resources

7 ELT Materials Using Process Drama

Hae-ok Park

It cannot be denied that developing language teaching materials requires knowledge of theories of second language acquisition and methodologies of language teaching. According to Maley (1995), writing instructional materials is an art, not a science. The following quote illustrates his thoughts on the development of L2 teaching materials, which requires a range of tacit knowledge:

> Writing instructional materials is certainly a complex and skilled task, involving a large number of decisions. It is my view that it is best seen as a form of operationalised tacit knowledge rather than an algorithmic set of fixed operations based on some kind of (mythical) objective, 'scientific' knowledge. This does not mean that we should turn our backs on the 'objective' knowledge and procedures available to us. But it does mean trusting our intuitions and beliefs. If a unit of material does not 'feel' right, no amount of rational persuasion will usually change my mind about it. (Maley, 1995: 220–221)

As Maley (1995) posits, developing ELT materials is not a simple undertaking. When it comes to talking about developing process drama materials for those learning an additional language, the process is still more complex and multilayered because, during a process drama, teachers must cope with a number of unexpected responses from the participants (Park, 2012).

Discussing teacher artistry in the implementation of a drama class, Dunn and Stinson (2011) emphasise that the process drama teacher should consider two levels of planning: macro and micro. Macro-level planning requires the selection of pre-texts and the preparation of a learning sequence. Micro-level planning requires in-the-moment artistry and the making of immediate decisions in the middle of a drama.

Given that process drama progresses with the improvised interactions and spontaneous reactions between teacher and students, writing process drama teaching materials appears at first a daunting task. This chapter therefore explores ways of developing L2 process drama teaching materials with the aim of widening and strengthening the application of process drama in L2 classrooms by integrating it with other L2 instructional techniques, such as task-based instruction and content and language integrated learning (CLIL). The first part of the chapter introduces the main features of process drama, and briefly explains the rationale of using process drama for teaching additional languages. The second part explicates the relationship between the principles of L2 materials development and the cornerstones of process drama; it explains how two well known L2 instructional techniques, task-based instruction and CLIL, can be integrated with process drama in the language classroom.

What is Process Drama?

How can we define process drama succinctly? According to Bowell and Heap (2013: 6), in a process-oriented drama approach 'performance to an external audience is absent but presentation to the internal audience is essential'. In a similar vein, O'Neill (1995: xvii) explains that the four main aspects of process drama are 'absence of script, an episodic structure, an extended time frame, and an integral audience' . As O'Neill points out, process drama progresses without a pre-written script; it develops with participants' spontaneous responses and interactions. It is also described as a drama approach in which teachers and students co-create an imaginary context to 'interact, experience, and develop their thinking and speaking skills' by negotiating and reflecting on each other's ideas and viewpoints (Park, 2012: 12). In fact, participants in process drama write 'their own play as the narrative and tension unfold in time and space and through action, reaction and interaction' (Park, 2012: 13).

Process drama originates from educational drama, specifically from drama-in-education, which uses drama techniques and conventions as the learning medium (Heathcote & Bolton, 1995; Park, 2012). Two leading pioneers of process drama, Dorothy Heathcote and Gavin Bolton, developed this method to teach curricular matters; therefore, it is often described as 'learning through drama' (O'Toole, 2009). Since teachers use this method to teach subject matter in the classroom, a final product 'performance' is not required in process drama. Instead, the most important aspect of process drama is that students learn through participating in each stage of the drama sequence; the process itself is learning (Fleming, 2000; Park, 2012).

What effect does this method have on L2 learning? According to Liu (2002), process drama has at least three types of function in a language classroom: cognitive, social and affective. Similarly, Kao and O'Neill (1998) set out the key aspects of drama approaches in the language classroom. They describe process drama as the most open form of communication and say that it provides 'fluency, authenticity, confidence, challenge, and a new classroom relation' (Kao & O'Neill, 1998: 16).

Studying the effectiveness of process drama in the language classroom by comparing teacher questioning in two different types of language classroom – process drama and regular English class – in a Korean EFL middle school, Park (2012) demonstrated that teacher and students used more referential-type questions during process drama than in the regular class. This shows that process drama provides more opportunities to use the target language in a more authentic context, as referential questions, in which the questioner does not know the answer, are considered more authentic than display questions, in which the questioner does know the answer (Long & Sato, 1983).

In fact, the number of research studies on the effects of L2 process drama is growing fast, and the findings demonstrate that process drama provides various benefits in language classrooms (e.g. Kao *et al.*, 2011; Kim, 2014; Lee, 2014; Park, 2010, 2012, 2013; Piazolli, 2011; Rothwell, 2011; To *et al.*, 2011); however, it is still difficult for L2 teachers who are interested in using it to find systematised and organised ways of planning process drama lessons. Planning L2 process drama is therefore discussed in the following section.

Process Drama and ELT Materials Development

The brief explanation about process drama in the preceding section will be readily understood by practitioners with experience as participants; however, to those without experience in a process drama class, it might be difficult to visualise what actually happens. Park (2012) notes that the majority of Korean in-service teachers of English who participated in her process drama training course cited the lack of process drama teaching materials and teacher training sessions as the factor most likely to hinder uptake of process drama in their classrooms. Indeed, it is rare to find process drama materials which guide practitioners. In L1 contexts, in contrast, there are a range of books which introduce how to plan process drama and which provide sample materials (e.g. Bowell & Heap, 2013; Fleming, 2000; Neelands, 2004; Neelands & Goode, 2000; O'Neill, 1995). For instance, Bowell and Heap (2013) state that a teacher should consider the following four cornerstones when developing process drama materials: play, learning in context, owning the learning, and symbolic representation of experience. Park (2012) describes the four cornerstones as follows:

> The first cornerstone is play. Children project themselves into a world through their dramatic playing; they practise life in the course of dramatic playing, and discover for themselves the boundary which exists between dramatic playing and reality. In fact, play is the innate predisposition of children to learn through dramatic playing. The second one is learning in context. This refers to learning takes place most effectively when it is contextualised. The third one owns the learning, and it suggests that learners who have a sense of ownership about their learning would have a greater

commitment to it, and as a result would gain more. Finally, the fourth cornerstone is using drama to represent life experiences symbolically and comment on them. (Park, 2012: 79)

However, unlike with L1 process drama, a prerequisite is understanding the principles of developing L2 teaching materials (Park, 2012, 2013). Emphasising the coincidence between the cornerstones of process drama (Bowell & Heap, 2013) and the principles of language materials development (Tomlinson, 2011), Park (2012) demonstrates the similarity of the two areas (see Table 7.1).

How can a teacher develop process drama materials? Bowell and Heap (2013) propose six planning principles: theme or topic (i.e. learning area), context, roles, frame, sign and strategies. They recommend that teachers

Table 7.1 Comparison of the four cornerstones of process drama and the principles of L2 materials development

Four cornerstones of process drama (Bowell & Heap, 2013)	Principles of L2 materials development (Tomlinson, 2011)
Play: the innate predisposition of children to learn through dramatic playing	Materials should achieve affective engagement
Learning in context: recognition that learning takes place most effectively when it is contextualised	What is being taught should be perceived by learners as relevant and useful Materials should help learners to learn in ways similar to the circumstances in which they will have to use the language Learners must be ready to acquire the points being taught (in terms of both linguistic, developmental readiness and psychological readiness)
Owning the learning: learners with a sense of ownership about their learning have a greater commitment to it and gain more as a result	Materials should require and facilitate learner self-investment (e.g. through giving learners responsibility for making decisions and through encouraging them to make discoveries about the language for themselves) Materials should maximise learning potential by encouraging intellectual, aesthetic and emotional involvement, which stimulates both right- and left-brain activities (through a variety of non-trivial activities requiring a range of different types of processing) Materials should take into account that learners differ in learning styles Materials should take into account that learners differ in affective attitudes (and therefore materials should offer variety and choice)
Symbolic representation of experience: humans use drama to symbolically represent life experiences and make comments on them	Materials should reflect the reality of language use Materials should expose learners to language in authentic use (ideally to a rich and varied input which includes unplanned, semi-planned,and planned discourse and which stimulates mental response) Materials should provide learners with opportunities to use the target language to achieve a communicative purpose

Adapted from 'Implementing process drama in an EFL middle school classroom: An action research project in Seoul, Korea', by H-O Park, 2012, p. 81. PhD thesis, Leeds Metropolitan University, UK.

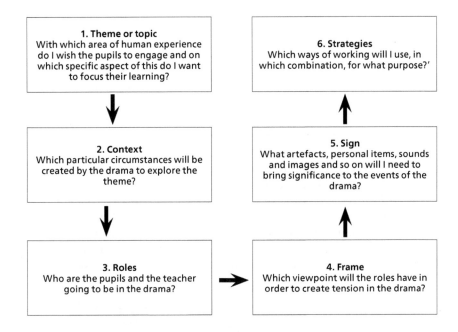

Figure 7.1 Principles of planning process drama. From *Planning Process Drama* by P. Bowell and B. Heap, 2013, p. 12. London: David Fulton.

seek answers to questions prior to finalising each principle (see Figure 7.1). For instance, in the first step, the theme or learning area of the drama should be decided. In this case, teachers should examine which area of human experience they want the students to learn about (e.g. Bowell & Heap, 2013; Heathcote & Bolton, 1995; Morgan & Saxton, 1987). Likewise, the other five planning principles require answers to questions.

In L2 process drama, however, students cannot respond as they might in their L1, due to limitations of language proficiency. When a teacher implements task-based instruction, similar problems can occur since both methods ask learners to react spontaneously. The following section explains how task-based instruction can be integrated into L2 process drama.

Process drama and task-based instruction

It was seen in the preceding section that the cornerstones of process drama and the principles of language teaching materials are similar in their rationales and functions in language teaching and learning arenas. In a similar fashion, the four cornerstones of process drama coincide closely with the rationale of using task-based instruction in the language classroom, as both methods prioritise the use of language in meaningful and authentic contexts and the completion of an activity to achieve a goal (Bachman & Palmer, 1996; Bygate *et al.*, 2001; Ellis, 2003; Nunan, 1989; Van Den Branden, 2006; Willis, 1996).

Brown posits that task-based instruction has received considerable attention from language teachers due to the growing importance of 'classroom interaction, learner-centred teaching, authenticity, and viewing the learner's own experiences as important contributors to learning' in an the context of learning an additional language (Brown, 2014: 237). In fact, the core concept of communicative language teaching (CLT), developing language learners' communicative competence, is fully represented in task-based language teaching (Brown, 2014).

Regarding the definition of 'task', Nunan explains that a range of definitions have been proposed, yet all have a common feature: a task involves communicative language use in which 'the user's attention is focused on meaning rather than linguistic structure' (Nunan, 1989: 10). In the following comment, Nunan explains that a communicative task is:

> a piece of classroom work which involves learners in comprehending, manipulating, producing or interacting in the target language while their attention is principally focused on meaning rather than form. The task should also have a sense of completeness, being able to stand alone as a communicative act in its own right. (Nunan, 1989: 10)

Classroom tasks are generally categorised as either 'real world' or 'pedagogical'. Tasks with a real-world justification ask learners to conduct in class something required in the real world (Nunan, 1989), and these are also called authentic tasks (Tomlinson, 2011). Examples of authentic tasks are 'answering a letter addressed to the learner, arguing a particular point of view, and comparing various holiday brochures in order to decide where to go for a holiday' (Tomlinson, 2011: ix). A task with a pedagogical rationale, on the other hand, requires learners to do things they would not do outside the classroom; it prepares them for real language use (Nunan, 1989). Examples of pedagogical tasks include 'completing one half of a dialogue, filling in the blanks in a story, and working out the meaning of ten nonsense words from clues in a text' (Tomlinson, 2011: xv). According to Willis and Willis, however, when planning a task-based lesson it is better to sequence a range of tasks than to provide a single task:

> So a task-based lesson would probably involve not a single task, but a sequence of tasks. These tasks relate to one another. The teacher-led introduction is a task in itself. It involves a genuine exchange of meaning, in which learners are required to process language for meaning. It also serves a priming function. (Willis & Willis, 2007: 21)

Target tasks, which mostly invite learners to engage in real-world events, follow after a range of priming tasks, which have a preparatory role (Willis & Willis, 2007). The sequencing of tasks (i.e. performing priming tasks in preparation for a target task) provides a rationale for planning an L2 process drama. Process drama progresses with a list of drama strategies/conventions, most of which require a preparatory stage analogous to priming tasks for a target task. For instance, prior to the drama strategies, a teacher could ask learners to create their role in the drama and prepare some questions to ask peers or the teacher. Meanwhile, the teacher monitors the learners to help them whenever they have problems. This preparatory activity is similar to a priming task, since its role is exactly the same as the role of a priming task in the task sequence of task-based language teaching. The teacher plays the role of monitor, facilitator or a resource during this preparatory stage (Spratt *et al.*, 2011).

Table 7.2 illustrates how an L2 process drama progresses through a series of priming and target tasks. The pre-text for the following process drama is based on the well known Aesop's fable 'The Boy Who Cried Wolf'. The drama starts when most of the villagers have lost their sheep in the wolf's attack and are holding David, the shepherd boy, responsible for the loss. David lives a poor life with his mother, who has terminal cancer. Unable to bear the pressure, David runs away, leaving only a sad letter to his mother. The first priming task asks students to create an identity as one of the villagers who has lost sheep in the attack. For this task, the students are given a name tag and a worksheet to create an identity as a villager: name, job, number of sheep lost and so on.

Owing to the learner training they did prior to the drama, the class recognises that a whole-group improvisation starts as soon as the teacher puts on a police cap. The teacher-in-role (TiR) as a police officer greets the villagers and asks everyone how many sheep they lost. The students answer from their worksheets completed during the priming task. In continuation, the TiR reads to the villagers David's letter. When the teacher takes off her cap, the class understands that the drama has ended and that the teacher is out of her role. To prepare for the next target task, hot-seating, two further priming tasks, role-on-the-wall and creating questions, can be conducted. The students co-create the character of David through the role-on-the-wall; it provides an opportunity to emphasise him being a lonely shepherd boy.

As seen in Table 7.2, one or two priming tasks are suggested prior to each target task, with the exception of writing-in-role, in which students are asked to write a title and brief summary of a newspaper article about the whole story they have developed. Learners, therefore, have opportunities to use language through various drama conventions, namely, target tasks. The core concepts of task-based instruction, which focuses on the use of language, meaning-oriented activity, task completion and priority of outcome, can be fully realised through L2 process drama because it progresses with teacher and student responses to a given pre-text, which commonly demands participants' active involvement. The next section explains how an L2 process drama works in harmony with CLIL.

Table 7.2 Types of process drama task for Korean secondary students: 'The Boy Who Cried Wolf and Its Epilogue'

Task type	Drama strategy	Procedure	Teacher's role	Students' role
Priming		Preparing for a village meeting		
Target	TiR[a] and whole-group improvisation	Village meeting is held to discuss the accident	Police officer	Villagers
Priming	Role-on-the-wall	Brainstorming David, the shepherd boy	Facilitator	Villagers and David
Priming		Creating questions for hot-seating	Facilitator	
Target	TiR and hot-seating	Interviewing Anna, David's mother	Host of TV programme	Reporters
Priming		Preparing for tableau	Monitor and resource	
Target	Tableau: group still image[b]	Representing wolf's attack with a still image	Facilitator	Villagers
Priming		Preparing an urgent hospital meeting	Monitor and resource	
Target	TiR and whole-group improvisation	Discussing Anna's situation and villagers' invasion of the hospital	Hospital director	Employees at the hospital
Priming		Preparing for the volunteers' meeting	Monitor and resource	
Target	TiR and mantle of the expert[c]	Students become an expert who volunteers to help David's family	Leader of the volunteers' group	Volunteering experts
Priming		Discussing David's decision	Monitor and resource	
Target	Spectrum of difference[d]		Facilitator	David's inner thoughts
Target	Writing-in-role	Each group selects a title of a newspaper article which is about the recent accident in the village	Monitor and resource	Reporters

[a] Teacher-in-role (TiR): The teacher manages the theatrical possibilities and learning opportunities provided by the dramatic context from within the context by adopting a suitable role in order to excite interest, control the action, invite involvement, provoke tension, challenge superficial thinking, create choices and ambiguity, develop the narrative, and to create possibilities for the group to interact in role. The teacher is not acting spontaneously but is trying to mediate the teaching purpose through involvement in the drama (Neelands & Goode, 2000: 40).

[b] Groups devise an image using their bodies to crystallise a moment, idea or theme; or an individual acts as sculptor to a group. Contrasting images are made to represent actual/ideal dream/nightmare versions (Neelands & Goode, 2000: 25).

[c] The group become characters endowed with specialist knowledge that is relevant to the situation, for example historians, social workers, mountain climbers. The situation is always task oriented and so expert understanding or skills are required to perform the task (Neelands & Goode, 2000: 34).

[d] This strategy requires group members to place themselves physically on an imaginary line linking two alternatives, indicating their preference through their choice of position. An open mind is indicated through placing oneself centrally; otherwise, stronger support is indicated by placement nearer one end of the line. This convention allows students to see the potential range of opinion within a group. With some groups it will be important to ask for the reasons for the choices made but, equally, with other groups the strategy can be set up so as to allow individuals the opportunity to make a statement without having to verbally defend their position (Neelands & Goode, 2000: 87).

Process drama and content and language integrated learning

The effects of using curricular content in a language classroom has been recommended by a range of academics who argue that subject areas are the most relevant and meaningful forms of content to learners (e.g. Widdowson, 1978). This idea has been concretely and systematically effectuated in language teaching in European countries since the 1990s under the name of content and language integrated learning (CLIL).

In fact, as briefly noted above, it is not a novel approach to use subject content in language classrooms: there have been a number of similar implementations in language teaching, such as immersion, content-based instruction, and sheltered instruction observation protocol (SIOP). Some researchers, therefore, consider CLIL an umbrella term for all the methods which incorporate content in language classroom instruction (e.g. Mehisto *et al.*, 2008). According to the pioneers of this approach, CLIL is defined as 'a dual-focused educational approach in which an additional language is used for the learning and teaching of both content and language' (Coyle *et al.*, 2010: 1). Some researchers assert that it is differentiated from previous attempts to use content in the language classroom by a range of innovative and systematic ideas and concepts, such as the 4Cs Framework of content, communication, cognition and culture (e.g. Bentley, 2010; Coyle *et al.*, 2010), or the language triptych, which 'has been constructed to take account for the need to integrate cognitively demanding content with language learning and using' (Coyle *et al.*, 2010: 36). Richards and Rodgers (2014) state that the difference between content-based instruction (CBI) and CLIL is that, unlike CBI, 'CLIL not only aims at stimulating multilingualism of all citizenship in the European community' but also seeks to conserve the independence and status of local languages. In reality, CLIL represents 'the development of English language skills in those who will use English as a lingua franca' (Richards & Rogers, 2014: 116), whereas CBI commonly represents immersion programmes in ESL settings. Moreover, as Coyle *et al.* contend, learners in CLIL classrooms are 'active participants in developing their potential for acquiring knowledge and skills (education) through a process of enquiry (research) and by using complex cognitive processes and means for problem solving (innovation)' (Coyle *et al.*, 2010: 5–6). The 4Cs Framework, which was designed to support the effective implementation of CLIL classroom practice, reinforces the innovative element of CLIL by integrating four contextualised building blocks. The following comment describes each component of the 4Cs Framework and its functions within a CLIL lesson.

The 4Cs Framework integrates four contextualised building blocks: content (subject matter), communication (language learning and using), cognition (learning and thinking processes) and culture (developing intercultural understanding and global citizenship). In doing so, it takes account of integrating content learning and language learning within specific contexts and acknowledges the symbiotic relationship that exists between these elements. (Coyle *et al.*, 2000: 41)

Analogously, process drama has been used to teach subject matter in classrooms. Since the pioneer of process drama, Dorothy Heathcote, initiated the use of drama techniques to teach subject areas such as history and maths (Heathcote & Bolton, 1995), it has been commonly used to teach subject content in classrooms. With her unique techniques, named 'mantle of the expert' and 'teacher-in-role', she transforms traditional teacher-dominated classrooms into learner-centred atmospheres (Kao & O'Neill, 1998; Park, 2012; Wagner, 1998). Emphasising her influential role in the area of curriculum design, O'Toole describes the grand and powerful influence of Heathcote as 'hurricane Heathcote' (O'Toole, 2009: 101) and acknowledges her influence on the education sector by stating that classroom drama would never be the same again after her appearance.

Students in process drama are given legitimate opportunities to research a subject area in the self-chosen role of expert. They could be a scientist, a detective, a teacher or even an explorer, depending on the drama, and carry out research to solve a given problem. Mehisto *et al.* set out the benefits of using drama in CLIL as follows:

> Content acquisition is enhanced through drama. Drama requires students to use their imagination and to visualise situations, processes and options. Imagination and visualisation build bridges from one's current state of knowledge to a new level of knowledge and understanding. Language acquisition is also enhanced through role-playing. In a role, students find and use language appropriate to a wide variety of circumstances. They communicate the words and thoughts of many different people to a wide range of 'others'. Their vocabulary, tone, expression, level of formality, speed of communication and ability to listen change and adapt to the drama being developed. As students engage emotionally they find words deep within themselves because the need to communicate is both immediate and compelling. (Mehisto *et al.*, 2008: 219)

As addressed above, drama strategies facilitate both content and language acquisition in an authentic and meaningful context. Common drama strategies used in the CLIL classroom are tableau(x), movement/word work, writing-in-role, role-on-the-wall, talking walls, hot-seating and drama for a science unit (Mehisto *et al.*, 2008).

Conclusion

The world changes, and with it so do classrooms. In 2007, when I started to train Korean in-service teachers of English in L2 process drama, the majority came to me after class with a serious but compassionate facial expression. They would typically say something like:

Well, I know what you are talking about, and I mainly agree with the effectiveness of process drama in L2 learning, but considering the reality of Korean secondary classroom contexts, it is far too unrealistic and difficult to implement. I am sorry to tell you this, but it is too idealistic for Korean public school contexts.

Around 10 years have passed, and I am still teaching in-service teachers and graduate students about process drama; however, the responses have changed enormously. The changes have been slow but continued. Now when I introduce process drama to in-service teachers, most of them have positive responses, and some even come to me and ask for teaching materials to use later in their classrooms. It is said that a growing number of Korean in-service teachers are getting interested in new types of instruction and curricula which allow them to organise their classes in more learning-centred ways, such as with the flipped-class ideology (Bergmann & Sams, 2012) or the free semester system. Learners become active and spontaneous in those classes, and the classroom atmosphere changes into a more democratic and cooperative environment than in traditional classrooms. In consideration of all these changes, I am confident that the Korean education environment is becoming more accommodating to the implementation of process drama.

References

Bachman, L. and Palmer, A. (1996) *Language Testing in Practice*. Oxford: Oxford University Press.

Bentley, K. (2010) *The Teaching Knowledge Test Course: CLIL Module*. Cambridge: Cambridge University Press.

Bergmann, J. and Sams, A. (2012) *Flip Your Classroom: Reach Every Student in Every Day*. Washington, DC: International Society for Technology in Education (ISTE).

Bowell, P. and Heap, B. (2013) *Planning Process Drama: Enriching Teaching and Learning* (2nd edn). London: Routledge.

Brown, D. (2014) *Principles of Language Learning and Teaching: A Course in Second Language Acquisition* (6th edn). New York: Pearson Education.

Bygate, M., Skehan, P. and Swain, M. (eds) (2001) *Researching Pedagogic Tasks: Second Language Learning, Teaching and Testing*. Harlow: Longman.

Colye, D., Hood, P. and Marsh, D. (2010) *Content and Language Integrated Learning*. Cambridge: Cambridge University Press.

Dunn, J. and Stinson, M. (2011) Not without the art!! The importance of teacher artistry when applying drama as pedagogy for additional language learning. *Research in Drama Education* 16 (4), 575–84.

Ellis, R. (2003) *Task-Based Language Learning and Teaching*. Oxford: Oxford University Press.

Fleming, M. (2000) Wittgenstein and the teaching of drama. *Research in Drama Education* 5 (1), 33–44.

Heathcote, D. and Bolton, G. (1995) *Drama for Learning*. Portsmouth, NH: Heinemann.

Kao, S. and O'Neill, C. (1998) *Words into World: Learning a Second Language Through Process Drama*. Stamford: Ablex.

Kao, S., Carkin, G. and Hsu, L. (2011) Questioning techniques for promoting language learning with students of limited L2 oral proficiency in a drama-oriented language classroom. *Research in Drama Education* 16 (4), 489–515.

Kim, Y-M. (2014) Implementation of process drama in Korean elementary schools. Master's thesis, International Graduate School of English, Seoul, Korea.

Lee, H-M. (2014) An action research on content and language integrated learning at elementary school in Korea. Master's thesis, International Graduate School of English, Seoul, Korea.

Liu, J. (2002) Process drama in second- and foreign-language classrooms. In G. Brauer (ed.) *Body and Language: Intercultural Learning Through Drama* (pp. 51–70). London: Ablex.

Long, M.H. and Sato, C.J. (1983) Classroom foreigner talk discourse: Forms and functions of teachers' questions. In H.W. Selinger and M.H. Long (eds) *Classroom Oriented Research in Second Language Acquisition* (pp. 268–285). Rowley, MA: Newbury House.

Maley, A. (1995) Materials writing and tacit knowledge. In C. Hidalgo, D. Hall and G.M. Jacobs (eds) *Getting Started: Materials Writers on Materials Writing* (pp. 220–239). Singapore: SEMEO Regional Language Centre.

Mehisto, P., Marsh, D. and Frigols, M.J. (2008) *Uncovering CLIL: Content and Language Integrated Learning in Bilingual and Multilingual Education*. Oxford: Macmillan.

Morgan, N. and Saxton, J. (1987) *Teaching Drama: A Mind of Many Wonders*. Portsmouth, NH: Heinemann.

Neelands, J. (2004) *Beginning Drama 11–14* (2nd edn). London: David Fulton.

Neelands, J. and Goode, T. (2000) *Structuring Drama Work* (2nd edn). Cambridge: Cambridge University Press.

Nunan, D. (1989) *Designing Tasks for the Communicative Classroom*. Cambridge: Cambridge University Press.

O'Neill, C. (1995) *Drama World*. Portsmouth, NH: Heinemann.

O'Toole, J. (2009) Drama as pedagogy. In J. O'Toole, M. Stinson and T. Moore (eds) *Drama and Curriculum: A Giant at the Door* (pp. 49–97). Milton Keynes: Springer.

Park, H-O. (2010) Process drama in the Korean EFL secondary classroom: A case study of Korean middle school classrooms. In B. Tomlinson and H. Masuhara (eds) *Research for Materials Development in Language Learning* (pp. 155–171). London: Continuum.

Park, H-O. (2012) Implementing process drama in an EFL middle school classroom: An action research project in Seoul, Korea. PhD thesis, Leeds Metropolitan University, Leeds, UK.

Park, H-O. (2013) Adapting classroom materials using process drama strategies. *Foreign Language Education* 20 (4), 91–120.

Piazolli, E. (2011) Process drama: The use of affective space to reduce language anxiety in the additional language learning classroom. *Research in Drama Education* 16 (4), 557–573.

Richards, J.C. and Rodgers, T.S. (2014) *Approaches and Methods in Language Teaching*. Cambridge: Cambridge University Press.

Rothwell, J. (2011) Bodies and language: Process drama and intercultural language learning in a beginner language classroom. *Research in Drama Education* 16 (4), 575–594.

Spratt, M., Pulverness, A. and Williams, M. (2011) *The TKT: Teaching Knowledge Test Course, Module 1, 2 and 3*. Cambridge: Cambridge University Press.

To, L.D., Chan, Y.P., Lam, Y.K. and Tsang, S.Y. (2011) Reflection on a primary school teacher professional development programme on learning English through process drama. *Research in Drama Education* 16 (4), 517–539.

Tomlinson, B. (2011) *Materials Development in Language Teaching* (2nd edn). Cambridge: Cambridge University Press.

Van Den Branden, K. (2006) *Task-Based Language Education: From Theory to Practice*. Cambridge: Cambridge University Press.

Widdowson, H. (1978) *Teaching Language as Communication*. Oxford: Oxford University Press.

Willis, D. and Willis, J. (2007) *Doing Task-Based Teaching*. Oxford: Oxford University Press.

Willis, J. (1996) *A Framework for Task-Based Learning*. Harlow: Longman.

8 Living in the Materials World: Why Literature Has a Place Here

Paul Hullah

Introduction and the Fourth Hunger

Despite the gradual ongoing marginalisation of literature in EFL curricula, symptomatic of the damaging 'dumbing down' and insidious 'infantilisation' of global education worldwide, research demonstrates that suitably selected, properly presented 'literary' texts can effectively re-engage and re-motivate jaded English L2 learners (Brown, 2000; Hullah & O'Sullivan, 1995; McCarthy & Carter, 1994). That literature and its themes can kindle and develop hitherto neglected critical thinking skills and linguistically empower learners has also been strongly suggested (Ahmad & Aziz, 2011; Hullah, 2003). Yet EFL educators electing to educate with literature are called upon to justify themselves in ways that persons advocating other sorts of lesson content are not, implying that, somehow, literature is not a *natural* choice of material to make, not the first port of call we should seek in stormy educational seas. I want here to consider and refute this supposition and hopefully alleviate some of the resultant 'stress' under which educators operate, and which the voicing of such misguided assumptions can cause (Hullah & Hoy, 2014).

I used to tell students that we don't find our future, our future finds us, but I would now amend that position. You can't just wait for things to happen. You have to actively engage with life, make positive undamaging meanings out of apparent mayhem. The 16th-century French essayist Michel de Montaigne said 'I discover myself more by accident than by enquiring' (Holbrook, 2010: 82), an enigmatic but disingenuous view: I think the discoveries happen most when we are consciously 'enquiring'. As Socrates reputedly declared, the 'unexamined life is not worth living' (Adler, 1997: 77). Self-evaluation need not be self-centred: self-awareness is an essential mechanism of defence and damage limitation when faced with difficulties and disasters (and equally when blessed with triumphs and prosperity). Lack of self-examination fosters *complacency*, a deleterious condition adjacent to inertia.

In active pursuit of survival and even success, we have to try to make good, educated choices. Free, creative choice is remedial, curative, motivating, and exemplified and interpretatively encouraged by literary texts. Literary texts (I will explain what I mean by 'literary' soon) can inspire and assist us to make better life decisions, while simultaneously alerting us to the emotive and rhetorical potencies of language. Both of these functions of literature, I want to argue, are desirable, *special* qualities that any worthwhile curriculum should contain and explore.

Philosophers of human consciousness argue that the urge to seek and find meaning (and to *create* it where none can be found) is essential and instinctive in sane individuals: a 'fundamental hunger arising out of the human condition'. This posited primeval desire relies on our making meaningful choices and has been termed our 'fourth hunger', after 'three obvious hungers: for survival; for pleasure; and for positive acknowledgement by real or imaginary others (internalised as self-esteem at being loved, lusted after, or knowing that one is not, or is not thought to be, useless)' (Tallis, 2006: 7). I believe that literature addresses this hunger (as religion used to for many and still does for some) and, to reiterate, will argue hereafter that literature in general and poetry in particular, if properly presented and meaningfully studied, can form a fecund and inspiring teaching resource that we must not allow to disappear from curricula.

Literaphobia

Many EFL teachers ask me, 'Why do you use literature?' 'Why *don't* you?', I reply. We might protest that, in an ideal world, we wouldn't need to justify what we do, but this isn't an ideal world (or, if it is, my own ideals aren't the ones it reflects). Anyway, justifying what we choose to teach and do *is* meaningful, for if we find we cannot rationalise our choices, it might be time to revise them. A colleague, alarmed to discover that poetry was my chosen poison in the shifting pedagogical apothecary, admonished me that I was treading on thinning ice, as 'poetry is a dying medium!' 'Then so, perhaps, is critical thinking?' was my response, for the two (poetry, and critical thinking), are closely related, as I intend to show.

I call the reticence and nervousness of many teachers and students regarding 'literary' materials 'literaphobia': a 'fear of literature'. My colleague Mike Pronko and I coined this term while concocting a theme for the 2012 Liberlit conference, the international forum for 'the promotion and defense of "literary texts"', of which we are co-founders (Hullah & Pronko, 2015). Liberlit challenges the way literary materials are overlooked, even actively discouraged, as an EFL teaching resource. The fact that literary texts are in danger of disappearing from textbooks and courses made us resolve to make a stand against the rising tide. Liberlit functions primarily as a society for teachers who believe that appropriately guided exposure to literature may significantly help L2 learners, and not erode their motivation in ways that certain other pedagogical approaches might (Hernandez, 2011; Hullah & O'Sullivan, 1996).

In 1996, I surveyed over 200 freshmen (English- and non-English majors) about to embark on 'General English' courses at universities across Japan. The survey was completed before the first class of the first term. (The results are presented in Hullah, 1997; and discussed in Hullah, 2003.) Respondents were asked (in Japanese) to give adjectives describing their feelings about 'poetry in English'. Eighty percent of students responded with adjectives of negative import: the most popular was 'difficult'. But in response to a subsequent question, over 70% of students admitted they had 'never' or 'hardly ever' read any English poetry (Bibby, 2012: 33). I suspect that teachers might react similarly if quizzed on using poetry in the EFL classroom: their reticence relies on some erroneous preconceptions that I want to dispute and hopefully dispel. Rob Waring, in his Liberlit 2012 keynote presentation, insisted that literature's chief enemy is 'its name' (Hullah & Pronko, 2015): a very valid point. As with cancer, the *name* is repulsive, hence we wish to shun the thing itself. Rebranding would be ideal but impractical, so here I will have to settle for explication.

Literary Texts and Their Usefulness

In his knowingly provocative but eminently sensible 1891 'Preface' to *The Picture of Dorian Gray*, Wilde famously declared that there is 'no such thing as a moral or an immoral book. Books are well written, or badly written. That is all' (Wilde, 1908: 5). If we accept this, and I can think of no conclusive reason why we should not, then, just as 'morality' might be said to be in the eye of the beholder, then so is 'literariness': there is no such thing as a literary or a non-literary text, except that a reader interprets it so. Texts are written in different styles (or registers, paroles, varieties of English, whatever we call it). That is all. And some of these styles can be called 'literary'. John Carey answers the question 'What is a work of art?' with the (far from flippant but, rather, supported by a lengthy and convincing thesis) reply: 'A work of art is anything that anyone has ever considered to be a work of art, though it may be a work of art only for that one person' (Carey, 2005: 29). I might similarly respond to the question 'What is a literary text?'

Liberlit offered a broad-church definition of literature as part of its original 'Manifesto', a revised version of which I give here:

> By 'literature', we mean interesting and engaging texts that use language
> in original, meaningful, memorable, emotive, playful, creative and careful
> ways to tell stories, convey impressions, express original opinions, pose

critical questions and openly provoke more than simplistic, pragmatic responses. Those texts could include poetry, novels, plays, movies, songs, TV shows, jokes, bloopers, advertising slogans, YouTube clips, blogs, tweets, or thoughtful writings on culture, society, or history. (Hullah & Pronko, 2015)

This definition formerly included the qualifier 'authentic': 'we mean ... authentic texts ... authentic writings'. But I now believe the condition of authenticity to be unnecessary and, in fact, meaningless. I explained this adjustment in an interview printed in the *Language Teacher*:

[A]nything can be a 'literary text' if it uses language, words, images, in ways allowing for interpretation beyond the literal. It's all in the presentation; provenance is irrelevant. If it makes my students think in mature critical ways, I don't care if a passage was penned by Shakespeare or the bloke who cleans the toilets. There's no exclusivity, no obligation to 'authenticity'. What's 'authenticity' anyway? Everything's authentic. Everything comes from somewhere. (Bibby, 2012: 33)

But my favourite definition of literature is one formulated by Carey, who succinctly defines it as 'writing that I want to remember – not for its content alone, as one might remember a computer manual, but for itself: those particular words in that particular order' (Carey, 2005: 173–174).

Is literature useful to educators, then? Poets appear unsure: 'Poetry makes nothing happen', wrote Auden, a Wildean maxim that might (ironically) appeal to objectors to the use of literature in EFL. Poetry epitomises literature: difficult, ambiguous, open to multiple interpretation, its 'meaning' not mediately clear. It 'makes nothing happen' because literature doesn't *make* things happen. People make things happen. People make choices and, as a result of these choices, good or bad things happen. How can literature affect this, if at all? Literature is where language becomes self-conscious, knowingly opaque, purposefully arranged to make us most aware of its affective, emotive aspects. Literature is a painless way of imposing ceremony, rituals, shapes, patterns upon the chaotic world and offering memorably expressed ideas in an attempt to make life more meaningful, less confusing. It makes maps that we can pass on to others so that they can learn from our versions of the world and begin to form their own. It can teach us, help us, heal us. It can *make us better*, in more ways than one. We can become what we read. Literature expresses life and the world to us, and offers us ways of explaining them, ways that we are free to concur or disagree with or, if we wish, ignore. Good literature survives because it speaks to every generation, tells us things that were not just true when it was written, but are now and will always be true. As Freud said, 'Everywhere I go I find that a poet has been there before me' (Nin, 1976: 14).

Poetry in Particular

Poetry invites us to think about words in ways we might not normally, automatically do. It makes language, ordinarily a transparent window to the world we wish to describe and communicate, opaque and important in itself. Marc Edmundson relates the tale of a fish swimming in the sea that is asked by an older fish, 'How is the water today?' 'What the hell is water?' replies the first fish (Edmundson, 2013). Language is like that, claims Edmundson: something that surrounds us and creates our world, but of which we spend most of our lives blissfully unaware. The most (perhaps the only) poetic act that many persons perform is the naming of a child: we want to know the meaning, history and connotations of the appellation we will bestow upon our offspring, hence the proliferation of *Naming Baby* books and websites explaining the etymology of proper names. The christening of animals demands similar study: the most famous racehorse in British sporting history was called Red Rum, a name chosen because it is the word 'murder' spelled backwards, and hence may signify a celebration of murder's opposite, life. Its alliteration of the initial 'r' sounds makes it very memorable too. A friend of mine named her dog 'Chappy' chiefly because, she explained, 'it sounds nice'.

A poet will put the same meticulous intensity of consideration into every single word of a poem, supremely aware of the meanings, connotations and melodic aural timbre of every lexical item chosen over other possible items, and will hope that readers appreciate these things too. Thomas Carlyle remarked on this correlation in 1832: 'all poetry ... is but a giving of names' (Dorsey, 1971: 4). For these reasons alone, I would propose poetry as a perfect medium in which L2 learners can hone and develop their ways with words, begin to be aware of the language they are learning at a deeper level, start *actively using language* rather than acting as a passive communicative conduit though which English words pass unconsidered.

Coleridge rightly defined poetry as 'the best words in their best order' (Coleridge, 1835: 84). Poets use language carefully – *sedulously* – in knowingly prominent creative ways to open and explode meaning. Poetry brings dead phrases and expressions back to life, makes words sensuous and more than just prosaic functional tools. Because poetry has (breakable, flexible) 'rules' and sets of inherited forms, it makes us aware and careful of how we express ourselves. Poetic expression reminds us that language can elevate, dignify, identify and beautify us as well as serve us. Literary texts stimulate us and challenge us intellectually, asking the questions that through the ages we ask ourselves. Rather than asking 'How do I get to the airport?', literature poses profound questions such as 'To be, or not to be?' Shakespeare is saying, how much is it worth staying alive when life is unbearable? The language is simple; the question is profound and timeless. Our response is a personal, free, inventive creative act.

I have always believed that my *raison d'être* as an educator is to *educate*: to draw out the latent potential of students who have memorised vocabulary and grammar, but whose linguistic creativity has been neglected. Utilitarian schooling and homogenous testing tell students that every problem has a right answer and a wrong answer. Poems can explode that limiting, reductive misconception by actively inviting each reader to export his or her own meaning from the text: poetry lets learners personalise L2. Poetry means different things to different people. There are no necessarily correct or incorrect answers. Instead, we have to *question*, think creatively and critically to make sense of it all. Poetry mirrors life in that important respect.

A Literature Syllabus?

The inclusion of literature in a syllabus *does not* necessitate that the course be classified as or labelled a literature course. This is of great importance, lest we invite and encourage the knee-jerk negative reaction alluded to by Waring and risk exacerbating literaphobia. A literary text best functions as a vehicle (see De Botton, 2013):

- to demonstrate the multifold expressive possibilities and potencies offered by language (and thus highly appropriate to EFL), and
- to serve as a vibrant and affecting repository of useful and engaging insights into a variety of human behaviours and mindsets that can develop life skills and give guidance (but never dogma) to readers faced with real-life dilemmas, difficulties and disasters, and even dreams and delights.

I will now proceed to demonstrate how a literary text might be presented and parsed in order to fulfil each of those two functions, by focusing firstly on some linguistic aspects and, thereafter, addressing methodological issues.

The linguistic challenge

A frequent objection to the use of literature in EFL is that it is 'too difficult'. My first riposte to this rather revealing objection would be: if the text you are teaching is 'too difficult' for your students, then either you have selected an unsuitable text and should abandon it and select another, or you are not teaching the text appropriately, or both. Learner needs and sensitivity to levels of maturity and linguistic ability are paramount. Text selection is vital and something that any competent teacher ought to be able to do (and, moreover, should be *allowed* to do) but, to a certain extent, to paraphrase a song, it ain't *what* you teach, it's *the way* that you teach it. A good teacher will be able to demystify and explicate even apparently complex study materials in a way that affords the learners in their classroom comfortable and meaningful access to those materials.

However, Hu and Nation (2000) admonish us that L2 learners must know '98–99%' of words in a text to be able to infer meaning. Waring agrees with them, and asserts that learners 'cannot guess the meaning of an unknown word from context if the surrounding text is too difficult' (Waring, 2001: 11). The consensus appears to be a 3000-word minimum vocabulary requirement for 'effective reading' (Hunt & Beglar, 2002). This surely precludes us from using literary texts? Not so. Fortunately, all our students have access to over 57,000 English words: it's called a diction-ary (Hornby *et al.*, 2013). Waring, who authored a book called *Getting Your Students To Use Their Dictionaries Effectively* (Waring, 2001), also advocates that L2 instruction (at least where 'vocabulary exercises' are concerned) 'should focus on deepening and internalising knowledge of words, not only the surface "form-meaning" level' (Waring, 2002: 12). The careful emotively and allusively charged employment of words in literary texts will clearly offer a vast reservoir of examples for teachers wishing to facilitate this 'deepen[ed] and internalid[ed] knowledge' of lexical items beyond a superficial level.

Of course, confidently to engage with, explicate or discuss a literary text in English, a student will require a certain level of linguistic com-petence. But that basic ability in language is a prerequisite to literary study, rather than what I would primarily seek to teach via a literary text. A good curriculum will ensure that courses are in place so that students receive sufficient scaffolding – competence in reading, writing and expressing opinions clearly – before they arrive at textual study proper. A student will learn many new vocabulary items from reading Tennyson's 'Ulysses' but that's not my prime aim in using that text in my class. If students come to me desiring solely to improve their TOEFL/TOEIC score, or brush up on their 'Business English' skills, I will gladly point them towards courses designed to do just that: courses specifically designed and paced to build up and consolidate appropriately graded chunks of vocabulary and classi-fied, calibrated grammatical patterns, answering techniques, test-taking strategies and so on. But if a student comes to me wanting to learn about life, art, culture, history, philosophy and society, and how these affect and effect ways in which people feel and think, then I will throw my door open to that student and pull down a book of poems from my shelf.

If a student tells me he or she is experiencing difficulties 'understand-ing' a poem, I tell that student that a poem is like an abstract painting: suggestively inviting our participation to construct meaningful encodings of its deliberately non-didactic content and provocative language and images. I tell them, 'Consult a translation of the poem into your own language if it helps you!' The sooner they can get into and connect with the text the better; then they can start exporting themes and ideas and processing them. I tell them not to worry, but to summon what Keats called 'negative capability' – the ability to know that there are aspects in everything we cannot fully comprehend and that we must not let this imperfect understanding be cause for unease or despair. Why? Because life is like that! In this elemental way, what I am defining here as 'literary' *mirrors* life. If you spend your life craving 100% understanding of everything in it, you'll have a miserable existence and likely go insane. You have to let it go. You have to abandon the quest for the perfect masterpiece and settle for the imperfect masterpieces that remain. Only then can you be content. Reading's like that too. We should read books as we read life. We can't expect to understand everything, nor should we, or that would be the end of things. Literature, like life, isn't a solvable scientific equation; it's an abstract work students can imagine into meaning, focusing on parts that communicate with them and, if necessary, ignoring bits they don't like or don't 'get'. This empowers them, puts them in control and leaves them no longer feeling guilty about having less than 'perfect' comprehension. L2 learners need that negative capability. They need to stop striving for perfection. Indeed, we all do.

Method madness

So, I hope, we can relax and be confident that our students will be capable of reading the (appropriately selected) literary texts we choose to place before them. The elephant in the room at this point, for many teachers reading this, will, I suspect, be the pragmatic query: but *how do you teach* it? Nowadays, we are being urged to be transparent: accountable for and methodical in all that we do inside the classroom. TEFL no longer stands for 'Teaching English for a Laugh', as it may have done in certain parts of the world some decades ago. It has become a regulated and systematised multimillion-dollar industry whose front-line employees (i.e. teachers) are (on the whole, one would hope) diligent and driven educators keen to identify the best, most effective ways to fulfil their self-chosen duty successfully to teach English as a foreign language. A spectrum of differing 'methodologies' has been debated and discussed, with this or that particular methodology drifting in and out of fashion with the passage of time: Grammar-translation, audiolingual, the silent way, communicative language teaching, total physical response, task-based learning, the lexical syllabus and so on, and so on (Richards & Rodgers, 2001).

But adherence (whether dictated or self-decreed) to this method madness, with its one-size-fits-all prescriptive implications, and any rigid adoption of one pedagogical strategy above all others, can be reductive and disabling, a straitjacket placed upon both agile-minded teachers and learners better regarded as individuals with differing goals and needs. There is no magic bullet. Between 1964 and 2015, the Canadian-American stage magician turned scientific sceptic James Randi's Educational Fund offered a cash prize, which latterly stood at $1,000,000, to anyone who could successfully pass his 'Paranormal Challenge' and, under scientific conditions, prove that they possessed 'supernatural powers' (Randi, 2015). Over 400 persons tried Randi's challenge; all failed. If I had a spare million dollars (which I do not), I would offer a similar challenge to proponents of one or other ELT methodology, gladly handing over the prize to anyone who could prove to me that his or her particular methodology is universally effective in all cases, including those in which other methodologies had been shown to fail. I am confident that my money, like Randi's, would stay in my pocket. An open-minded and eclectic commonsensical approach to methodology, mindful of learner needs and diligently adapted and revised whenever necessary, is preferable.

The Way That You Teach It

There will be more for both teacher and students to say about some texts than about others. As already stated, text selection is crucial: all else hinges upon and proceeds from it. Seasoned teachers know this anyway, based upon a personal catalogue of blissful and/or bitter experiences directly related to materials or textbooks they have chosen (or been ordered) to use down the years. So, which poems to choose? The Irish poet William Yeats famously said that only one thing is 'certain' of poets: 'we are too many' (Yeats, 1921: 33). It is likewise with poems. There are too many, and the majority of them are (for a variety of reasons: archaic and/or obscure lexis being a main one) neither good for EFL instruction, nor 'good' in any sense at all. Much of what passes for poetry nowadays is not poetry at all, at least to the ears and eyes of those of us old and/ or inquisitive enough to be aware of how good true poetry can be. The shallow, banal, creatively impoverished stuff that so often poses as poetry these days (akin to 'musak': I call it 'poe-zak', with the half-pun on the mind-numbing happy-drug Prozac fully intended) can, to listener-readers craving the emotional and mental stimulation that true poetry delivers, be at best an experiment in endurance and at worst an instrument of torture.

True poets create poetry for at least two important reasons: they feel a desire to express something worth expressing in a new and memorable way, and they possess a profound love of language that they are able inventively, respectfully and consistently to demonstrate. With too many 'poets', however, (a) the 'something' that is expressed, even once we have worked out (or been confidently told by a critic) what it is, is obscure or trivial or simply old-hat and of interest to no one except the poet himself or herself, and (b) the no-doubt once genuine 'love' of language has translated itself on the printed page as derivative pretentiousness or simply verbal affecta-tion, linguistic ostentation.

Many of my own early poems were undeniably guilty of both the above trespasses (no doubt many would argue that my more recent efforts are too). I once did a poetry reading in New York, after which a man approached me and started, 'I really like your poems', only to continue, 'I mean, I like that ones that are *about something*'. I now regard his seemingly bathetic comment as one of the most perceptive and constructive pieces of criticism I have ever received, and I have tried to act upon it. I mention it here because I think it relevant to text selection: poems that are obviously *about something* (rather than poems which are primarily histrionic introspective navel-gazing clad in lexical acrobatics) are the best sort of poems to choose for an EFL class. Poems with a clearly identifiable, easily accessible and learner-appropriate subject matter *at literal level* are the best poems to use.

Example 1

Here is a poem I use with EFL learners of varying ages and ability levels that has always been effective. It is a haiku, by the contemporary British poet John Cooper Clarke:

> To convey one's mood
> In seventeen syllables
> Is very diffic.
> (Cooper Clarke, 2015)

Ninety percent of this text's lexical items are in the *Oxford 3000* list:

> ... a list of the 3000 most important words to learn in English ... carefully selected by a group of language experts and experienced teachers as the words which should receive priority in vocabulary study because of their importance and usefulness. (*Oxford 3000*, 2015)

This means that the poem qualifies, in *Oxford*'s reckoning, as an 'intermediate text' (*Oxford Text Checker*, 2015). The term 'syllables' is the only word not in the Oxford 3000 list: a word it would be not difficult, and in fact very useful to teach to L2 learners for its meta-textual significance.

This clever poem succeeds by way of a linguistic trick that, if considered in context (out of 'haiku' context it wouldn't work so well), can disclose insight regarding the relationship between expression and language and form, and comparative cultural differences between traditional European and Asian attitudes as expressed in literary texts. Being a modern European poet, thus attuned to discursive modes of writing inherited from Wordsworth (all 13 books of *The Prelude*) through Tennyson (all 63 sections of *In Memoriam*) to Eliot (the symphonic movements of *Four Quartets*), Clarke is (knowingly and ironically) ideologically uncomfortable and artistically compromised as he attempts to inhabit the Japanese haiku form, with its enforced brevity, its strict 5–7–5 17-syllable confines (which should of course be explained to learners unfamiliar with the haiku discipline). In persona as speaker-poet, Clarke is deliberately missing a main point of haiku poetry: 'mood' is conveyed not by the poet (who must remain absent from a genuine haiku) but rather by objective minimalist presentation of an image or snapshot scene, described but not discussed. In haiku, the poem, not the poet, will 'convey'. Hence the difficulties and feelings of cultural alienation (that sense that haiku are, somehow, *weird*) that Westerners experience when first encountering authentic haiku poetry, feelings expertly rendered by Clarke's witty and well executed poem. Best of all for the EFL teacher, the poem succeeds or fails, at first reading, by way of its carefully selected lexis, in fact by use of a single (non-)word: 'diffic'. (If the final word were 'tricky', how less effective would the poem become?) This usefully highlights the expressive potency inherent to word choice, and shows how form can be manipulated to add meaning to the content of utterance. (Word-count restrictions on text messages and tweets, with which today's L2 learners are very familiar, might present similar issues.) I have found that presentation and subsequent discussion of this skilful little piece works to great effect with Asian learners of English of all ages, instigating, if taught properly, pertinent and animated classroom debate as to differences in native and L2 expression.

It should be stressed here (if it is not already clear) that EFL teachers wishing to use poetry should feel no pressure to restrict primary material selection to texts from an established literary 'canon', though many items from that canon may be eminently usable. Perhaps the most important defining and liberating characteristic of a literary text is *openness*, non-dogmatism. 'We hate poetry that has a palpable design upon us', wrote John Keats in 1821, and we would be correct to despise a fixed set menu of writings permitted the title of 'literature' for the same reason (Scott, 2002: 86). The 'established canon' (which, of course, is far from fixed but, rather, endlessly evolves and revises itself over time) is full of texts with unproblematic vocabulary and grammar. There are countless instances of writing, phrased in lexis neither difficult nor old, that can be used in EFL: hundreds of short poems by Wordsworth, Tennyson, Christina Rossetti, Blake, Yeats, Larkin, even Eliot, that, presented properly, can be first-rate teaching resources. I cannot think of a single 'canonical' author from the last two centuries who didn't write at least a few grammatically and lexically straightforward short poems (or standalone extractable sections from longer works).

Example 2

I will illustrate this claim with a poem written by that most 'canonical' of English authors, William Wordsworth (Wordsworth, 1807: 44). The poem is untitled, but is usually known as 'My heart leaps up' or 'The rainbow'. Here it is in full:

My heart leaps up when I behold
A rainbow in the sky:
So was it when my life began;
So is it now I am a man;
So be it when I shall grow old,
Or let me die!
The Child is father of the Man;
I could wish my days to be
Bound each to each by natural piety.

Ninety-three percent of the words in this poem are in the *Oxford 3000*. Two crucial words are not – 'behold' and 'piety' – but the fact that these terms will thus warrant additional instructional attention is beneficial and certainly not detrimental to the poem's efficacy for L2 learners. The first seven lines of the poem are clear: the speaker is moved by contemplation of a rainbow, recalling that he or she felt similarly in youth, and hopes always to be so affected, deducing that childhood feelings and experiences contribute to our identity and attitudes in adulthood, something that he or she clearly regards as a good thing. Five of these seven lines have an identical rhythm (iambic tetrameter, but no need to confuse the students with that): eight syllables in bi-syllabic units making four strong beats (de-DUM de-DUM de-DUM de-DUM), and this adds to the memorability of the piece and shows that the writer cared about sound as well as meaning. The two lines which deviate from the eight-syllable pattern, the shorter second and sixth lines, do so for good reasons, and I have often found that students can deduce these reasons for themselves: the second line is curtailed to leave the reader space to contemplate its sentiments in the same way that the speaker contemplates the rainbow, and the sixth line gives us sudden silence instead of words after 'die!', to emphasise the finality of death and imitate the silence thereafter. The poet thus uses rhythm not only for memorability but also to dramatically enhance meaning: *how* things are said is as important as what is said.

The first and seventh lines of the piece are worthy of special attention. The use of word 'behold', probably unfamiliar to most EFL learners, is significant. Why 'behold' and not the more predictable 'see'? Well, firstly, a two-syllable word was needed to set up the core tetrameter, so 'see' would have fallen short. But there is another reason. 'Behold' is, firstly, an archaic term most usually connotatively associated with biblical discourse; that is, it carries overtones of spiritual, religious experience that the simpler 'see' does not. Furthermore, 'behold' is parsable into 'be' plus 'hold': the speaker does not just 'see' the rainbow, but muses and meditates upon it (*holds* it in his or her mind) and connects with it (can almost be said to become or *be* one with it). Printed and online translations of this poem (which students should feel free to consult) often translate 'behold' into a simple verb meaning 'see' (Japanese translations almost always do). This simplification can be used to demonstrate the difficulty of translating poetry (since poems depend on very particular word selection), the way that 'poetry' itself (as Frost defined it) is 'that which is lost … in translation' (Brooks & Warren, 1961: 74).

Elsewhere, it pays to notice that, rather than tell us the emotion experienced, the speaker invites a reader to deduce it: the speaker's 'heart leaps up', intimating a potential variety of feelings (joy, surprise, awe, even fear). The seventh line of the poem works neatly as a cloze exercise, with the three nouns initially elided from the line and listed separately, to gauge students' understanding of the preceding sestet. This aphoristic line can also be used further to demonstrate how careful ordering of words can increase semantic effect: meaningfully recasting (here by simple inversion) an unremarkable phrase in basic lexis (the man is father of the child) can be a potent expressive device. Such 'tricks' are beloved of poets, but are well within the grasp of many L2 learners.

The poem's final two lines are, admittedly, tricky and, for a very low-level class, could be omitted without serious loss of effect. It might be useful to remember that an original meaning of the term 'religion' was 'binding' (hence the word 'bound'), and to note the unusual coupling of 'piety' (denoting belief rather than systematised religion) with 'natural', conveying the speaker's reverence for nature (of which the rainbow is a metaphor) itself.

In all these aspects, the poem demonstrates language being sedulously selected and meticulously arranged in order to create cognitive and emotive impact that augments and reinforces meaning: *how* things are said shapes what is said, and learners can immeasurably empower themselves by realising this and progressing accordingly. For teachers desiring to delve further thematically, Wordsworth's 'I wandered lonely as a cloud' (85% in *Oxford 3000*) and the 'For I have learned … my moral being' section of 'Tintern Abbey' (90% in *Oxford 3000*) are recommended. (Wordsworth expresses the same themes throughout his career in different ways.) With minimum ingenuity, poems such as these and their themes can be directed towards issues with which L2 learners of any age and level can comfortably connect.

Pop Song Lyrics

For teachers nervous of 'poetry proper', for whatever reason, certain modern popular song lyrics seem to me an appropriate resource, especially for lower-level learners. They fit well our fluid definition of a 'literary' text, as they tend to use language (words, images, sounds, poetic devices such as irony, punning, alliteration) in suggestive, creative ways, and raise questions as much as attempt to answer them. But songs can be straightforward and immediate (ideally without being shallow), less lexically dense and less cryptic than many formal written poems, whose explication can admittedly takes time and patience. Besides, the vast majority of young learners will be far more acquainted with (thus more initially receptive to) pop music than with poetry. Written poetry and song words are related and do many similar things with language, but with pop lyrics teachers can more quickly cut to the chase, the chase being learner response and personalisation of exported meaning.

In fact (and this will hopefully further demonstrate my 'ain't what you teach but the way you teach it' credo), at the precise time of first composing this paragraph, a very pleasant pop song has burst onto my radio: 'Vehicles & Animals', by the British band Athlete (from the 2003 album of the same name). Investigating, I find that in the first half of this song, the speaker affectionately describes a small male child who is most content when playing alone with his toys: his 'vehicles and animals'. In the latter half of the lyric, the central titular 'vehicles and animals' image is extended into an ambiguous metaphor for the modern human condition, where 'vehicles' might symbolise physical manmade possessions and technology, and 'animals' signify the natural world (as the rainbow in Wordsworth's poem signified nature). 'We've got our vehicles and animals,/ So we will be all right...'. The vocabulary and grammar of the song are unproblematic (99% of words in *Oxford 3000*!) and it expresses thought-provoking, profound sentiments in a manner stylistically most associated (as I have associated it in this chapter) with written poetry. 'There are moments of escape for every one of us,/ And the beauty in the times that we create', the speaker observes, concluding that, if as adults we stay in touch with childhood's innocent awe and remember the importance of 'play', then we can be untroubled by the issue of growing up: 'There's no need for us to go back in time/ Because we've found our open eyes...'.

I can easily conceive of using this song in the EFL classroom (and no doubt I will soon be doing so) as a catalyst to lively debate as to what we regard as important in our lives, how we should negotiate a balance between progress and tradition, science and the spiritual, innocence and maturity, and how our attitudes change (or don't change) as we grow older. In this latter aspect, 'Vehicles & Animals' most clearly connects with Wordsworth's poem of the rainbow experience: in both pieces the importance of maintaining a connection, in adulthood, with childhood experience, re-finding the 'open eyes' of childhood wonder, is emphasised by vivid (metaphorical) presentation of a genuine memory/experience. Another contemporary pop song, Keane's 'Somewhere Only We Know' (also 99% in *Oxford 3000*), from the 2004 album *Hopes and Fears*, also effectively echoes and complements the Wordsworth poetry referred to above, especially when presented together with its provocative official video.

Blueprint

My aim here is to be suggestive rather than prescriptive, but I have found that the following eight-stage pattern of activities can form an appropriate adaptable blueprint for class presentation of literary texts (each stage can be done as either written or spoken activity, or a mixture of both):

(1) pre-reading (warm-up, introduction of text theme);
(2) word check (present and explain problematic vocabulary);
(3) text (cloze activity, listening, reading aloud);
(4) comprehension (true/false, simple queries: text only);
(5) response (key phrases, characters, images, ideas from text, facilitated by queries such as 'What is described and/or analysed in the text?', 'How does the speaker connect what is described to his or her situation?', 'What new insight(s) does the speaker achieve and/or the text offer?');
(6) personalise/emotionalise (relate text to teacher and/or student personal experiences or insights);
(7) discussion/debate/essay/presentation (return to text theme);
(8) review/conclusion (return to text itself).

Conclusion

We are cognitively and emotionally engaged by literary texts, and the intellectually capable L2 learners we endeavour to educate need to be similarly affected by and engaged in their language-learning experience. Both of these processes should and can be pleasurable. Awareness of language's potency, beyond a functionally communicative level, is beneficial to learners. To achieve control of language's several registers, to recognise and master its affective/effective aspects in the manner exemplified by poets, is to become a rounded and proficient user of language with radically amplified expressive capabilities.

I recently received an email from a Japanese former student of mine who currently lives in London. He wrote:

> I want to thank you for introducing me [*sic*] English poetry and literature. It changed my life. When I talk with native speakers here, they don't only know I can speak English. They also know who I am.

Thus affirmed, I have argued in this chapter for the inclusion of literary materials in effective EFL curricula, with the disclaimer that certain preconceived notions of literature require reconsideration for these times. Properly to comprehend the special nature of literature as a resource is to achieve a profounder perception of teaching and learning that is itself both improving and enlightening. Literary materials can focus and activate L2, not in ideal but in practical ways. Literary content should not supplant, replace or compromise other EFL materials, but rather develop, reinforce and enhance them. Ideally, an EFL curriculum's constituent parts should combine to nurture students to a point where they feel empowered to make confident choices regarding the direction of their own learning, providing options from which they can select once that power to choose is instilled. In terms of an English curriculum, this will entail a systematic building up of the four skills, with skills ideally used together and not in isolation (Debate, rather than Speaking in one room and Listening in another), followed by a gradually integrated second tier of varied content-based courses including literary texts.

Language has many registers, and the more of these that L2 learners can confidently inhabit, the better for everyone. Literary language, so judiciously selected, so lovingly pruned, is one of these registers, and to deprive learners of access to it is to disable and emasculate their expressive potential. They may not choose to use it in most everyday situations, but to have it in their locker as an available option in special circumstances will make them more linguistically competent and complete. The singular parole that identifies a text as literary transcends lexis. It involves sounds, tones, imagery, metaphor, symbolism, irony, inter-textualities and narratives, all of which coexist to anchor, reinforce and enhance purposefully arranged themes and ideas. The idiosyncratic 'grammar' of literature resides in its rhetorical properties, management of constituent elements, relationships to inherited genres, styles and forms, and how all these can function meaningfully to explore (and, ideally, challenge) philosophical, ontological, political, artistic, moralistic, sociological and cultural positions. Thus, I have argued, L2 learners 'knowing' 99% of a literary text's vocabulary is *not* an essential prerequisite to understanding and the exportation of *meaning*, be it emotive or ontological or heuristic or all of these. The ideas behind literature speak as loudly as its actual words. Critical thinking and extracurricular life skills are valuably nurtured by judiciously chosen, appropriately presented, thematically expounded literary texts, and thus I advocate the maintenance (in both senses of this term) of literary texts in any meaningful English curriculum.

References

Adler, M.J. (1997) *Aristotle for Everybody: Difficult Thought Made Easy*. New York: Touchstone.

Ahmad, F. and Aziz, J. (2011) Students' perception of the teachers' teaching of literature. *British Journal of Arts and Social Sciences* 1 (1), 31–51.

Bibby, S. (2012) Simon Bibby interviews literature specialist Paul Hullah. *Language Teacher* 36 (5), 31–34.

Brooks, C. and Warren, R.P. (1961) *Conversation on the Craft of Poetry*. New York: Holt, Rinehart and Winston.

Brown, K.J. (2000) What kind of text, for whom and when? Textual scaffolding for beginning readers. *Reading Teacher* 53 (4), 292–307.

Carey, J. (2005) *What Good Are The Arts?* London: Faber and Faber.

Coleridge, H.N. (ed.) (1835) *Specimens of the Table Talk of the Late Samuel Taylor Coleridge*. London: J. Murray.

Cooper Clarke, J. (2015) 'Haiku.' Retrieved from http://johncooperclarke.com/?p=37.

De Botton, A. (2013) *Art as Therapy*. London: Phaidon.

Dorsey, J.M. (1971) *Psychology of Language: A Local Habitation and a Name*. London: Center for Health Education.

Edmundson, M. (2013) The ideal English major. *Chronicle of Higher Education*. Retrieved from http://chronicle.com/article/The-Ideal-English-Major/140553.

Hernandez, P.S. (2011) The potential of literary texts in the language classroom. *Odisea* 12, 233–243.

Holbrook, P. (2010) *Shakespeare's Individualism*. Cambridge: Cambridge University Press.

Hornby, A.S., *et al*. (eds) (2013) *Oxford Advanced Learner's Dictionary* (8th edn). Oxford: Oxford University Press.

Hu, M. and Nation, P. (2000) Unknown vocabulary density and reading comprehension. *Reading in a Foreign Language* 13 (1), 403–430.

Hullah, P. (1997) Language learners reading literary texts. Paper presented at the Japanese Association for Language Teaching (JALT) National Conference, Hamamatsu.

Hullah, P. (2003) L2 learner attitudes to ELT textbooks. *Language Teacher* 27 (9), 13–17.

Hullah, P. and Hoy, T. (2014) Appraisal and review of role perception and job satisfaction among expatriate English-teaching communities in Japan and Thailand. *Journal of Meiji Gakuin University Faculty of English* 129, 45–61.

Hullah, P. and O'Sullivan, B. (1995) The effect of text type on learner written performance. Paper presented at the Regional English Learning Center (RELC) International Seminar, Singapore.

Hullah, P. and O'Sullivan, B. (1996) Using 'modern' literary texts in the language classroom. *Guidelines* 18 (1), 43–57.

Hullah, P. and Pronko, M. (2008) Liberlit Manifesto. Retrieved from http://www.liberlit.com/liberlit-manifesto.

Hunt, A. and Beglar, D. (2002) Current research and practice in teaching vocabulary. In J. Richards (ed.) *Methodology in Language Teaching: An Anthology of Current Practice* (pp. 258–266). Cambridge: Cambridge University Press.

McCarthy, M. and Carter, R. (1994) *Language as Discourse: Perspectives for Language Teaching*. London: Longman.

Nin, A. (1976) *In Favor of the Sensitive Man, and Other Essays*. New York: Hardcourt Brace.

Oxford 3000 (2015) Retrieved from http://www.oxfordlearnersdictionaries.com/ wordlist/english/oxford3000.

Oxford Text Checker (2015) Retrieved from http://www.oxfordlearnersdictionaries.com/ oxford_3000_profiler.

Randi, J. (2015) James Randi Educational Foundation. Retrieved from http://web.randi.org/the-million-dollar-challenge.html.

Richards, J. and Rodgers, T. (2001) *Approaches and Methods in Language Teaching* (2nd end). Cambridge: Cambridge University Press.

Scott, G.F. (ed.) (2002) *Selected Letters of John Keats* (revised edn). Princeton, MA: Harvard University Press.

Tallis, R. (2006) Art (and philosophy) and the ultimate aims of human life. *Philosophy Now* 57, 7–9.

Waring, R. (2001) *Getting Your Students to Use Their Dictionaries Effectively*. Tokyo: Oxford University Press.

Waring, R. (2002) Basic principles and practice in vocabulary instruction. *Language Teacher* 26 (7), 11–13.

Wilde, O. (1908) Preface. In *The Picture of Dorian Gray*. Leipzig: Bernhard Tauchnitz.

Wordsworth, W. (1807) *Poems, in Two Volumes* (Vol. 2). London: Longman.

Yeats, W.B. (1921) *Four Years*. Churchtown: Cuala Press.

9 ICT Integration in Second Language Materials: Challenges and Insights

Dat Bao and Xiaofang Shang

Scholarly Interest in the Role of Technology in Course Materials

Over the past several decades, the dimension of language learning materials has been extended to embrace the involvement of technological and online resources (see, for example, Garton & Graves, 2014; Harwood, 2010; Tomlinson, 2011). The developments in technology that began in the 1980s continue to affect ELT materials and practice today (Dudeney & Hockly, 2012), and resources need to be constantly upgraded to catch up with new technologies such as videoconferencing, YouTube, Facebook, Twitter, blogs and mobile phones (Tomlinson, 2011), CD-Rom, 3D games, audios, videos, emails and other types of media. Among the key benefits of the use of computers and the internet are the richness of available resources (such as multimedia activities and web-based readings), the interactive nature of online materials (such as emails and web chats), the international context of language use (Muehleisen, 1997) and many online tools for fostering all kinds of linguistic competence (Liou, 2000).

A number of impact reports from Europe demonstrate learners' positive feelings about the use of ICT in education (Balanskat *et al.*, 2006; Korte & Hüsing, 2006). In particular, second language materials derived from information technology have a number of characteristics that make them distinctive from the traditional printed text and image:

- Resources available on the internet possess qualities such as fast access, and being current, authentic and abundant (Jonassen *et al.*, 1999).
- Since internet resources are available at all times, they allow for autonomous and self-regulated learning.
- Due to easy accessibility and sharing, they also provide conditions for peer collaboration, such as idea exchange and team projects, not only in the classroom but also in learners' own time and at their own pace through emails and web chats.

- ICT tools such as forums and Adobe Connect allow teachers to provide guidance and make comments on learners' work, either individually or collectively, without having to be present in person (Kumar & Tammelin, 2008).

Arguably, intelligent use of technology should make teaching easier, more enjoyable and more effective. Unfortunately, theoretical discourse regarding the use of ICT in language education has not gone very far. When browsing through 80 course evaluation journal articles and book chapters, we encountered very few that actually made reference to technology in language materials. Moreover, even these mentions do not discuss how ICT works but only acknowledge, in a sentence or two, the increased integration of technology in teaching (Demir & Ertas, 2014; Litz, 2005) and the need for students to acquire information through technology. Furthermore, when the above materials are reviewed or evaluated, it seems that the efficiency of pedagogy and technology-related materials are perceived as two separate categories, without much discussion of their mutual connection. There is not much analysis of how the implementation of ICT assets is informed by pedagogical research. While academic scholars and education systems express interest in and appeal for the use of ICT in English coursebooks, theories regarding the integration of ICT into English teaching materials remain surprisingly minimal.

Discussions on the role of technology in language education tend to focus on the logical assumptions and expected outcomes of ICT rather than analysis of approaches to the integration of technology. For example, there have been claims that the use of the internet has been innovative (Liou, 2000; Shetzer & Warschauer, 2000), that web tools are widely integrated into teaching materials (Yang, 2001), that the web provides 'greater access to a world of knowledge' (Dudeney & Hockly, 2012: 539), that the internet provides a new learning environment (Muehleisen, 1997) and enhances linguistic proficiency (Lee, 2000), that ICT serves to increase motivation (Grabe & Grabe, 2004), that technology makes learning more convenient (Attewell *et al.*, 2009) and that technology has changed language learning in interactive, collaborative and communicative ways (Kern & Warschauer, 2000), among many other affirmations of the positive outcome of ICT in language education. Despite such optimistic views about *what* happens, the discourse regarding *how* ICT has been implemented in a procedural and pedagogical sense to tap into second language acquisition remains fairly slim, with the exception of (according to Voogt, 2008b) a number of small-scale research studies in the classroom. While the implementation of technology has been increasing in quantity, scholars are expressing concern with the lack of brilliant practice in supporting learning (see, for example, Becta, 2008; Tearle, 2003; Yang, 2012).

Current Challenges in ICT Integration in Second Language Materials

Immature ICT pedagogy in second language teaching

An ICT impact report conducted in Europe in 2006 showed that teachers were struggling to embrace pedagogical concepts that maximise the potential of ICT (Korte & Hüsing, 2006). Although a number of research studies have looked at the effect of technology in second language education, such as peer feedback in chat environments (Morris, 2005), the role of IT in teacher development (Richards, 2005) and the entertainment value of software in L2 learning (Purushotma, 2005), theorisation will need a stronger empirical foundation and there have been appeals for further research to be conducted on the use of technology in language learning, so that ICT-based pedagogy can be strengthened (Voogt, 2008b).

Coursebooks should play a role in easing this struggle. With regard to materials evaluation, there have been appeals for consideration of the new changing era (Brown, 1995; Cunningsworth, 1995; Harmer, 1991; Hismanoğlu, 2011; Sheldon, 1988) and for ICT to be vibrantly taken into account (Dudeney & Hockly, 2007) to reflect modern-day pedagogical contexts.

Besides, ICT use in language education is not a stand-alone endeavour but is closely connected with many institutional, administrative, financial, instructional, technical and individual factors that need to be networked with available tools and resources to bring the optimal impact to learning (Piotrowski & Vodanovich, 2000; Tammelin, 2004). Due to this broad picture, the incorporation of technology in teaching and learning requires thoughtful collaborative work. Teachers will need to make tremendous efforts to train themselves in technological skills as well as to spend a great deal of time in preparing tasks and ways to make technology work along the lines of their pedagogical repertoire. Such timing, hard work and commitment create a challenge for teachers' successful use of technology, considering the fact that ICT training alone is insufficient to boost teaching quality (Albion, 2001; Cuban, 2001; Ertmer, 1999).

Disconnection between ICT and learner styles

Learners' perceptions of and attitudes towards the use of technology in second language learning represent another challenge that ELT materials developers should look into. Many communities of L2 learners around the world have been accustomed to face-to-face interaction and do not believe in the efficiency of online language courses in relation to verbal skills development, for example. In fact, learner preferences play a role in how materials can be developed. According to Kumar (2007), highly verbal learners might feel isolated by intensive use of ICT, while reticent learners might internalise online written participation as a safe environment for articulating their thoughts. Coursebook writers, therefore, might consider recommending both online learning and face-to-face options within the same learning activity, so as to cater for more than one group of learners. For example, a task that involves a discussion or debate between two characters could be conducted in a meeting or via email exchanges, or even both, which would reflect communication in the real world. In other words, course materials need to incorporate a number of ways to connect ICT resources with students' learning preferences, which should be pedagogically strategic and well justified rather than serve as a convenient add-on tool.

The lack of support for teacher preparation

It is uncommon to find coursebooks that provide teacher training in ICT as one of their components and most of the time teachers are expected to develop ICT pedagogy autonomously. Unfortunately, to connect online resources with the textbook can be a mystifying task that requires teachers to have a clear understanding of pedagogical principles, technological competence, willingness to make experimental effort and sufficient available time. In reality, not many teachers are able to invest in ICT development and their cautious attitude towards the pedagogical value of technology represents a real challenge. As Nim Park and Son (2009) observe, when teachers' ICT ability is limited, it is hard for them to develop a positive attitude towards the use of technology in the classroom. This situation requires materials to provide teachers with essential skills and experiences so as to convincingly demonstrate how ICT can enhance classroom processes. After all, teachers' need for practical experience with ICT is greater than their need for academic literature that provides knowledge in that respect. As Timucxin (2006) implies, a technological tool may produce a different effect that anticipated when it comes to actual implementation in concrete situations.

Disengagement between ICT resources and the existing curriculum

The discourse on ICT use by teachers indicates a lack of pedagogical support from the curriculum. Course materials play a role in teachers' optimal use of ICT because all aspects of teaching and learning per-formance, including ICT tools based on curriculum requirements, are reflected in the material. According to Voogt (2008b), teachers' freedom in creative integration of technology is often restricted by the slow revision of curriculum content and the narrow scope of assessment programmes. For instance, many curriculum developers do not consider allocating time for teachers to experiment with IT applications (Cuban, 2001) and teachers often suffer from a lack of guidance from the curriculum in what technology tools to select for their everyday teaching practice (Hinostroza *et al.*, 2008). In addition, the pressure to cover the prescribed curriculum content and to prepare students for examinations often limits the teacher's flexibility to make creative use of IT.

The coursebook, as a teachers' manual, might provide creative technological ideas and suggest useful online resources to help teachers perform their classroom teaching productively without having to spend the extra time and energy searching for relevant tools and selecting resources. It would be unreasonable for the coursebook to give only content while leaving the ICT implementation task for teachers to struggle with on their own. Scholars have expressed concern regarding how teachers 'have to go beyond their immediate means' (Voogt, 2008b: 128) when they wish to integrate technology in every lesson. The implementation of online resources for classroom teaching requires both teaching flexibility and conformity with the broader content of the curriculum. This process needs to be well supported by administrative effort, including, for example, the updating of CD-Roms, the purchase of relevant equipment, a systematic bank of specific resources related to the curriculum, allocated time for teaching preparation, and teacher training in the use of tools required for such ICT application.

Ways of Integrating ICT in Course Materials

In the rest of this chapter we would like to offer a number of insights and recommendations for coursebook developers to improve the quality of their design.

Taking a leading role in ICT use

Coursebooks, first of all, might take a leading role in incorporating ICT into language teaching and learning. There have been appeals for technology to be more frequently and comprehensively integrated into every aspect of the classroom process rather than merely to serve as additional tools (Bax, 2003; Hismanoğlu, 2011). In this endeavour, materials writers might consider how the use of ICT can enhance language practice in a way that compensates for some weaknesses in coursebooks. The shortcomings often found in coursebooks include the representation of unrealistic language models, limited cultural understanding and poor contextualisation of language use (Richards & Renandya, 2002).

Inspiring teachers' positive attitude towards technology

Coursebooks should inspire teachers and shape their proactive attitude towards the use of technology in classroom teaching. One common challenge to the incorporation of technology in the classroom comes from teachers with conventional practice who rely heavily on the textbook, who employ ICT only as an occasional add-on tool (Blin & Munro, 2008), who lack ICT training and support from the system (Hu, 2009; Mumtaz, 2000; O'Mahony, 2003; Wang, 2007) and who are reluctant to switch from a teaching to a facilitating role (Morrison & Navarro, 2012). Such narrow circumstances in teaching need to be broadened through more well organised support. A technology-integrated classroom process will have the conditions to develop if coursebooks can assist teachers in trying out new ideas (Redmond *et al.*, 2005; Nim Park & Son, 2009) through increasingly positive experiences and enhanced computer skills (Egbert *et al.*, 2002; Kim, 2002).

Providing technological guidance for teachers

Coursebooks need to provide specific guidance for teachers in implementing ICT tools to conduct classroom activities. In fact, teachers' need for technical support has been regularly highlighted (Hu & McGrath, 2011; McGrath, 2007) and it has been argued that technology can make a positive difference in teacher roles, learner roles and the impact of tasks on the learning process (Loveless & Ellis, 2001). To make this possible, coursebooks should consider how teacher and learner beliefs interact with the introduction of technological tools rather than solely attempt to apply what computers can do. As Albion and Ertmer (2002) imply, computers must act in a constructivist rather than authoritative manner, which means that one should look beyond the inherent features of technology into the basis of teacher knowledge and expertise.

Coursebooks should provide convincing examples of how the use of technology can bring more excitement to language learning. A number of research studies have indicated that if teachers perceive ICT as motivating learners as well as enhancing the quality of pedagogy and curriculum, they will be more willing to implement technology in their classroom practice (see, for example, Cuban, 2001; Doering *et al.*, 2003; Kumar & Tammelin, 2008; Russell *et al.*, 2003). Besides, materials should not treat all learners as one homogenous group who use ICT in the same way but they need to provide options for learners with various learning styles and interests, so that they can select the kind of tools they enjoy the most. As Hennessy *et al.* (2010) suggest, technology on its own cannot motivate teachers to apply it in their everyday teaching, but course materials need to present pedagogical options in connection with ICT use.

Another reason for providing diverse alternatives has to do with the question of workplace constraints. One cannot assume that ICT tools are available across all educational contexts, as limited ICT resources are inherent to many school systems. With this in mind, coursebooks should include suggestions for adapting ICT resources to local circumstances (Convery *et al.*, 2006). Any implementation, after all, needs to be understood within the ecology of expectations and practices in individual institutes (Eraut, 2010; Hammond, 2014; Hodkinson & Hodkinson, 2003).

Assisting teacher training in ICT

Coursebooks need to support teacher training and development in ICT use. In the everyday practice, many teachers are reluctant to employ technology in the classroom not only because they hold little belief in the impact of ICT tools but also because they do not have a strong ICT competence. To enable the optimal use of technology requires teachers to make the extra effort and without support from coursebooks and the school curriculum it is unrealistic to expect such effort. In fact, the challenge facing teachers in ICT use in the classroom cannot be underestimated, considering much of the literature has emphasised the need for good modelling and years of experience in achieving a fully integrated ICT classroom practice (Atkins & Vasu, 2000; Blin & Munro, 2008; Kuure et al., 2015; Li & Walsh, 2011; Picciano, 1994; Sheingold & Hadley, 1990; Ziegler et al., 2009).

Motteram (2011) provides a helpful example of building a blog or mobile phone application as a pedagogical way of enhancing language practice. If a textbook presents these ideas in its lessons, it should also provide a procedure, such as giving instructions to the teacher in setting up a blog or installing an application. Once teachers have learned or mastered the skills of using a blog and can see its operation in learning, materials can be considered to be pedagogically helpful, and to represent a small step forward in the incorporation of ICT in language teaching.

Modifying teacher roles in the classroom

Coursebooks should modify teachers' role in the classroom. As learning facilitators, teachers are expected to perform a wide range of tasks, including selecting resources, organising learning, motivating students, reflecting critically on the learning circumstance and adapting various technology possibilities to suit all of those needs. To do so requires teachers to have mastered a number of ICT tools, to be aware of their impact on education and to be able to adjust their teaching by optimising the impact of technology. This process of migrating from a conventional way of teaching to an updated approach in the ICT era will transform students' learning experience, but it requires more than just some ICT knowledge; rather, it requires a whole new style of teacher participation, in research, frequent reflection and enriching experiences. It also demands of teachers the ability and willingness to allocate time in developing ICT knowledge and skills (Pelgrum, 2001; Shah & Empungan, 2015), the ability to relate the goals of education to the effective use of ICT (Zepp, 2005) and a certain degree of commitment to research into how technological resources can enhance their inherent teaching repertoire (Ghasemi & Hashemi, 2011).

Suggested Principles for Integrating Technology in L2 Materials and Pedagogy

Assisting learners in selecting learning resources

The use of ICT is frequently linked with learner autonomy but it is not a very helpful attitude to leave learners to their own arbitrary use of technology without much guidance. Since the range of resources available on the internet is vast and very mixed in terms of relevance, to decide what is useful can be daunting for learners. It is therefore the teacher's job to communicate to learners what types of materials are pedagogically helpful so as to assist them in their selection. For example, depending on individual tasks, the teacher can encourage students to focus their choices on either content or form of the language, on educational values and entertaining effects, on familiar content or novel tools, on social relationships or intercultural interactions, on individual effort or teamwork, on consistent information and contradicting ideas, on revision of already learned structures or new language input, on information collection or problem solving, on mutual communication or personal reflection, as well as on various aspects of the language (such as grammar analysis, pronunciation practice, vocabulary building) and various degrees of challenge (such as learning space, complexity of materials and levels of proficiency). Once learners are aware of what is expected of them in the search for and choice of their learning materials, the task becomes highly manageable and the teacher can always make comments on such processes through acknowledging learner effort, praising choices and employing those in classroom activities so that learners feel their engagement has made a worthwhile contribution in the teaching and learning process. It is also important to note that the nature and choice of ICT in language learning should be connected with learners' needs, aims, styles, strategies and preferences (Richards, 2005).

Encouraging learners' self-regulation of ICT resources

Learners should be encouraged and guided to exercise control over their own learning with regard to the use of multimedia (linear, non-interactive) and hypermedia (non-linear, interactive) resources that serve learning. Such resources might range from texts to graphics, from sound to visuals, from still images to videos, from non-network software to web content, from real-time interaction to blog discussion; and this wealth of materials can be utilised both in class as learners collaborate with peers and beyond class as they engage in small projects to produce L2 output.

Teachers then can learn from this process and take note of learners' abilities to handle their own choices. They can also document learners' favourite ways of learning as enriched by information technology.

Promoting teacher–learner collaboration in the use of ICT

The above varieties of materials and methods of learning as generated by learner participation are worth noticing as they can help to build the teacher's bank of ICT resources, some of which might have been overlooked before these tasks were assigned to learners. We believe in teacher–learner collaboration in the use of technology in language education, based on the understanding that learners with interest and experience in the use of technology will provide inspiration and ideas for the teaching profession.

Gathering teachers and learners' experiences to inform materials development

Effective incorporation of ICT in language teaching requires considerable input from practitioners' everyday experimentation with technological tools and such hands-on knowledge can contribute tremendously to coursebook writers' expertise and production. Little in the literature has documented such trial-and-error reflection on a sufficiently systematic basis to lay a pedagogical foundation for the development of language teaching materials. With this type of exercise to inform materials writing, instead of leaving the use of ICT to teacher's themselves, writers will be in a better position to integrate technological tools into the heart of the coursebook. At present, collaboration between practitioners and materials developers is not commonly heard of in research-based publications. For example, a number of teachers with a constructivist teaching approach have utilised more sophisticated applications of software in simulation and data logging (Becker, 2000), for example, and such observations are often not communicated to course writers for enhancing the quality of ICT use in textbooks.

Conclusion

Although various views on ICT use in language education expressed in this chapter confirm many scholars' enthusiastic attitude towards the value of technology, the overall actual picture of ICT use has not been overly optimistic. Research shows that ICT implementation often takes place slowly (Pelgrum & Anderson, 1999) due to a gap between ICT policy and actual teaching practice. For example, many curricula, while stressing the need to employ technology, fail to provide instructional guidance (Goodison, 2002) and thus ICT implementation easily gets neglected by teachers as an optional undertaking. In addition, some programmes do not show an understanding of school cultures (Olson, 2000), nor do they take into account teacher perspectives and workplace constraints on the use of technology (Hennessy *et al.*, 2005).

Many a discussion of the contribution of ICT 'has been caught up in a largely aspirational and "inevitable" discourse' (Hammond, 2014: 194) and is sometimes characterised by an aspiration more to keep up with modern technological capabilities than to gain fundamental pedagogical understanding and justification (Rushby & Seabrook, 2008). It seems that second language materials have a long way to go, not only in providing ICT guidance for teachers but in making ICT use efficient in a way that would not otherwise take place without ICT integration. For example, the accompanying ICT components in many textbooks, such as software packages, tend to serve self-study rather than to support classroom learning (Hismanoğlu, 2011) and seem to be an additional materials bonus rather than meaningful integration that would enrich the learning process (see, for example, Wong, 2011). Besides, the types of challenges in ICT use include a wide range of factors, many of which go beyond the control of textbook developers, such as ICT training for teachers, a sophisticated support system, the development of ICT pedagogy, teachers' attitude and commitment, workplace constraints, and stronger empirical research into the efficiency of ICT integration in language learning.

Many training programmes require teachers to develop ICT ability by focusing solely on the technical skills rather than on how to adapt technology across various teaching circumstances (see, for example, Cai & Zhang, 2008; Zhao & Xu, 2010). When the training is over, teachers are expected to return to their schools and autonomously apply ICT to the prescribed coursebook. This task becomes challenging without the opportunity for a discussion on such application during the training and without guidance on how to connect technology with the prescribed curriculum. If course materials writers realise this dilemma and make an effort to weave technology ideas into the course development process, teachers will not have to struggle with the heavy burden mentioned above but can be inspired to employ workable ideas in their everyday teaching until this process becomes a natural part of their job.

Not unlike the need for collaboration and support in any other dimension of education, vibrantly implemented information technology in language teaching and learning requires the collective participation of various parties, including students, teachers, parents, academic theorists, teacher trainers, education policy makers, school facility providers, funding bodies, curriculum developers and coursebook writers. The challenges that have been highlighted in many systems have included the shortage of ICT infrastructure, lack of investment in teacher training in ICT use, lack of connectedness between technology and relevant curriculum content, community inclusion for sustainability, the cost of ICT ownership (Kozma & Vota, 2014), the lack of connection between courseware and the national standard and assessment practice (Harding, 2001) and a lack of research into the positive impact of ICT use on student performance (Dynarski *et al.*, 2007). In particular, there is the need to look further into the connections among 'the intended, the implemented and the attained curriculum' (Voogt, 2008a: 115) as well as the need to update and reinforce the entire school support system and logistics services (Young, 2003).

The use of ICT in a task should be recognised as effective, in a way that would not be so without such technological tools or online resources. In order for such impact to be well justified, it is essential to specify the aim of every task in relation to the ICT tool which serves that aim. As Pich and Kim (2004: 316) explain, we 'want students to use technology flexibly and creatively. We want them to be able to size up a task, recognise how technology might help them fulfil the task, and then use the technology to do so'. After all, the incorporation of ICT should be seen as an instrument rather than an ability and its major purpose in language education is to facilitate learning beyond what has been carried out without ICT support.

References

Albion, P.R. (2001) Some factors in the development of self-efficacy beliefs for computer use among teacher education students. *Journal of Technology and Teacher Education* 9 (3), 321–347.

Albion, P.R. and Ertmer, P.A. (2002) Beyond the foundations: The role of vision and belief in teachers' preparation for integration of technology. *TechTrends* 46 (5), 34–38.

Atkins, N.E. and Vasu, E.S. (2000) Measuring knowledge of technology usage and stages of concern about computing: A study of middle school teachers. *Journal of Technology and Teacher Education* 8 (4), 279–302.

Attewell, J., Savill-Smith, C. and Douch, R. (2009) *The Impact of Mobile Learning: Examining What It Means for Teaching and Learning*. London: Learning and Skills Network.

Balanskat, A., Blamire, R. and Kefala, S. (2006) *The ICT Impact Report: A Review of Studies of ICT Impact on Schools in Europe*. Retrieved from http://unpan1.un.org/intradoc/groups/public/documents/unpan/unpan037334.pdf.

Bax, S. (2003) CALL-past, present and future. *System* 31 (1), 13–28.

Becker, H.J. (2000) Findings from the teaching, learning, and computing survey: Is Larry Cuban right? *Education Policy Analysis Archives* 8 (51). doi: http://dx.doi.org/10.14507/epaa.v8n51.2000.

Becta (2008) *Harnessing Technology: Next Generation Learning 2008–14*. Retrieved from http://webarchive.nationalarchives.gov.uk/20101102103654/publications.becta.org.uk/display.cfm?resID=37348&page=1835.

Blin, F. and Munro, M. (2008) Why hasn't technology disrupted academics' teaching practices? Understanding resistance to change through the lens of activity theory. *Computers and Education* 50, 475–490.

Brown, J.D. (1995) *The Elements of Language Curriculum: A Systematic Approach to Program Development*. Boston, MA: Heinle and Heinle.

Cai, L. and Zhang, W.L. (2008) 从教育生态学的视角看信息技术与课程整合的' 高原期' 现象 [Analysing the plateau period of the integration between ICT and curriculum: An educational ecological perspective]. 现代教育技术 [*Modern Educational Technology*] 18, 5–7.

Convery, A., Mavers, D., Lewin, C. and Somekh, B. (2006) *ICT Test Bed Action Research Reports Cross-Case Analysis December 2006.* Manchester: ICT Test Bed.

Cuban, L. (2001) *Oversold and Underused: Computers in the Classroom.* Cambridge, MA: Harvard University Press.

Cunningsworth, A. (1995) *Choosing Your Coursebook.* Oxford: Heinneman.

Demir, Y. and Ertas, A. (2014) A suggested eclectic checklist for ELT coursebook evaluation. *Reading Matrix: An International Online Journal* 14 (2), 243–252.

Doering, A., Hughes, J. and Huffman, D. (2003) Preservice teachers: Are we thinking with technology? *Journal of Research on Technology in Education* 35 (3), 342–361.

Dudeney, G. and Hockly, N. (2007) *How to Teach English with Technology.* Harlow: Pearson Longman.

Dudeney, G. and Hockly, N. (2012) ICT in ELT: How did we get here and where are we going? *ELT Journal* 66 (4), 533–542. doi: 10.1093/elt/ccs050.

Dynarski, M., Agodini, R., Heaviside, S., Novak, T., Carey, N., Campuzano, L. and Sussex, W. (2007) *Effectiveness of Reading and Mathematics Software Products: Findings from the First Student Cohort.* Washington, DC: US Department of Education, Institute of Education Sciences.

Egbert, J.L., Paulus, T.M. and Nakamichi, Y. (2002) The impact of CALL instruction on classroom computer use: A foundation for rethinking technology in teacher education. *Language Learning and Technology* 6, 108–126.

Eraut, M. (2010) Knowledge, working practices and learning. In S. Billet (ed.) *Learning Through Practice* (pp. 37–58). London: Springer.

Ertmer, P.A. (1999) Addressing first- and second-order bariers to change: Strategies for technology integration. *Educational Technology, Research and Development* 47 (4), 47–61.

Garton, S. and Graves, K. (2014) Materials in ELT: Current issues. In S. Garton and K. Graves (eds) *International Prespectives on Materials in ELT* (pp. 1–15). Basingstoke: Palgrave Macmillan.

Ghasemi, B. and Hashemi, M. (2011) ICT: Newwave in English language learning/teaching. *Procedia – Social and Behavioral Sciences* 15, 3098–3102. doi: http://dx.doi.org/10.1016/j.sbspro.2011.04.252.

Goodison, T.A. (2002) Learning with ICT at primary level: Pupils' perceptions. *Journal of Computer Assisted Learning* 18, 282–295.

Grabe, M. and Grabe, C. (2004) *Integrating Technology for Meaningful Learning* (4th edn). Boston, MA: Houghton Mifflin.

Hammond, M. (2014) Introducing ICT in schools in England: Rationale and consequences. *British Journal of Educational Technology* 45 (2), 191–201. doi: 10.1111/bjet.12033.

Harding, R. (2001) What have examinations got to do with computers in education? *Journal of Computer Assisted Learning* 17, 322–328.

Harmer, J. (1991) *The Practice of English Language Teaching.* London: Longman.

Harwood, N. (2010) Issues in materials development and design. In N. Harwood (ed.) *English Language Teaching Materials: Theory and Practice* (pp. 3–30). New York: Cambridge University Press.

Hennessy, S., Harrison, D. and Wamakote, L. (2010) Teacher factors influencing classroom use of ICT in sub-Saharan Africa. *Itupale Online Journal of African Studies* 2 (1), 39–54.

Hennessy, S., Ruthven, K. and Brindley, S. (2005) Teacher perspectives on intergrating ICT into subject teaching: Commitment, constraints, caution, and change. *Journal of Curriculum Studies* 37 (2), 155–192.

Hinostroza, J., Labbé, C., López, L. and Iost, H. (2008) Traditional and emerging IT applications for learning. In J. Voogt and G. Knezek (eds) *International Handbook of Information Technology in Primary and Secondary Education* (pp. 81–96). New York: Springer.

Hismanoğlu, M. (2011) The integration of information and communication technology into current ELT coursebooks: A critical analysis. *Procedia – Social and Behavioral Sciences* 15, 37–45. doi: http://dx.doi.org/10.1016/j.sbspro.2011.03.048.

Hodkinson, P. and Hodkinson, H. (2003) Individuals, communities of practice and the policy context: School teachers' learning in their workplace. *Studies in Continuing Education* 25 (1), 3–21.

Hu, Z. (2009) ICT, teacher development and the reform of college English in China: An implementation study. Doctoral thesis, University of Nottingham.

Hu, Z. and McGrath, I. (2011) Innovation in higher education in China: Are teachers ready to integrate ICT in English language teaching? *Technology, Pedagogy and Education* 20 (1), 41–59. doi: 10.1080/1475939X.2011.554014.

Jonassen, D.H., Peck, K.L. and Wilson, B.G. (1999) *Learning with Technology: A Constructivist Perspective.* Upper Saddle River, NJ: Merrill.

Kern, R. and Warschauer, M. (2000) Theory and practice of network-based language teaching. In M. Warschauer and R. Kern (eds) *Network-Based Language Teaching: Concepts and Practice* (pp. 1–19). New York: Cambridge University Press.

Kim, H. (2002) Teachers as a barrier to technology-integrated language teaching. *English Teaching* 57 (2), 35–64.

Korte, W.B. and Hüsing, T. (2006) *Benchmarking Access and Use of ICT in European Schools 2006: Results from Head Teacher and A Classroom Teacher Surveys in 27 European Countries. Vol. 2: eLearning Papers.* Retrieved from http://www.ictliteracy.info/rf.pdf/Use%20of%20ICT%20in%20Europe.pdf.

Kozma, R.B. and Vota, W.S. (2014) ICT in developing countries: Policies, implementation, and impact. In J.M. Spector, M.D. Merrill, J. Elen and M.J. Bishop (eds) *Handbook of Research on Educational Communications and Technology* (4th edn) (pp. 885–894). New York: Springer.

Kumar, S. (2007) Professor use, facilitation, and evaluation of asynchronous online discussions in on-campus courses. In C. Montgomerie and J. Seale (eds) *Proceedings of EdMedia: World Conference on Educational Media and Technology 2007.* Chesapeake, VA: Association for the Advancement of Computing in Education (AACE).

Kumar, S. and Tammelin, M. (2008) *Integrating ICT into Language Learning and Teaching.* Retrieved from https://www.researchgate.net/profile/Swapna_Kumar/publication/255583982_INTEGRATING_ICT_INTO_LANGUAGE_LEARNING_AND_TEACHING/links/540333ea0cf2c48563b02ae0.pdf.

Kuure, L., Molin-Juustila, T., Keisanen, T., Riekki, M., Livari, N. and Kinnula, M. (2015) Switching perspectives: From a language teacher to a designer of language learning with new technologies. *Computer Assisted Language Learning,* 1 July, 1–12. doi: 10.1080/09588221.2015.1068815.

Lee, K.W. (2000) Energizing the ESL/EFL classroom through Internet activities. *Internet TESL Journal* 6 (4), 1–4.

Li, L. and Walsh, S. (2011) Technology uptake in Chinese EFL classes. *Language Teaching Research* 15 (1), 99–125. doi: 10.1177/1362168810383347.

Liou, H.C. (2000) Conceptualization and implementation of an English learning website which bridges TEFL theories and practices. Paper presented at the 4th International Conference on Multimedia Language Education, Taipei, Taiwan.

Litz, D.R. (2005) Textbook evaluation and ELT management: A South Korean case study. *Asian EFL Journal* 48, 1–53.

Loveless, A. and Ellis, V. (2001) *ICT, Pedagogy and the Curriculum: Subject to Change.* London: Routledge Falmer.

McGrath, I. (2007) Textbooks, technology and teachers. In O. Alexander (ed.) *New Approaches to Materials Development for Language Learning* (pp. 343–358). Bern: Peter Lang.

Morris, F. (2005) Child-to-child interaction and corrective feedback in a computer mediated L2 class. *Language, Learning and Technology* 9 (1), 29–45.

Morrison, B.R. and Navarro, D. (2012) Shifting roles: From language teachers to learning advisors. *System* 40, 349–359.

Motteram, G. (2011) Developing language-learning materials with technology. In B. Tomlinson (ed.) *Materials Development in Language Teaching* (2nd edn) (pp. 303–327). New York: Cambridge University Press.

Muehleisen, V. (1997) *Projects Using the Internet in College English Classes. Vol. 3: The Internet TESL Journal.* Retrieved from http://iteslj.org/Lessons/Muehleisen-Projects.html.

Mumtaz, S. (2000) Factors affecting teachers' use of information and communications technology: A review of the literature. *Journal of Information Technology for Teacher Education* 9, 319–331.

Nim Park, C. and Son, J.-B. (2009) Implementing computer-assisted language learning in the EFL classroom: Teachers' perceptions and perspectives. *International Journal of Pedagogies and Learning* 5 (2), 80–101. doi: 10.5172/ijpl.5.2.80.

Olson, J. (2000) Trojan horse or teacher's pet? Computers and the culture of the school. *Journal of Curriculum Studies* 32, 1–8.

O'Mahony, C. (2003) Getting the information and communication technology formula right: Access + ability = confident use. *Technology, Pedagogy and Education* 12, 295–311.

Pelgrum, W.J. (2001) Obstacles to the integration of ICT in education: Results from a worldwide educational assessment. *Computers and Education* 37 (2), 163–178. doi: http://dx.doi.org/10.1016/S0360-1315(01)00045-8.

Pelgrum, W.J. and Anderson, R.E. (eds) (1999) *ICT and the Emerging Paradigm for Life Long Learning: A Worldwide Educational Assessment of Infrastructure, Goals and Practices.* Amsterdam: International Association for the Evaluation of Educational Achievement.

Picciano, A. (1994) *Computers in the Schools: A Guide to Planning and Administration.* New York: Merrill, Macmillan.

Pich, A. and Kim, B. (2004) Principles of ICT in education and implementation strategies in Singapore, the province of Alberta in Canada, the United Kingdom, and the Republic of Korea. *Journal of Educational Technology Systems* 32 (4), 315–335.

Piotrowski, C. and Vodanovich, S.J. (2000) Are the reported barriers to Internet-based instruction warranted? A synthesis of recent research. *Education* 121 (1), 48–53.

Purushotma, R. (2005) Commentary: You're not studying, you're just.... *Language, Learning and Technology* 9 (1), 80–96.

Redmond, P., Albion, P.R. and Maroulis, J. (2005) Intentions v reality: Pre-service teachers' ICT intergration during professional experience. Paper presented at the 16th International Conference of the Society for Information Technology and Teacher Education (SITE 2005), Phoenix, USA.

Richards, C. (2005) The design of effective ICT-supported learning activities: Exemplary models, changing requirement, and new possibilities. *Language, Learning and Technology* 9 (1), 60–79.

Richards, J.C. and Renandya, W.A. (eds) (2002) *Methodology in Language Teaching: An Anthology of Current Practice.* Cambridge: Cambridge University Press.

Rushby, N. and Seabrook, J. (2008) Understanding the past – illuminating the future. *British Journal of Educational Technology* 39 (2), 198–233.

Russell, M., Bebell, D., O'Dwyer, L. and O'Connor, K. (2003) *Teachers' Beliefs About the Use of Technology: Enhancing the Use of Technology for New and Veteran Teachers.* Boston, MA: Boston College, Technology and Assessment Study Collaborative.

Shah, P.M. and Empungan, J.L. (2015) ESL teachers' attitudes towards using ICT in literature lessons. *International Journal of English Language Education* 3 (1), 201–218.

Sheingold, K. and Hadley, M. (1990) *Accomplished Teachers: Integrating Computers into Classroom Practices.* New York: Bank Street College of Education, Center for Technology in Education.

Sheldon, L.E. (1988) Evaluating ELT textbooks and materials. *ELT Journal* 42 (4), 237–246.

Shetzer, H. and Warschauer, M. (2000) An electronic literacy approach to network-based language teaching. In M. Warschauer and R. Kern (eds) *Network-Based Language Teaching: Concepts and Practice* (pp. 171–185). New York: Cambridge University Press.

Tammelin, M. (2004) *Introducing a Collaborative Network-Based Learning Environment into Foreign Language and Business Communication Teaching: Action Research in Finnish Higher Education*. Retrieved from https://helda.helsinki.fi/handle/10138/19988.

Tearle, P. (2003) ICT implementation: What makes the difference?. *British Journal of Educational Technology* 34 (5), 567–583.

Timucxin, M. (2006) Implementing CALL in an EFL context. *ELT Journal* 60 (3), 262–271.

Tomlinson, B. (2011) Introduction: Principles and procedures of materials development. In B. Tomlinson (ed.) *Materials Development in Language Teaching* (2nd edn) (pp. 1–31). New York: Cambridge University Press.

Voogt, J. (2008a) IT and curriculum processes. In J. Voogt and G. Knezek (eds) *International Handbook of Information Technology in Primary and Secondary Education* (pp. 115–116). New York: Springer.

Voogt, J. (2008b) IT and curriculum processes: Dilemmas and challenges. In J. Voogt and G. Knezek (eds) *International Handbook of Information Technology in Primary and Secondary Education* (pp. 117–132). New York: Springer.

Wang, Y. (2007) Information literacy that teachers need in the information age [in Chinese]. *Education Technology Resources* 1 (2), 13–15.

Wong, P. (2011) Case study: Singapore. In UNESCO 2011 (ed.) *Transforming Education: The Power of ICT Policies* (pp. 37–66). Paris: United Nations Educational, Scientific and Cultural Organization.

Yang, H. (2012) ICT in English schools: Transforming education? 1. *Technology, Pedagogy and Education* 21 (1), 101–118.

Yang, S.C. (2001) Integrating computer-mediated tools into the language curriculum. *Journal of Computer Assisted Learning* 17, 85–93.

Young, S.S.C. (2003) Integrating ICT into second language education in a vocational high school. *Journal of Computer Assisted Learning* 19, 447–461.

Zepp, R.A. (2005) Teachers' perceptions on the roles on educational technology. *Journal of Educational Technology and Society* 8 (2), 102–106.

Zhao, J. and Xu, F. (2010) The state of ICT education in China: A literature review. *Frontiers of Education in China* 5 (1), 50–73. doi:http://dx.doi.org/10.1007/s11516-010-0006-1.

Ziegler, G., Eskildsen, L., Coonan, C.M., Ludbrook, G., Bottin, C. and De Matteis, P. (2009) *Recommendations for Optimising Language Teacher Training in Europe*. Retrieved from http://www.ciep.fr/sites/default/files/atoms/files/semlang-recommandations-pour-optimisation-formation-des-enseignants-de-langues.pdf.

10 Mining Online L2 Learning Resources: From SLA Principles to Innovative Task Design

Flora D. Floris, Willy A. Renandya and Dat Bao

The Need for a Method to Manage Online Materials

With the rapid growth of computer applications, communication technologies and open-access information on the internet, online resources have now become an indispensable source of second language (L2) classroom materials. However, this wealth of materials varies greatly in quality and so requires thoughtful selection and creative modification to produce optimal learning impact. Although modern technology has increased flexibility in both course content and modes of delivery (McLoughlin & Oliver, 2000), such flexible practice might need well theorised, creative management to become maximally helpful in teaching and learning. As the availability of online L2 resources has enormously increased the range of choice, the key questions have become how to choose well and how to put those choices to good use. To acquire this understanding would mean making a step forward in pedagogy and materials.

Similarly to Hicks and Turner (2013), who suggest a remixing of pedagogy to meet the context of a digital age, in this chapter we discuss and propose ways to select, process and perhaps innovatively modify L2 resources that are available online. This chapter presents six L2 acquisition principles and discusses how they can productively serve as a guide for the selection of online materials. These points are then illuminated further through concrete examples to show how online materials can be used in the teaching of macro language skills – listening, speaking, reading and writing. To strengthen the quality of those choices, a number of innovative ideas are recommended to remove classroom learning as far from conventional, typical and dull ways of L2 learning as possible. The chapter concludes with recommendations on how teachers and materials writers can develop further tasks and activities based on online resources.

Today's students are increasingly living what Swenson *et al.* (2006) refer to as digital-media-saturated lives. Most are exposed to internet-based information, are familiar with a computerised environment and are accustomed to the use of digital communication from an early age. They engage in online activities. They use the internet to search for information, find new friends, play games, upload pictures, publish blogs and so forth. This context requires teachers and materials developers to incorporate technology into their teaching activities in ways that engage and motivate learners. One can take advantage of the vast number of resources that are freely available on the internet and exploit them for L2 teaching purposes. Many websites contain potentially useful language teaching materials that learners can easily access, but they need guidance in doing so. The resources range from sites designed specifically for teaching English as a foreign or second language (EFL/ESL) to sites offering authentic texts, images, audio and video podcasts and digital tools.

It is important to remember that, in general, online resources are not ready to be used but a great deal of work needs to be done for optimal teaching and learning impacts. The success of the integration of the internet in a language classroom depends on how appropriate the selected sites are for the intended context and how they are employed to achieve teaching objectives. Both teachers and coursebook writers need to decide how to harness online resources to facilitate language development.

When selecting internet resources for classroom instruction, one might like to consider some principles of second language acquisition (SLA) as guidance. Without judicious use of online resources, it would be hard ensure that optimal L2 learning will take place in the language classroom. We discuss in this chapter six of these principles which SLA and ELT experts (e.g. Ellis, 2005; Tomlinson, 2012) believe to be important when teachers select and adapt L2 teaching materials.

First Principle: Comprehensible Input

Input plays a very important role in language acquisition. SLA scholars recommend that learners are exposed to the target language in a communicative context (Wong, 2005). Such exposure provides opportunities for learners to observe the linguistic features of the target language and to make sense of what they hear or see. Input helps build learners' vocabulary, develop their understanding of grammar and as a result improve their overall language proficiency. A large quantity of input is probably better than less, but not all types of input are considered equally valuable. Krashen (1985) argues that good input is comprehensible, which might mean making it easy to understand either by modifying it or by using contextual props.

Renandya (2011) states that good input for L2 learners has to meet the following requirements:

- It has to be comprehensible.
- It has to be abundantly and reliably available.
- It has to be frequently encountered.
- It has to contain language features that are slightly beyond the learners' current level.
- It has to contain language features that engage the learners' attention.
- It has to be meaningful and interesting

Ensuring access to abundant and comprehensible input is clearly one of the major tasks that language teachers need to accomplish. According to Krashen (2005), English teachers can ensure access to good input by maximising the use of the target language inside their classrooms and by providing multiple opportunities for students to get input outside the classrooms. Encouraging students to do their independent reading and viewing outside the classroom will ensure that they get sufficient language input for their continued language development.

One of the great features of the internet is the instant access to various written, audio and audio-visual input in English. BookBox, one of the YouTube educational channels (http://www.youtube.com/user/bookboxinc/featured), for example, offers highly interesting digital short stories that can be used for extensive reading, listening or viewing activities (Figure 10.1). All stories provided are narrated, synchronised with audio and visual elements, and presented in clearly structured and highly visual ways. They are only about five minutes long, and input that is highly contextualised and is easy to comprehend. The same-language subtitling (SLS) feature (Figure 10.2) is also provided on this website.

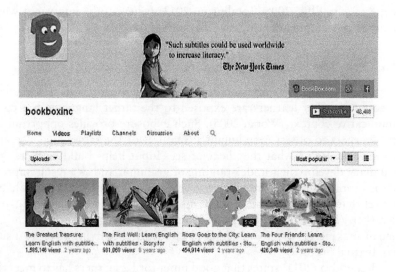

Figure 10.1 BookBox's frontpage

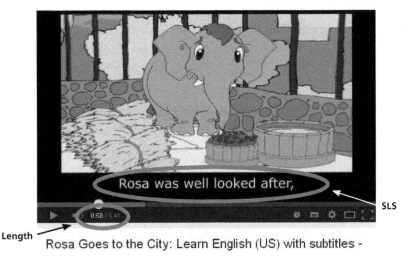

SLS

Length

Rosa Goes to the City: Learn English (US) with subtitles -

Figure 10.2 BookBox's 'Rosa goes to the city'

It helps learners read along at a comfortable pace while listening to the recording of the same short story. The text they see and the sound they hear reinforce each other in perfect synchronisation (Kothari & Takeda, 2000). The language-learning benefits of SLS, according to King (2002) in relation to learning English, include the following:

- increased motivation to learn English, especially to listen to the English dialogues in movies;
- enhanced reading and listening skills;
- deeper understanding of English context-bound expressions;
- improved word-recognition skills;
- enhanced vocabulary and pronunciation skills;
- faster reading speed.

Breaking News English (http://www.breakingnewsenglish.com) is another internet website that can be used to provide extensive target language input for L2 learners (Figure 10.3). The site presents authentic current news stories that are put into seven difficulty levels, from elementary to advanced. The news stories are typically 250–300 words long and they cover a wide range of topics. For classroom teachers or learners who need more practice in language development, Breaking News English provides some exercises (along with answer keys). The site also provides a listening link which enables learners to listen to the recorded reading of the news text and download the audio if needed. The listening speed can be adjusted across five levels, from slowest to fastest (Figure 10.4).

Figure 10.3 Breaking News English's front page

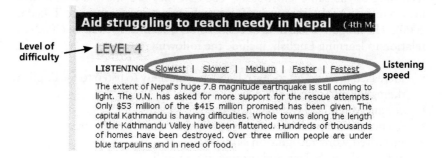

Figure 10.4 Example of a news story on Breaking News English

The design of Breaking News English allows learners to do simultaneous reading and listening of the text. This makes reading and listening activities easier while at the same time it helps learners to gain full understanding of the reading texts provided. In the long run, as stated by Kuhn and Stahl (2000), this mode will help L2 learners to gain significant improvement in several reading areas, including comprehension.

One innovative way of making this task more rewarding is to create follow-up sub-tasks to invite both written to verbal responses to the video. Coursebooks might provide handouts with opportunities for learners to interact further with what they watch, for example to think of a moral for the story, share their own experiences, imagine they are characters in the story and say how they would act differently, or suggest how a person might behave if the same event took place in another culture.

Another creative way of exploiting this task is to pause selected frames in the video, capture still images and print them out on flashcards. The flashcards are then shared among learners for a variety of learning purposes, such as identifying vocabulary or sounds, memorisation of specific language, checking comprehension, making comments on selected details in the video, capturing major syntactic structures for more practice, and so on. All of these can be learned among peers with teacher guidance. These flashcards can also be used as a formative assessment tool during the lesson or in any of the next sessions when the need arises to recall previously learned information.

Access to a great deal of comprehensible target language input is believed to be one of the key instruments in language learning. With the help of technology, teachers can provide extensive and meaningful input through the use of freely available internet resources such as BookBox and Breaking News English. Generally, the beauty of such websites, as well as its graded levels and the convenient choices of both texts and levels, is the result of hard work on the part of a design team. However, it has to be said that many of the tasks on Breaking News English that follow the news are rather conventional, with mainly gap-filling and word-matching exercises, and even the section 'Write your own questions' regrettably leaves the discussion to learners without much guidance, motivating strategies, or any inspirational, affective stimulus. If ELT materials writers are to recommend this website for language practice, it may be helpful to include follow-up tasks that tap into learners' imagination, creativity, multiple senses and the desire to share individualised ideas; otherwise, the use of these online resources risks becoming humdrum, routine-based learning.

Second Principle: Saliency

Saliency is related to input. To acquire the target language, learners need both input and notice of the input received. In order to acquire pragmatics competence, for example, one must notice both linguistic forms and the relevant contextual features. Noticing alone does not mean that learners will automatically acquire the target language but it is an essential starting point for acquisition. Input that gets noticed receives a deeper level of processing, which in turn increases its likelihood of being incorporated into L2 learners' developing linguistic system.

Skehan (1998) observes that the more prominent a language form is in the input, the greater is the chance that it will be noticed, while the less salient a form is – such as a bound or unstressed morpheme, or a grammar feature that does not carry much meaning (e.g. the third person singular) – the less likely it is to be noticed. As stated by Schmidt (1993: 195) in his 'noticing' hypothesis, 'target language forms will not be acquired unless they are noticed and one important way that instruction works is by increasing the salience of target language forms in input so that they are more likely to be noticed by learners'.

Teachers can help their learners to notice various language forms by having a wide range of possibilities for the classroom activities, such as input flooding and textual enhancement (Sharwood-Smith, 1993). Input flooding is defined by Sharwood-Smith (1993) as the enrichment of input by artificially increasing the number of the target forms while maintaining a communicative focus and without overtly drawing attention to the target form. Textual enhancement is a technique of manipulating the typo-graphical features of a written text such as using larger fonts or coloured words, underlining, bold type or capitalisation, to attract students' attention and make them conscious of particular language features.

In the past, marker pens were used to highlight paper documents; to point out important issues or information on printed papers. Nowadays teachers can use a variety of online annotation tools, such as Marker.to (http://marker.to), to enhance the noticeability of certain language features in the input materials. The applications can be used in diverse ways to highlight important language features in online text on a website so as to increase their noticeability. Feedback can be further enhanced through a combination of tools beyond the options for textual enhancement noted above. One creative technology-based approach of providing feedback is to tap into learners' multisensory experience (see, for example, Oliver *et al.*, 2004). This approach, as we visualise it, can be performed through various tools such as: Word editing functions for learners to read; video-captured commentaries for learners to watch and listen; virtual reality space for peer interaction; and software-based engines for self-correction, to name a few. Recent discourse in creative technology has shown how learners can build more integrated, immersive experiences through computers using all of these methods and in various combinations.

Images available on the internet can also be used to highlight the meaning of vocabulary words. Pixabay (http://pixabay.com), for instance, provides over 390,000 public-domain images. Some words (as tags) are presented with each picture that capture the essence of the image (Figures 10.3 and 10.5). The picture can thus assist learners' memory and it is the combination of image and words that touches on noticeability.

The concept of noticing and saliency is very important in ESL/ESL classrooms. Schmidt (1995: 20) proposes that 'SLA is largely driven by what learners pay attention to and notice in target language input and what they understand the significance of noticed input to be'. Therefore, it is important for teachers to help learners notice language features or items in order to acquire them.

Learning in the digital age has changed the structure of narratives, to become what Bañares-Marivela and Rayón-Rumayor (2016) refer to

Bird, Flying, Soaring, Soar, Fly   **Winter, Cold, Snow, Forest**

Figure 10.5 Example of a public-domain picture on Pixabay (http://pixabay.com), with tags: soaring bird; and winter scene

as 'multimodal narratives', whereby image–word interrelated expression not only enhances communication of meaning but also promotes readers' interaction with texts. Empirical research conducted by Bao (2017) demonstrates a tendency among today's students to make use of both mediums in their creative writing. In his study, 107 students in China and Thailand were given the choice to use either or both tools, that is, visual images and/or words, to develop an essay about their life aspirations. Sixty-seven of the students (63%) chose to integrate both together, in a variety of innovative combinations. For example, while some students employed both means to express the same idea, others used the two tools separately for sharing different thoughts. While some kept pictures and texts separate in their essay, others wove them together. Arguably, the relationship between visual texts and words is more complex than it seems.

Third Principle: Frequency

'Children acquiring their first language take between 2 and 5 years to achieve full grammatical competence, during which time they are exposed to massive amounts of input' (Wells, 1985; cited in Ellis, 2005: 11). Similar amounts of input are needed regularly over the same period to develop L2 competence. Without this amount and frequency of language input, it is simply not possible to master a language.

The third SLA principle discussed here deals with the frequency of input because frequency of encounters determines what gets learned (Renandya, 2013). Input frequency affects the processing of phonology and phonotactics, reading, spelling, lexis, morphosyntax, formulaic language, language comprehension, grammaticality, sentence production and syntax (Ellis, 2002).

That frequency affects language acquisition is not hard to fathom; this essentially means that the more times learners are exposed to or experience something, the stronger the memory of that experience they are likely to build. Thus, when a language feature appears frequently, it will be more easily noticed and integrated into the interlanguage system (Schmidt, 1990). Some highly successful Chinese learners involved in a study by Ding (2007) reported that after doing extensive reading and listening for a period, they began to learn and internalise numerous fixed expressions in English. Later on, 'when they speak English, lines from movies [referring to movie captions] often naturally pop out, making others think of their English as natural and fluent' (Ding, 2007: 275).

All online reading and listening texts can serve as suitable materials for extensive reading and listening. What teachers need to do is to encourage their L2 learners to increase their reading and listening frequency and/ or read and listen to the same texts repeatedly, inside or outside the classroom. Online versions of newspapers might be appealing, and such sites can be especially valuable if readers are able to compare different presentations of the same news item.

Another website that might be useful for the third principle of SLA is Lyrics Training (http://lyricstraining.com), which features emedded YouTube music videos of popular songs and their lyrics. As a video begins to play, learners are invited to complete a gap-fill exercise using the song's lyrics, which appear underneath the video (Figure 10.6). The difficulty level

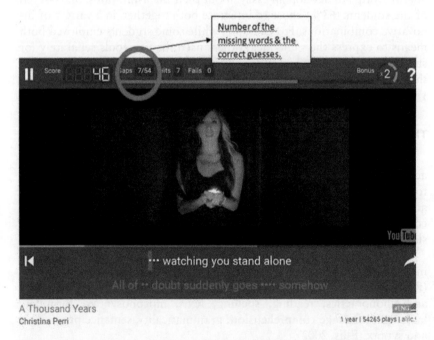

Figure 10.6 Screenshot from the Lyrics Training website: a game at the 'intermediate' level of difficulty for the song 'A Thousand Years', by Christina Perri (http://lyricstraining.com/play/christina-perri/a-thousand-years/H3ymUHgUk3#)

can be set by the learner: beginner, intermediate, advanced or expert. The video will not continue until the missing word is filled in, so learners are encouraged to listen attentively to the lyrics. The backspace key can be used to repeat a line. In addition, the 'Karaoke' mode and 'Withdraw' button are available for those who wish to preview the lyrics or to see any words that elude them. Learners can listen their favourite songs while improving their pronunciation, listening kills and vocabulary use. The website also records learners' progress, which can give users a sense of achievement. The key thing, though, is that learners get to hear the song repeatedly, thus increasing the frequency of exposure to the language input.

It seems clear that frequency of encounters can facilitate and accelerate the acquisition process. More input means more frequent encounters with L2 words and language features, which in turn leads to students being able to develop their word-recognition skills. According to Ellis (2002), when learners process the same idea multiple times, the span of processing reduces each time. This 'practice increment' suggests that learners' perceptual and motor systems improve as experience is accumulated. As L2 learners improve their receptive skills, they gradually find that their productive language skills also develop, enabling them to express themselves both in speech and in writing more accurately, fluently and appropriately.

Although there is no doubt that the target language being reviewed and recycled will stay in the learner's long-term memory, materials developers cannot simply rely on frequency alone for learners' overall L2 development. Other factors that may contribute to this process might include, for example, affective commitment, cognitive challenge, amusing content, a variety of contextual choices and novel ways to stimulate learner curiosity. An example of how learners can be helped to escape the humdrum routine of vocabulary overuse is shared on Teaching English, a joint British Council/BBC website. One innovative task, presented on the page 'Headlines: Recycling vocabulary creatively' (https://www.teachingenglish.org.uk/blogs/chrysapap/headlines-recycling-vocabulary-creatively), encourages learners to experiment with a visible thinking approach. In the task, towards the end of a topic discussion, learners are encouraged to collect some of the most essential words related to the content. With these words, each learner then attempts to compose a newspaper-type headline to summarise the essence of the topic. In many cases, the struggle to create headlines can lead to alternative ideas that can become catchy slogans or can engage the class in deeper thinking.

Fourth Principle: Automaticity

Automaticity in language learning refers to 'those properties of behavior that reflect the individual's ability to perform very rapidly and with little or no (conscious) effort' (Segalowitz, 2013: 53). SLA scholars believe that some transitions, for example from explicit to implicit

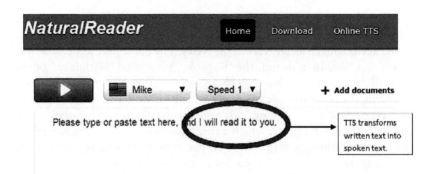

Figure 10.7 Natural Reader's front page

knowledge or from declarative to procedural knowledge, depend on the extent to which one's 'linguistic processes become automatized' (Lim & Godfroid, 2014: 2). Enough opportunities should be given for students to achieve automatisation. Learning processes should entail a transition from attentive to automatic mode (DeKeyser, 2007).

Text-to-speech (TTS) applications such as Natural Reader (http://www. naturalreaders.com) and voice-recording such Vocaroo (http://vocaroo. com) can be used to assist students to develop automaticity. First, teachers assign students a reading passage and ask them to study it carefully. Next, they ask their students to use Natural Reader to practise reading aloud the assigned passage (Figure 10.7). TTS applications will read the text in accordance with a preferred talking speed and voice. Students then follow the model's reading style (this includes the speaker's pronunciation, tone and so on). After listening to and modelling the speaker, students read the text aloud and record it using Vocaroo (Figure 10.8) or a recording device on their smart phones. When they complete their recording, they save it, share it as a link in an email or website or send it as a file, and ask their peers and teacher to give feedback.

Juel (1991) says that automaticity is mostly derived from repeated practice and drilling. With the help of the internet, such regular practice can be done inside and outside the classroom in a meaningful and interesting fashion. When the practised materials are interesting enough for learners to make personally meaningful connections with them, learners are more likely to be motivated to spend longer in repeated practice of language skills.

Fluency, which refers to both speaking and writing abilities, can be developed through constant practice that involves speed in creation and in response. To make such rehearsal more interesting, tasks can be set within a time frame, for example a set period in which learners have to write or type non-stop. For instance, within five minutes, learners have to come

Figure 10.8 Vocaroo's front page

up with as many ideas as possible without caring much about whether those ideas are connected. Many educators believe that sometimes even the silliest idea may contain the seed of a worthwhile topic. Once a list of ideas (each of which can be a sentence or a phrase) has been created, each learner then studies it and picks out the most inspiring thought as a topic. Based on this topic, the learner then begins to improvise a presentation, work with a peer to role-play a discussion, or develop that idea into a piece of writing to be read aloud to the class. One of the authors of this chapter has used such tasks in many classroom sessions and the result was often more rewarding than anticipated, in terms of both learning effect and an enjoyable class atmosphere.

Fifth Principle: Social Interaction

Studies on language learning reveal that L2 learners need both extensive input in the target language and opportunities to produce or to use the language. Swain (1995, 2005), a strong proponent of the output hypothesis, believes that there is no better way to test one's language knowledge or competence than to interact with other people – to communicate in the target language. In Swain's point of view, L2 learners need meaningful opportunities to practise language at their level of language competency in order to produce comprehensible output. By producing output, learners move from semantic to syntactic language processes, generate feedback from their interlocutors and notice the gap between what they want to express and what they can express. This in turn will help learners to consolidate their language knowledge, and to develop more fluency and automaticity in their oral and written language production.

Social media such as Facebook, Twitter, Blogger and Skype can serve as excellent platforms for L2 learners to produce their 'output': to present ideas, to share information and to interact with their peers, teachers or other English-speakers around the globe. When used appropriately, social media can become a valuable interactive teaching/learning tool.

Figure 10.9 shows how a Facebook group is used to share information about the latest Indonesian government's education policy to change the national curriculum. The thread was initiated by one of the teachers of English Education Business (EEB) of Petra Christian University in Surabaya, Indonesia. As can be seen, some students became involved and posted comments.

Skype (http://education.skype.com) is another tool that provides some features that make it possible for users to meet and work together with users in other parts of the world (see Figures 10.10 and 10.11). One of its features enables students to meet their favourite authors; and another feature combines online games with real communication activities.

Figure 10.9 Thread from the Facebook group set up by English Education Business (EEB) of Petra Christian University in Surabaya, Indonesia (http://www.facebook.com/groups/EEB.PCU)

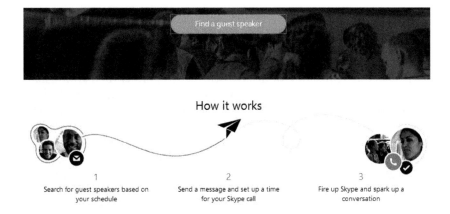

Figure 10.10 Skype's 'Guest Speaker' facility

Figure 10.11 An educational game on Skype

SLA scholars generally agree that learner output has a beneficial role in L2 acquisition. Comprehensible input alone is not sufficient to ensure that learners develop sufficient proficiency in the target language. L2 learners need to be engaged in a variety of input- and output-based activities so that they can develop effective receptive and productive skills. The social media can be a powerful tool that teachers can exploit to provide learners with ample opportunities to interact socially with others using their newly acquired language.

For output to achieve a novel, entertaining learning effect, materials writers can create more creative tasks that connect learners' personal thinking with existing social media tools. Since the purpose of these tools is networking and interaction, task designers may consider putting learners in different shoes for diverse perspectives, rather than always have learners remain themselves. One such example is provided by Jenkins and Dillon (2014) in the design of their Facebook-based activity. The task requires each learner to develop for him/herself a fictitious Facebook identity – someone of a different gender, race, age, living location and culture. Various Facebook members then start making friends to exchange information, interact and discuss issues of shared concern. The task taps into a number of learning facilities, including the practice of reducing personal inhibition to open up, playing with novel content, exploring multiple assumptions and viewpoints, and walking in the shoes of others. All of these denote learning through imagination and creativity.

Sixth Principle: Motivation

Supporting learners' orientation to L2 learning, motivation is one of the most important variables that determine achievement in language acquisition. Motivated learners are more enthusiastic, goal-oriented, committed, persistent and confident, and, as a result, tend to be more successful in their learning. They are willing to work hard to achieve their goals and do not easily give up. Motivation in L2 learning is so important that an L2 scholar claims that motivation alone is sufficient for ensuring that L2 learners achieve a working knowledge of the target language (Dörnyei, 2001). Learner motivation can be elevated through the use of entertaining materials that allow learners to connect with their own lives. Motivation can also be enhanced through tasks and activities that are cognitively challenging and affectively appealing. Only when students are fully engaged will language learning be optimal (Renandya, 2014; Tomlinson, 2012).

Efforts to use computer-mediated tools for authentic, motivating communication have been made since 1980s (Beauvois, 1997; Pennington, 1996) with such tools as chatrooms, bulletin boards and email (Kelm, 1998; Salaberry, 2001), among others. Despite this, the question of *how* technology can have a motivating effect on L2 learners remains an unsettled issue, simply because technology itself cannot function without thoughtful choices and specific pedagogical arrangement. For example, research by Holland *et al.* (1999) found that a speech-enabled interactive technology can improve learners' motivation and output. Salaberry (2001) also emphasises the need for technological tools and resources to be both well contextualised and pedagogically sound.

One dimension of motivation is enjoyment. Teachers and materials developers can motivate learners is by inviting them to have fun through games-based learning activities. Games are likely to be motivating when they are amusing and challenging; at the same time they provide opportunities for their players to produce meaningful language in real contexts. They can be used to provide practice in all language skills. According to McFarlane *et al.* (2002), games lower anxiety, enable students to acquire new experiences in learning a new language, add variation to the regular classroom activities and create a relaxed classroom atmosphere.

The internet provides a vast array of free games that can be brought into the classrooms. Some of the games on the ESL Games website (http://www.eslgamesplus.com) are designed so that students will learn English grammar, vocabulary, sentences, listening and pronunciation while playing. Figure 10.12 shows one example. The game itself focuses on prepositions (for, in, to, from, by, at, on, since, with) in an adaptation of the game 'spin the wheel'.

Another idea to motivate students is to ask them to work on digital collaborative projects, for example to create stories as a group. Digital storytelling has been widely used in the classroom because it brings numerous language-learning benefits. Barrett (2006) argues that stories combine different aspects of learning pedagogy, including: student engagement, reflection for deeper learning, technology integration and project-based learning.

In creating digital stories, students can use Story Creator (http://myths.e2bn.org/create) or ZooBurst (http://www.zooburst.com). These websites provide free images and sounds that can be customised to illustrate stories.

Figure 10.12 Example of an English-language game from the ESL Games website http://www.eslgamesplus.com/preposition-interactive-grammar-game-for-esl-wheel-game

Figure 10.13 Digital collaborative project: 'Little Red Riding Hood 2.0', produced by students on Zooburst (http://www.zooburst.com/zb_books-viewer. php?book=4c7b261baa0d2)

When they finish their stories, learners are able to share them and receive feedback. Figure 10.13 shows part of an example story created and shared on ZooBurst.

Motivation is vital in language learning as it energises, directs and sustains behaviour so that learners will have the drive to go through the learning process and acquire the target language. Well developed materials play a key role in sustaining motivation. Bringing digital games and digital projects into the classroom can spark English language interest and increase learners' motivation.

Suggested Activities for ELT Materials and Pedagogy

Technology and the internet have become an integral part of society. Generation Z obviously has embraced it as an indispensable part of life. It is therefore essential to integrate technology into lesson plans, keeping in mind that traditional classroom methods have served us well in the past but might disengage students from the learning process. A pool of diverse web resources can be used in a countless number of ways for language teaching. The 'Hero' teaching activities sketched out below for intermediate students can be done using the free internet resources described in this chapter. Since it might take more than one session to carry out all the recommended activities, we suggest that these can be selected and adapted according to various classroom situations.

'Hero' teaching activities

Brainstorming: Principle 5 – social interaction

Learners are asked to brainstorm who is a hero to them, what kinds of deeds a hero would do and whether a hero should be a famous person or even should be a person at all.

Watching the video: Principle 1 – comprehensible input

Learners watch the video 'The first well', available on BookBox (http://www.youtube.com/watch?v=a4uLfei-0kU), which is about a warrior trying to find water to save his kingdom.

Defining 'hero': Principle 6 – motivation

From the above as a stimulus, questions are raised whereby class members attempt to define in their own way what makes someone a hero. Such definitions can range from being formal to light-hearted jokes. For example, one might say 'A hero is a person who saves his or her country from invaders' while another might suggest 'Whoever buys me a Gucci bag is my hero'. This exercise is a chance to laugh and learn.

Reading texts: Principle 1 – comprehensible input

Learners are given one or more reading texts about heroes. Figure 10.14 presents an example of an online passage, entitled 'World mourns Nelson Mandela'. Both the reading text and the audio, from the Breaking News English site, are level 3 (intermediate).

World mourns Nelson Mandela (8th December, 2013)

South Africans and people from all over the world are mourning the death of Nelson Mandela. In South Africa, thousands of people gathered in Johannesburg and Soweto to say goodbye to their country's first ever black president. They danced, sang, cried and prayed for the man they loved. Mr Mandela died aged 95 on Thursday after months of illness. South Africa's President Jacob Zuma broke the news of Mr Mandela's death in a late-night speech on TV. Mr Zuma said: "Our nation has lost its greatest son." Mr Mandela spent most of his life campaigning for equal rights in South Africa. He spent 27 years in jail before becoming South Africa's president in 1994.

Leaders from all over the world heaped praise on Mr Mandela. His long-time friend Archbishop Desmond Tutu said: "God was so good to us in South Africa by giving us Nelson Mandela." US President Barack Obama said: "He achieved more than could be expected of any man. Today, he has gone home." UN Secretary-General Ban Ki-moon called him "a giant for justice and a down-to-earth human inspiration". He added: "Nelson Mandela showed what is possible for our world and within each one of us if we believe, dream and work together for justice and humanity." British Prime Minister David Cameron tweeted: "Nelson Mandela was a hero of our time. A great light has gone out in the world."

Figure 10.14 'World mourns Nelson Mandela', from the Breaking News English website (http://www.breakingnewsenglish.com/1312/131208-nelson-mandela-a.html), used as an intermediate reading text

Figure 10.15 Graphic from 'Roselle's finest hour', a touching story about a dog, from the Reader's Digest website (http://www.rd.com/advice/pets/heroic-dogs)

Discussion: Principles 2 and 3 – saliency and frequency

Learners now work in pairs or small groups to choose 3 out of 20 questions available on the 'Nelson Mandela discussion' section of the Breaking News English website (http://www.breakingnewsenglish. com/1312/131208-nelson-mandela.html). This story relates not only to Mandela's movement in South Africa but to human rights and the elimination of discrimination across the globe. Mandela remains an enduring source of inspiration. In selecting and answering these questions, learners will need to refer to the text, a process that allows for both the noticing of key language and reading the same words again.

Another suggestion for a story is 'Roselle's finest hour' (see Figure 10.15), a touching story about a dog who saved its blind owner, Michael, by leading him out of danger when the World Trade Center were destroyed on 11 September 2001. This real anecdote is not only motivating as a text but also useful for developing narratives and coming up with the moral of events, as can be seen in the excerpt below, from the Reader's Digest website:

> Michael kept a tight grip on Roselle's harness, using voice and hand commands, as they ran to a street opposite the crumbling tower. The street bounced like a trampoline, the sky rained debris, and 'a deafening roar' like a hellish freight train filled the air. Hours later, Michael and Roselle made it home safely.
>   In the months that followed, Michael became a spokesperson for Guide Dogs for the Blind, the organization that had trained Roselle. Together, they spread their message about trust and teamwork'.
> (Retrieved from http://www.rd.com/advice/pets/heroic-dogs)

Speaking and reading: Principles 3 and 5 – frequency and social interaction

Learners are invited to look up internet resources by themselves and find a written text they like about heroes. They then upload the text onto

Natural Reader (http://www.naturalreaders.com), which is an online 'copy, paste and edit' tool that converts any written text into spoken words. Learners can use their own voice to read the edited text aloud for peer sharing and discussion.

Recording: Principles 3 and 5 – frequency and social interaction

Learners record their reading using Vocaroo (http://vocaroo.com/). The recording is then downloaded and passed on to the teacher or peers for feedback. If the class has a Facebook group (http://www.facebook.com) or uses a learning management system such as Edmodo (http://www.edmodo.com), they can upload their recordings to the site.

Videoconferencing: Principles 1 and 5 – input and social interaction

The class can organise a videoconference using Skype (http://education.skype.com). Guest speakers can be invited, such as the Education Director at the Livingston County War Museum and veterans from World War II, Korea, Vietnam, Grenada, Iraq and Afghanistan (refer to http://education.skype.com/users/79168-livingstoncountywarmuseum). The purpose of this videoconference is to give learners an opportunity to communicate with some living heroes.

Interviewing: Principles 1, 4 and 5 – comprehensible input, automaticity and social interaction

Learners work in pairs or small groups to interview one of the guest speakers to find out his or her personal background, achievements and hopes for the future. The communication can happen through email, Skype or other social media.

Developing an online book: Principles 1, 3 and 5 – comprehensible input, frequency and social interaction

Based on the interviews, pairs or groups of learners can develop an online book that informs readers about the interviewee. ZooBurst (http://www.zooburst.com) can be used to create a five-minute presentation. An example of a short biography of Nelson Mandela is available at http://www.zooburst.com/zb_books-viewer.php?book=zb01_4f3d123c59de4.

Learners, in groups, can do library research on local heroes. They then share their results via ZooBurst digital books so that the teacher and peers can access the books to give comments.

Developing a video story: Principles 1, 3 and 5 – comprehensible input, frequency and social interaction

Alternatively, based on their self-made content from the above project, learners can create a digital (video) story honouring the hero and his or her memorable achievements. Each video lasts for about five minutes, and presents the hero's personal background, achievements and hopes for the future. The video can be created using free software such as Microsoft Photo Story or Microsoft Movie Maker. An example of a video describing a sports hero is available at http://www.teachertube.com/video/olympic-hero-photostory-49846.

Feedback: Principles 1, 3 and 5 – input, frequency and social interaction

Learners then share the video online to invite comments from their teacher and peers. Their work can be uploaded via a Facebook group (http://www.facebook.com) or a learning management system such as Edmodo (http://www.edmodo.com).

Conclusion

Technology and internet-based materials make up a major part of language learning in the 21st century as they offer unlimited possibilities to enrich second language instruction and facilitate second language acquisition. Such support enables classroom activities not only to focus on grammar rules or vocabulary but also to gain access to real-world issues, authentic materials and collaborative problem-solving tasks. With thoughtful application, the internet represents a powerful tool to see that 'language learning is an act of creativity, imagination, exploration, expression, construction, and profound social and cultural collaboration' (Fereira, 2006: 3).

Second language tasks can make use of multimedia elements and online environments to encourage learners' apprenticeship of the real discourse communities around the world. Such practice also helps cultivate essential skills and abilities that are needed for success in today's professional and personal pursuits. Gone are the days when textbooks and teachers were the only medium or source that facilitated language learning. The World Wide Web offers tremendous innovative potential to support teaching and learning. Viewed in this light, the focus of technology integration should be on 'learning with technology' rather than 'learning from technology', as the former allows for more empowered learning (Kingsley, 2006, cited in Mohanty, 2011: 99). The internet thus should be viewed as a platform that allows interaction and engagement in meaningful creative activities that explore users' potential. Furthermore, teaching digital natives is not simply about learning technology but also about engaging learners with innovative use of technology so that they become critical thinkers and problem solvers (Theodosakis, 2001).

Younger learners will almost all be familiar with how the web works and feel comfortable with such technology. Equipped with such resources, today's L2 materials developers can expand their repertoire to assist language learners in many novel fashions. Such endeavour requires previous generations of teachers and course writers to be fully prepared to migrate into the digital world (Prensky, 2001).

This chapter has addressed a complex theme that aligns online resources and SLA theories with creativity. We have discussed the theory-informed selection and innovative adaptation of internet-based materials with SLA principles in mind. Putting these broad themes together in one discussion like this is something of a venture into an unusual playground. Our advice for teachers and materials developers does not represent a final set of rules. The SLA principles employed in this discussion are not guidelines written in stone but will constantly expand as empirical research proceeds. Internet-based materials can be a double-edged sword that can either encourage teacher creativity or constrain it, depending whether one is willing to adapt or lazily adopt what is available. With the awareness that SLA research outcome at the moment is still poorly connected with efforts in materials development, we hope the discussion opens a dialogue for more connection with current debates that link technology with both creativity and SLA research.

It is important to keep in mind that technology alone cannot make decisions for educators. To achieve maximum pedagogical potential, choices and implementation will need to be creatively made not by software but by human-ware. The integration of online resources into second language teaching needs to be continually connected with research into second language acquisition. In the meanwhile, we encourage materials developers to selectively and creatively engage with internet resources by keeping in mind how learners can achieve better learning outcomes through multiple senses and with enjoyment.

Ever since artificial intelligence became an education issue of concern in the 1950s (Bobrow & Brady, 1998), scholars have been curious about its connection to creativity. One might wonder about the extent to which computers and ICT applications can assist educators in decision making. Could an application be invented that can help teachers select the optimal materials to release humans from the burden of complex thinking? There is as yet no clear answer. Computers cannot yet replicate the specific mental properties of a creative teacher and no computerised system can generate innovative pedagogical ideas. Although computers have been programmed to compose music, write poetry, make paintings and react to human questions, to be able to respond to a constantly changing, complex classroom setting with a wide range of sociocultural, political, economic and educational factors will require the experienced judgement of a creative human mind.

References

Bañares-Marivela, E. and Rayón-Rumayor, L. (2016) Multimodal narratives and iPad in second language teaching. *Multiculturalism and Technology-Enhanced Language Learning*, 57–79.

Bao, D. (2017) Learner drawing as connected with writing: Implications in ELT pedagogy and materials development. *European Journal of Applied Linguistics and TEFL* 6 (1), 27–47.

Barrett, H. (2006) Researching and evaluating digital storytelling as a deep learning tool. *Technology and Teacher Education Annual* 1, 647.

Beauvois, M.H. (1997) Computer-mediated communication(CMC): Technology for improving speaking and writing. In R.M. Terry (ed.) *Technology Enhanced Language Learning* (pp. 165–184). Lincolnwood, IL: National Textbook Company.

Bobrow, D.G. and Brady, J.M. (1998) Artificial intelligence 40 years later. *Artificial Intelligence* 103 (1–2), 1–4.

DeKeyser, R.M. (2007) Introduction: Situating the concept of practice. In R.M. DeKeyser (ed.) *Practice in a Second Language: Perspectives from Applied Linguistics and Cognitive Psychology* (pp. 1–18). Cambridge: Cambridge University Press.

Ding, Y.R. (2007) Text memorization and imitation: The practices of successful Chinese learners of English. *System* 35 (1), 271–280.

Dörnyei, Z. (2001) *Motivational Strategies in the Language Classroom*. Cambridge: Cambridge University Press.

Ellis, N.C. (2002) Frequency effects in language processing. *Studies in Second Language Acquisition* 2 (24), 143–188.

Ellis, R. (2005) Principles of instructed language learning. *Asian EFL Journal* 7 (3), 9–24.

Fereira, E.P. (2006) The role of technology in language teaching and learning. *Humanising Language Teaching* 8 (3). Retrieved from http://www.hltmag.co.uk/may06/less01.htm#C1.

Hicks, T. and Turner, K.H. (2013) No longer a luxury: Digital literacy can't wait. *English Journal*, 58–65.

Holland, V.M., Kaplan, J.D. and Sabol, M.A. (1999) Preliminary tests of language learning in a speech-interactive graphics microworld. *CALICO Journal* 16 (3), 339–359.

Jenkins, J.J. and Dillon, P.J. (2014) Facebook, identity, and deception: Explorations of online identity construction. In *Cases on Communication Technology for Second Language Acquisition and Cultural Learning* (pp. 5–8). Hershey, PA: IGI Global.

Juel, C. (1991) Beginning reading. In R. Barr, M.L. Kamil, P.B. Mosenthal and P.D. Pearson (eds) *Handbook of Reading Research* (pp. 759–788). New York: Longman.

Kelm, O.R. (1998) The use of electronic mail in foreign language classes. In K. Arens (ed.) *Language Learning Online* (pp. 141–154). Austin, TX: Daedalus Group.

King, J. (2002) Using DVD feature films in the EFL classroom. *Computer Assisted Language Learning* 15 (5), 509–523.

Kothari, B. and Takeda, T. (2000) Same language subtitling for literacy: Small change for colossal gains. In S.C. Bhatnagar and S. Schware (eds) *Information and Communication Technology in Development* (pp. 176–186). New Delhi: Sage.

Krashen, S. (1985) *The Input Hypothesis: Issues and Implications*. New York: Longman.

Krashen, S. (2005) Is in-school free reading good for children? Why the National Reading Panel report is (still) wrong. *Phi Delta Kappan* 86 (6), 444–447.

Kuhn, M.R. and Stahl, S.A. (2000) *Fluency: A Review of Developmental and Remedial Practices* (CIERA Rep. No. 2-008). Ann Arbor, MI: Center for the Improvement of Early Reading Achievement.

Lim, H. and Godfroid, A. (2014) Automatization in second language sentence processing: A partial, conceptual replication of Hulstijn, Van Gelderen, and Schoonen's 2009 study. *Applied Psycholinguistics*. Retrieved from http://journals.cambridge.org/article_S0142716414000137.

McFarlane, A., Sparrowhawk, A. and Heald, Y. (2002) *Report on the Educational Use of Games*. TEEM (Teachers Evaluating Educational Multimedia). Retrieved from http://www.teem.org.uk/publications/teem_gamesined_full.pdf.

McLoughlin, C. and Oliver, R. (2000) Designing learning environments for cultural inclusivity: A case study of indigenous online learning at tertiary level. *Australasian Journal of Educational Technology* 16 (1), 58–72.

Mohanty, S. (2011) Global perspectives, local initiatives: Reflections and practices in ELT. Retrieved from http://www.nus.edu.sg/celc/research/books/3rdsymposium/097to106-seemita.pdf.

Oliver, N., Garg, A. and Horvitz, E. (2004) Layered representations for learning and inferring office activity from multiple sensory channels. *Computer Vision and Image Understanding* 96 (2), 163–180.

Pennington, M.C. (1996) The power of the computer in language education. In M.C. Pennington (ed.) *The Power of CALL* (pp. 1–14). Houston, TX: Athelstan.

Prensky, M. (2001) Digital natives, digital immigrants. *On the Horizon* 9 (5), 1–6.

Renandya, W.A. (2011) Extensive listening in the second language classroom. In H.P. Widodo and A. Cirocki (eds) *Innovation and Creativity in ELT Methodology* (pp. 28–41). New York: Nova Science.

Renandya, W.A. (2013) The role of input- and output-based practice in ELT. In A. Ahmed, M. Hanzala, F. Saleem and G. Cane (eds) *ELT in a Changing World: Innovative Approaches to New Challenges*, (pp. 41–52). Newcastle upon Tyne: Cambridge Scholars.

Renandya, W.A. (2014) *Motivation in the Language Classroom*. Alexandria, VA: TESOL International Association.

Salaberry, M.R. (2001) The use of technology for second language learning and teaching: A retrospective. *Modern Language Journal* 85 (1), 39–56.

Schmidt, R. (1990) The role of consciousness in second language learning. *Applied Linguistics* 11, 129–158.

Schmidt, R. (1993) Consciousness, learning and interlanguage pragmatics. In G. Kasper and S. Blum-Kulka (eds) *Interlanguage Pragmatics* (pp. 21–42). Oxford: Oxford University Press

Schmidt, R. (1995) Consciousness and foreign language learning: A tutorial on attention and awareness in learning. In R. Schmidt (ed.) *Attention and Awareness in Foreign Language Learning* (pp. 1–63). Honolulu, HI: University of Hawaii, National Foreign Language Resource Center.

Segalowitz, N. (2013) Automaticity. In P. Robinson (ed.) *The Routledge Encyclopedia of Second Language Acquisition* (pp. 3–57). London: Routledge.

Sharwood Smith, M. (1993) Input enhancement in instructed SLA: Theoretical bases. *Studies in Second Language Acquisition* 15, 165–179.

Skehan, P. (1998) *A Cognitive Approach to Language Learning*. Oxford: Oxford University Press.

Swain, M. (1995) Three functions of output in second language learning. In G. Cook and S. Barbara (eds) *Principle and Practice in Applied Linguistics* (pp. 125–144). Oxford: Oxford University Press.

Swain, M. (2005) The output hypothesis: Theory and research. In E. Heinkel (ed.) *Handbook of Research in Second Language Teaching and Learning* (pp. 471–483). Mahwah, NJ: Lawrence Erlbaum.

Swenson, J., Young, C.A., McGrail, E., Rozema, R. and Whitin, P. (2006) Extending the conversation: New technologies, new literacies, and English education. *English Education* 38 (4), 351–369.

Theodosakis, N. (2001) *The Director in the Classroom: How Filmmaking Inspires Learning*. Boston, MA: Tech4Learning.

Tomlinson, B. (2012) Materials development for language learning and teaching. *Language Teaching* 45 (2), 143–179.

Wong, W. (2005) *Input Enhancement: From the Theory and Research to the Classroom*. New York: McGraw-Hill.

Part 3: Improving ELT Materials Through Teacher and Learner Involvement

11 Localising the Genre-Based Approach: Lessons for Materials Development from Thailand

Rajeevnath Ramnath

This chapter highlights the current state of language teaching materials in terms of the texts and tasks that are used in the high schools of Thailand, before showing how the genre-based approach was used as an attempt to change the texts and tasks in EFL materials with a group of Asian students in a master's in ELT programme at an international university in Thailand. The project aimed to widen the scope of texts by tapping into teachers' creativity in order to break away from materials which have stemmed from structuralism.

The materials development project was carried out in two courses. Firstly, the student-teachers wrote narrative, recount and argumentative texts in the Theory and Practice of Reading and Writing course and converted their narratives into teaching materials in the Materials Development course in the MA-ELT programme. I will explain the phases of this project after discussing the current state of English teaching materials in many EFL settings, and then specifically in the Thai context.

The Current State of English Teaching Materials

Maley (2010) laments that a pedagogy of expectation tends to rule education systems across the world, as opposed to a pedagogy of expectancy. A pedagogy of expectation, with predictable outcomes, forces everyone to conform to the system; a pedagogy of expectancy allows teachers and learners join hands in discovering learning. Unfortunately, most language teaching materials are designed to meet pedagogical 'expectations'. Owing to the unwanted attention to results and examinations, the joy of learning is replaced by conformity to some unknown standard distanced from the learners' sociocultural context. Market need has forced materials writers to publish coursebooks for impressive grades rather than for learning experience. This is quite true in the Thai context, where learning English is often connected to passing entrance examinations or finding lucrative jobs in multinational companies and in international business. Not many people teach English for an appreciation of the beauty of the language through creative modes of expression. The real value of learning English is removed from the teaching/learning process. Teachers are under tremendous pressure to complete their syllabus and ensure learners gain high scores in institutional, standardised gate-keeping tests. Therefore, teaching is subordinated to testing. As Ralph Waldo Emerson said:

> We are students of words: we are shut up in schools, and colleges, and recitation-rooms, for ten or fifteen years, and come out at last with a bag of wind, a memory of words, and do not know a thing. (Cited in Williamson & Null, 2008: 381)

Since teaching is dependent on tests, many courses tend to teach the test rather than the language itself. Teaching materials are highly confined to test needs or, in other words, teaching tends to predict tests, thereby taking away the pleasure of learning a language through a process of discovery. Teaching or preparing learners to tackle tests leads to memorisation of language rules as opposed to understanding and application of the rules in real-life situations.

Maley (2003) rightly points out that language teaching materials tend to exclude a lot of interesting texts such as folktales, poems, advertisements, film scripts, one-act plays, one-liners, proverbs, literary letters and excerpts from diaries. Maley (1989), Maley and Duff (2005, 2007), Carter (1996), Carter and Long (1987), Collie and Slater (1987), McRae (1991, 1992, 1996), Cook (1996) and Tomlinson (1994) have published rich resources for exploiting creative and imaginative texts in the language classroom. On the other hand, textbooks include expository texts or texts which are artificially written and adapted from authentic sources and which focus on language points rather than engaging content.

Language teaching materials should aim to promote a Freirean approach (Wallace, 2003), to 'empower learners with the knowledge of the world' (Freire, 1970) rather than training learners for examinations. Activities in textbooks often focus on vocabulary and grammar, and feature multiple-choice questions in addition to literal comprehension questions (Nuttall, 1982) as opposed to activities that are likely to be relevant to learners' sociocultural context. Masuhara (2003), Aebersold and Field (1997), Wallace (2003) and Tribble (1996) point out that many textbooks treat reading and writing skills as language lessons instead of focusing on comprehension and fluent production of language. The excessive attention to language points is likely to force EFL learners to concentrate on each and every word in the texts (Masuhara, 2003), thus making foreign language reading a tedious activity.

Day and Bamford (1998), Hedge (1988), and Maley and Duff (2005, 2007) advocate the use of multidimensional/sensory activities, such as project work, orchestrating a poem into a song, converting a short story into a one-act play, creative writing, drama performance, visualisation, drawing and storyboards, as these are likely to cater to a wider range of learning styles. Constant exposure to such activities is likely to sharpen learners' language and critical sensibilities, which in turn will have a positive influence on test scores.

English teaching materials in Thailand

It is surprising to note that despite the increase of English teaching in schools and in other domains, the English proficiency of the vast majority of Thais remains poor. According to Bolton (2008), Thailand is almost at the bottom of the table in terms of TOEFL scores in South East Asia. English is a compulsory language starting from primary 1 (children aged six years or over). It is divided into four levels: level 1 is preparatory; level 2 is for beginners, children who are in primary school; level 3 is expanding or lower secondary; and level 4 is upper secondary education. Biyaem (1997) states that teachers and learners face a great deal of challenge. For teachers, the main problems are lack of proper training, heavy teaching loads and large classes, usually with unmotivated learners. It is worth noting that technology and resources in many of the institutions are far from adequate and teachers are often under pressure to prepare learners to pass various tests and examinations. Therefore, teaching for the tests is the main goal of English courses rather than fluent communication or interaction leading to the experience of language through appreciation which will eventually lead to acquisition.

Although there could be several cultural reasons for Thais' poor proficiency in English, the discussion in this chapter is restricted to high-school textbooks. A recent evaluation of high-school textbooks by Jivavorranun (2015) showed a clear lack of variety in terms of genres and questions. The evaluation assessed the dominant genres of the reading passages and reading questions in four textbooks meant for high schools in Thailand. The organisation and linguistic features of the materials were analysed using Derewianka's (1990) framework and the analysis of questions was based on Nuttall's (1982) types of questions. Literal comprehension questions were dominant in the textbooks, but inferential and reorganisation questions were dominant in the entrance tests. It is interesting to note that both the textbooks and the tests excluded questions that would involve appreciation, interpretive and personal responses. A brief discussion of the findings will highlight the limitations of high-school materials in terms of the genres and the dominant types of questions. The sample of textbooks analysed included *ICON 2* (Freeman *et al.*, 2004), *Mega Goal 2* (Santos & O' Sullivan, 2010), *Moving Up: Critical Reading 2* (Fotheringham, 2010), *Reading Adventures With Writing 2* (Lieske & Menking, 2013) and *Weaving It Together 2* (Broukal, 2009):

- *ICON 2*. The units consist of a reading passage with activities for listening, speaking, reading, writing, vocabulary and grammar. Each reading passage is at least one page a long and has at least one pre-reading question followed by post-reading questions which require short answers. This book has 12 texts, of which eight (67%) are information reports. There are 27 (46%) literal comprehension questions out of a total number of 59 questions.
- *Mega Goal 2*. Each unit contains at least one passage, which is less than two pages. The material involves listening, speaking, reading and writing. The material has eight (67%) information reports out of 12 texts and 60 (61%) out of 99 items are literal comprehension questions.
- *Moving Up: Critical Reading 2*. This book focuses only on reading and each unit is divided into two chapters. The material includes 140 post-reading questions, out of which 111 (79%) are literal comprehension questions, based on 13 (65%) information texts from a total of 20 texts.
- *Reading Adventures With Writing 2*. The first part of each unit of this textbook contains a reading passage and the second part deals with writing. There is at least one pre-reading question and the post-reading section has multiple-choice questions, ordering, matching and true/false items. Out of 16 texts, 11 (69%) are information reports and 59 (61%) out of 96 questions are literal comprehension questions.
- *Weaving It Together 2*. This book has eight units with two chapters in each unit and each chapter has a reading passage. The reading section includes 120 (69%) literal comprehension questions out of a total of 173 questions and seven (44%) out of 16 texts are information reports.

The findings showed that information reports (61%, or 47 out of 76 texts) and literal comprehension questions (95%, or 538 out of 567 questions) were dominant in all the materials, with minor variation in terms of distribution across the materials. There is no evidence of argumentative texts in the materials and there are three narratives (out of 76 texts) in the five textbooks. The materials do not include questions that require learners' interpretation in the reading section. However, most of the materials include personal response and inferential questions, in addition to the literal comprehension questions.

A Genre-Based Approach to EFL Materials Development: A Project in a Master's in ELT Programme

Considering the above findings, I decided to change the focus of materials in terms of texts and tasks through the Theory and Practice of Reading and Materials Development courses in the MA-ELT programme, which is offered to pre-service Asian teachers from several disciplines. I encouraged the course participants to write a fictional narrative apart from writing argumentative, recount and information genres in the Reading and Writing course. They read authentic texts in English, such as newspaper reports, fiction and comic strips drawn from diverse cultural contexts. I gave them a number of texts on issues related to Asia. The following comments from the journal presentations are useful to understand the role of reading in the course:

> Reading helps to improve my vocabulary and writing style. I note down when I come across interesting words. I try to remember new vocabulary and try them in my writing. (Student 1)

> I have difficulty to express my ideas and emotions in accurate words and sentences because I did very little reading and writing before coming here. (Student 2)

> These days my parents and family members are shocked to see me reading [student's comment in the journal for the Book Review assignment]. I enjoy my book and don't even take care of my favourite dogs. (Student 3)

> Today's activity was on writing a 60-word story in class and this is the first time I'm doing creative writing. I find it so interesting that I don't want to stop. (Student 4)

It is worth noting that journal-based presentations and peer discussions helped the course participants to reflect on their progress as writers, to evaluate others' work and to accept opinions. The following observations from students' journals are useful to substantiate this point:

> Although feedback helps me understand my own writing, sometimes I think my classmates will mistake me for being critical. Also am not sure what I say is correct or not. (Student 5)

> I think my friend writes better than me. Her vocabulary is very good. Has great ideas too. (Student 6).

The following section gives a brief overview of the genre-based approach and the curriculum cycle as used in the Theory and Practice of Reading and Writing course.

Genre-based approach: An overview

The term 'genre' originally referred to the genres of literature. However, according to Bradford-Watts (2003), in recent years it has become multidisciplinary, drawing on linguistics, sociology, anthropology and psychology. Genre experts focus on the participants' relationships as the basis of language use. Three broad schools of genre theory are identified in the literature (Hyland, 2003). Firstly, the rhetoric approach is based on the premise of post-structuralism, rhetoric and first language composition studies. This approach explores the relationship between the type of text and the rhetorical situation (Hyland, 2003). The focus here is on the rhetorical aspects of texts. Secondly, the ESP approach has a more linguistic orientation and sees genre as a class of structured communication events used by certain specific groups or communities who share similar goals and purposes (Bhatia, 1991; Swales, 1990).

The third approach is based on Halliday's (2004) systemic functional linguistics (SFL). Genre in this model/approach is considered as something which is purposeful, interactive and sequential, and depends on the nature of different genres in terms of text organisation and lexico-grammatical features, which are context specific. This approach is used in the curriculum cycle (Martin & Rose, 2003), which integrates listening, speaking and reading before producing drafts of writing. This approach shares common characteristics with the task-based approach, which focuses on language as a functional tool for negotiating meaning for useful goals. The writers become aware of the purpose of writing, target audience/possible readers, organisation and linguistic features of the text. The course participants in this study went through the stages of the curriculum cycle in which they read widely (reading) around the topics, examined similar genres (modelling) through discussions (listening and speaking) and group work before writing.

According to Shape and Thompson (1998) (cited in Foley, 2012), the curriculum cycle or teaching/learning cycle aims to integrate the four skills of language; in addition, this cycle can be incorporated into communicative language teaching (CLT). The curriculum cycle draws from Vygotsky's (1978) view that higher thinking processes, including language, arise as a consequence of human interaction.

The first stage of this cycle, 'field knowledge' or 'field building', is meant to prepare the context or the fieldThe main idea of this stage is to build control of the field or topic by talking about it. A range of activities that provide opportunities for students to talk about the topic would be included at this step, such as reading widely on the topic and discussing the lexico-grammatical features, depending on the learners' needs.

In the second stage, 'modelling', the explicit focus is on the genre in which the students will be writing. At this stage, models of the genre will be given to students for analysis. This stage exposes students to the selected genre, which allows them to familiarise with the text type.

The third stage is the 'joint construction'. Here, the teacher serves as a facilitator in helping the students to construct a model of the genre. The overall knowledge of the field, content and text organisation is stressed by the teacher, to help students practise what they have learned, with teacher guidance.

The teacher scaffolds in order to encourage learners to apply the knowledge from modelling and teacher input. The main objective of this stage (independent construction) is to reflect and apply ideas learnt in the earlier stages to produce an acceptable piece of writing (Martin, 1992).

The genre-based approach was chosen as most of the participants had learned or taught writing as a linguistic product. In other words, the course participants were familiar with 'writing to learn' (Tribble, 1996) tasks rather than 'learning to write', in which the writing focuses on the texts as opposed to the process or the reader. The teachers often viewed students' work as examiners as opposed to 'audience' or empathisers (Tribble, 1996). However, in the genre-based approach, writing has a functional purpose where the teacher is a member of the audience rather than an examiner of compositions or assignments.

The theoretical underpinnings of the genre-based approach were discussed in the course and the students were expected to write assignments in different genres such as information recount, argument, and narrative (an original story in 1500 words, with a title, characters, narrator, point of view and a clear end) by following the organisation and linguistic features of the narrative genre suggested by Derewianka (1990: 41). The organisation guidelines for the writing practice will include orientation (who, when, where and what in any order), complication (the series of events that lead to problems or conflicts in the story) and finally resolution (where there is an attempt to resolve the conflict).

The linguistic features of the writing practice will include students' ability to use a variety of verbs and processes in the past tense, words related to time, descriptive language to create images in the reader's mind, dialogue and point of view. It is worth noting that the students wrote in the genres listed above by following the four stages of 'field building', 'modelling', 'joint construction' and 'independent construction' of the teaching/learning cycle discussed in this chapter. However, only the structure of a narrative showing the organisation and language features is given here, as it is the main focus of this chapter.'

Overview of narratives produced in the course

The narratives had to be revised in several areas in terms of grammar, usage, organisation, character development and descriptions of people, places and things. The narratives were improved by expanding the nominal group (Halliday, 1994), which is a grammatical unit to express descriptions. It is widely accepted that the ability to compose a complex nominal group is a mark of control and maturity in writing. The writers also became aware of the need to use a wide range of processes (verbs) in narratives.

Some of the writers used the present tense instead of the past tense and showed a tendency to repeat words and structures instead of synonyms and hyponyms, which are characteristic of interesting narratives. In the early stages, the writing was primarily in the first person, but later some of the writers showed control over point of view, which altered speech patterns in the narratives from direct to indirect speech to reflect interactions among characters. Finally, the writers realised the importance of ending their narratives with some sort of resolution. It is worth mentioning that it was hard for some of the course participants to resolve the conflicts and provide an interesting end to their work as some of the writers did not have the experience of reading and analysing narratives in their earlier education.

Materials writing project

The course participants decided to use the narratives which they wrote in the Theory and Practice of Reading and Writing course as texts for developing materials in the Materials Development course. The activities included personal response questions, visualisation, rewriting parts of texts, characterisation, compare and contrast, argumentative writing, diary/blogs, drawing illustrations, acting out texts and creative writing. The course participants had to use their narratives with reading and writing activities for EFL learners. Initially, the participants had problems in creating original activities for a group of unknown students. At this stage, they needed assistance with ideas, but later the quality of their activities improved. Suggestions were given for various types of activities, like predicting, brainstorming, informal discussion with or without pictures. The following activities designed by the course participants break the tradition of using multiple-choice questions and literal comprehension questions, which are common in EFL coursebooks (as indicated at the start of this chapter).

Reading activities (student 7)

- In the first paragraph, the writer is setting the scene. Where do you think this story is taking place? Draw a picture of the setting based on your understanding.
- Discuss the message of the story with your group members.

Writing activities (student 7)

- Write a diary entry recording your personal response to the story in about 100 words.

- If you look at the story as a metaphor, what do you think it might refer to? Explain in 100 words.

Reading activities (student 8)
- Draw a picture to describe the setting of the story.
- Describe the hen's character with three adjectives. Share them with your friends.

Writing activities (student 8)
- Imagine yourself as one of the character in the story. Would you make the same choice as that character? Give your opinions.
- From the line 'The old man was quiet for a while, then he slapped his leg and exclaimed "I know what we can do. My Dear Wife, tomorrow we can kill our hen and use its meat to prepare food for the monk"' continue the story with another paragraph of about 100 words to give it a different ending.

Feedback

I started off with a discussion on the strengths of their work before pointing out the weaknesses of their activities in terms of Nuttall's (1982) taxonomy and Tribble's (1996) idea of 'writing to learn' and 'learning to write'. The participants had to rephrase and edit the questions for clarity in many instances. The course ended after a lot of writing, rewriting and evaluating.

I would like to share a few comments about the course from the students' journals:

> I learnt good lessons and also laughed a lot in this course ... you were kind enough to give us a second chance to rewrite our activities. Really appreciate your hard work for the last assignment. (Student 9)

> This assignment is not only process-oriented, but also product-oriented. We exchanged interesting and relevant activities from each other. (Student 10)

Conclusion

This chapter has shown ways to extend the scope of language teaching materials by moving away from the tradition of using information texts with literal comprehension questions or multiple-choice items. I tried to widen the scope of materials with the belief that teachers' creativity will lead to learners' creativity. I believe that if teachers develop materials, they are likely to be better motivated to teach from those materials. The objective is to achieve learner motivation through teacher motivation. It is worth highlighting that encouraging teachers to write stories and convert their creative works into materials will add to their self-esteem as creative writers and as language teachers.

I found that the reading component of the course had an impact on the course participants in terms of strengthening their knowledge. It is unlikely the participants would otherwise have read the materials which they read for the writing tasks. Needless to say, regular engagement in reading and writing will create better teachers of reading and writing, who will also likely be more critical and knowledgeable. I stressed the importance of reading by providing a range of texts for the course partici-pants, as well as taking them through the stages of writing texts in various genres. This is the main highlight of this approach which I demonstrated to the course participants so that they will be equipped to implement this approach in their teaching situations in Thailand and elsewhere. Using the texts the students read as a model for their writing reinforces the nexus between reading and writing (Stotsky, 1983) and helps in the reconstruc-tion of knowledge.

Based on my experience, encouraging Asian students to undertake creative writing in English allows them to reflect on their use of English and even become confident users of the language (Ramnath, 2009). It was interesting to see even the so-called 'weak' students trying to produce an acceptable piece of work. Creative writing has the potential to give fresh insights into language use, apart from distracting teachers from the monotony of teaching the rules of the language and marking students' as-signments and tests. The tasks and activities which I have suggested in this chapter are likely to cater to all learning styles, such as visual, auditory, kinaesthetic and tactile, in contrast to traditional teacher-centred ap-proaches. The activities are 'meaning' focused and the questions are not restricted to literal comprehension. Finally, the project ended with a note of advice to the participants to pilot, revise and improve their materials whenever they have an opportunity to teach a group of learners.

References

Aebersold, J.A and Field, M.L. (1997) *From Reader to Reading Teacher*. Cambridge: Cambridge University Press.

Bhatia, V. (1991) A genre-based approach to ESP materials. *World Englishes* 10 (2), 153–166.

Biyaem, S. (1997) Learner training for a changing world: Educational innovation for sus-tainable development, Third UNESCO-ACEID International Conference, Bangkok.

Bolton, K. (2008) English in Asia, Asian Englishes and the issue of proficiency. *English Today* 24 (2), 3–13.

Bradford-Watts, K. (2003) What is genre and why is it useful for language teachers? *JALT Journal*. Retrieved from publications.org/tlt/articles/2003/05/index.

Broukal, M. (2009) *Weaving It Together 2*. Bangkok: Cengage Learning Asia/Thai Wattana Panich.

Carter, R.A. (1996) Look both ways before crossing: Developments in the language and literature classroom. In R.A. Carter and J. McRae (eds) *Language, Literature and the Learner* (pp. 1–15). London: Longman.

Carter, R.A. and Long, M. (1987) *Web of Words*. Cambridge: Cambridge University Press.

Collie, J. and Slater, S. (1987) *Literature in the Language Classroom: A Resource Book of Ideas and Activities*. Cambridge: Cambridge University Press.

Cook, G. (1996) Language play in English. In J. Maybin and N. Mercer (eds) *Using English: From Conversation to Canon* (pp. 198–227). London: Routledge.

Day, R. and Bamford, J. (1998) *Extensive Reading Activities for Teaching Language*. Cambridge: Cambridge University Press.

Derewianka, B. (1990) *Exploring How Texts Work*. Newtown: Primary English Teaching Association (PETA).

Foley, J.A. (2012) *Unscrambling the Omelette. Second Language Acquisition: Social and Psychological Dimensions*. Bangkok: Assumption University Press.

Fotheringham, B. (2010) *Moving Up: Critical Reading 2*. Bangkok: World Com/Thai Wattana Panich.

Freeman, D., Graves, K. and Lee, L. (2004) *ICON 2*. Bangkok: McGraw Hill/ Thai Wattana Panich.

Freire, P. (1970) *Pedagogy of the Oppressed*. New York: Continuum.

Halliday, M.A.K. (1994) *An Introduction to Functional Grammar*. London: Edward Arnold.

Halliday, M.A.K. (2004) *Introduction to Systemic Functional Linguistics*. London: Continuum.

Hammond, J., Burns, A., Joyce, H., Brosnan, D., Gerot, L., Solomon, N. and Hood, S. (1992) *English for Social Purposes: A Handbook for Teachers of Adult Literacy*. Sydney: National Centre for English Language Teaching and Research, Macquarie University.

Hedge, T. (1988) *Writing*. Oxford: Oxford University Press.

Hyland, K. (2003) Genre-based pedagogies: A social response to process. *Journal of Second Language Writing* 12 (1), 17–29.

Jiravorranun, T. (2015) A study of reading genres and questions in English textbooks, O-NET and GAT examinations. Unpublished master's thesis, Assumption University, Bangkok.

Lieske, C. and Menking, S. (2013) *Reading Adventures With Writing 2*. Bangkok: Cengage Learning Asia/Eduzone.

Maley, A. (1989) Down from the pedestal: Literature as resource. In R.A. Carter, R. Walker and C.J. Brumfit (eds) *Literature and the Learner: Methodological Approaches* (pp. 10–24). Basingstoke: British Council.

Maley, A. (2003) Inputs, processes and outcomes in materials development: Extending the range. In J. Mukundan (ed.) *Readings on ELT Materials 1*. Serdang: Universiti Putra Malaysia Press.

Maley, A. (2010) Towards an aesthetics of ELT. *Advances in Language and Literary Studies* 1 (1), 4–28.

Maley, A. and Duff, A. (2005) *Drama Techniques: A Resource Book of Communication Activities for Language Teachers*. Cambridge: Cambridge University Press.

Maley, A. and Duff, A. (2007) *Literature*. Oxford: Oxford University Press.

Martin, J.R. (1992) *English Text: System and Structure*. Amsterdam: John Benjamins.

Martin, J.R. and Rose, D. (2003) *Working With Discourse: Meaning Beyond the Clause*. London: Continuum.

Masuhara, H. (2003) Developing materials for reading skills. In B. Tomlinson (ed.) *Developing Materials for Language Teaching* (pp. 340–364). London: Continuum.

McRae, J. (1991) *Literature With a Small 'l'*. Basingstoke: MEP/Macmillan.

McRae, J. (1992) *Wordsplay*. Basingstoke: Macmillan.

McRae, J. (1996) Representational language learning: From language awareness to text awareness. In R.A. Carter and J. McRae (eds) *Language, Literature and the Learner* (pp. 16–40). London: Longman.

Nuttall, C. (1982) *Teaching Reading Skills in a Foreign Language*. London: Heinemann.

Ramnath, R. (2009) Creative writing: Exploring the underexplored. *Asian Journal of Literature Culture and Society* 3 (2), 39–49.

Santos, M.D and O' Sullivan, J.K. (2010) *Mega Goal 2*. Bangkok: McGraw Hill/Thai Wattana Panich.

Stotsky, S. (1983) Research on reading/writing relationships: A synthesis and suggested directions. *Language Arts* 60, 627–642.

Swales, J. (1990) *Genre Analysis*. Cambridge: Cambridge University Press.

Tomlinson, B. (1994) *Openings*. London: Penguin.

Tribble, C. (1996) *Writing*. Oxford: Oxford University Press.

Vygotsky, L.S. (1978) *Mind in Society*. Cambridge, MA: Harvard University Press.

Wallace, C. (2003) *Reading*. Oxford: Oxford University Press.

Williamson, A and Null, J.W. (2008) Ralph Waldo Emerson's educational philosophy as a foundation for cooperative learning. *American Educational History Journal* 35 (2), 381–392.

12 Fostering Self-expression: Learners Create Their Own Visuals

Dat Bao

The Need for Learners' Contribution in Visual Resources

Visual illustrations in ELT materials for a long time have been the work of expert artists and photographers who are commissioned to support the content developed by course writers. Sensible as it sounds, this process is massively a top-down practice as it draws a boundary between the supplier who distributes images and the user who receives them without any say over whether a picture seems culturally irrelevant or poorly pedagogical. To address such dominance, this chapter argues that language coursebook activities can arrange for learners to be involved in a process of drawing pictures to express individualised meaning. If learners are recognised as rightful negotiators of their own learning, materials writers might consider occasionally liberating them from the heavy reliance on the illustrations provided by the coursebook. This can be realised by inviting learners to create their own visuals as a way to share voices and perspectives.

Research conducted by Bao (2006, 2017) shows that many English coursebooks tend to control the direction in which learners are supposed to respond, such as simplifying reality without building an in-depth discussion or interpreting the world they see. In many cases, visuals neither stimulate critical thinking nor push imagination forward but tend to spoon-feed learners with ideas that constrain autonomy. Some pictures restrict multiple senses and intelligences by showing learners what to see rather than inviting them to find and by asking learners to witness without much emotional engagement. Others neglect logical intelligence as they ignore learners' reasoning skills and ability to create connections among events. Some fail to promote interpersonal intelligence by not offering the learner the opportunity to walk in the shoes of others. Many tasks overlook intrapersonal intelligence by not allowing learners to analyse issues, feelings or dilemmas themselves. Such examples run on indefinitely, Pictures allocate information in domineering ways that restrain learners' self-expression.

The Main Functions of Visuals in Course Materials

An overview of the literature over the past two decades reveals seven major functions in the use of visuals:

(1) *To convey notions.* Coursebook visuals play the role of presenting concepts (Kang, 2004), developing conceptions (Arif & Hashim, 2009), conveying messages (Canning-Wilson, 2000), clarifying meanings (Mannan, 2005) and building relations between words (Canning-Wilson, 2000).

(2) *To construct knowledge.* Coursebook visuals assist learners in vocabulary retention (Peterson, 2004; Clark & Lyon, 2004; Hendricks, 2005; Altun, 2015), memory (Clark & Lyon, 2004; Watkins *et al.*, 2004), acquisition of linguistic expressions (Tomalin, 1991) and connection of learning content (Clark & Lyon, 2004).

(3) *To increase attentiveness.* Coursebook visuals arouse learner curiosity (Mayer & Moreno, 2000), capture attention, build motivation (Bradshaw, 2003), maintain learning interest and stretch concentration span (Canning-Wilson, 2000).

(4) *To organise discussion.* Coursebook visuals support the generation of ideas (Adoniou, 2015), language processing (Canning-Wilson, 1998), interpretation of meaning (Arif & Hashim, 2009) and persuasive effect (Barry, 2001).

(5) *To support learning.* Coursebook visuals promote student learning (Anglin *et al.*, 2004), mental scaffolding (Fang, 1996), reading competence (Carney & Levin, 2002) and the learning of the four macro language skills (Stoller, 1992).

(6) *To support pedagogy.* Coursebook visuals perform well in introducing lesson themes (Tomalin, 1991), giving paralinguistic cues (Canning-Wilson & Wallace, 2000), economising the teaching task (Brinton, 2001), contextualising language (Mukherjee & Roy, 2003) and promoting aesthetic appreciation (Fang, 1996).

(7) *To increase resources.* Online digital visuals are characterised as free-of-cost materials (Snelson & Perkins, 2009) with high accessibility (Snelson & Perkins, 2009) and the ability to build learners' confidence in speech (Shrosbree, 2008).

In a nutshell, visual images in course materials have made teaching and learning easier and more convenient by capturing learner attention, demonstrating vocabulary concepts, explaining linguistic features, providing practice of the four skills, illustrating lesson content and stimulating classroom discussion. Despite all this, the guidance for visual use in most coursebooks remains controlling. With discussion topics being specified by the writer, the illustrative visual serves as a pointer to that content rather than stretch beyond it. As a result, learners are not trained to produce their own meaning independently; nor are they encouraged to articulate their thoughts in a detached manner from the designated content when necessary.

The effect of visuals remains deficient because they does not support learners' high-order thinking facility. The discourse so far has not produced any indication of how visuals can inspire learners' original ideas, push imagination further, stimulate reflection on their own experiences, encourage differing viewpoints, promote awareness of social issues, facilitate judgement and encourage learners' self-initiated debate. Instead, learners play a submissive role as content followers without being able to come up with their own issues of interest. Learners find little room to become proactive agents of their own learning.

Learners' Need for Meaning Making

Learner voice matters, not only in adjusting pedagogy but also in improving materials quality. Respecting learner voice requires materials to foster learners' ability to generate opinions to discuss ideas in depth and to explore their own thoughts. One practice that makes the learning process highly productive is the opportunity to express oneself divergently, which, according to Saracho (2012), is closely connected to creativity.

Creativity starts at an early age among humans and tends to reduce as one ages, especially if such skills are not properly nurtured through upbringing and education. Creative behaviour is often spontaneous, original and self-expressive (Isenberg & Jalongo, 2001; Saracho & Spodek, 2013). When students enter school, they bring with them a background in reading not only words but also pictures – drawings, cartoons, comics, illustrations, animated visuals – and such experiences with images should be taken more seriously. Many educators with rich experience working with children have agreed that open-ended materials such as play-dough, blocks, sand and self-initiated drawings can stimulate alternatives and have great potential to generate rich learning. A review of how scholars discuss learner-generated visuals can shed some light on such potential.

Discourse on Learners' Drawings

The literature in education has acknowledged that, from an early age, drawing pictures represents a practice of language use connected to both spoken and written forms. Vygotsky (1978) refers to children's drawings as graphic speech and Newkirk (1989) regards drawing as a writing ability in itself. Malchiodi (1998) observes that drawings provide one with the potential to convey metaphors. Over the past six decades, many scholars who have conducted research into students' visual-creating skills have concluded that drawing can serve as:

- a 'method of conveying ideas as surely as language' (Sibley, 1957: 6);
- a kind of visual awareness which children have more than adults (McDermott, 1974);
- a representation of artistic cleverness (Gardner, 1980; Goodnow, 1977);
- a rehearsal for writing (Grave, 1983);
- a form of encoding meanings (Sulzby, 1990);
- a way to develop a viewpoint (Jacobs & Tunnel, 1996);
- a demonstration of ability to see the world (Jacobs & Tunnel, 1996);
- 'a constructive process of thinking in action' (Cox, 2005: 123);
- an expression of engagement (Einarsdottir *et al.*, 2009);
- the representation of one's learning environment (Nedelcu, 2013);
- an expression of identity (Schaenen, 2013).

In many cases, adults' assumption about students' needs and preferences can be misleading and damaging to their learning (Keddie, 2000). This is particularly true when learners' views are excluded from pedagogical practice. Such lack of trust in students' ability demonstrates pedagogical subjectivity and poor collaboration in research. Carl Jung (1939: 285) once made a statement that somehow conveys the depth of such understanding: 'If there is anything that we wish to change in the child, we should first examine it and see whether it is not something that could better be changed in ourselves'.

In recent decades, there have been appeals for educators to believe in students as social actors (Wyness, 2000), experts on their own lives (Mason & Urquhart, 2001) and legitimate research informants (Neale, 2004). Since drawing is an important means of communication (Nedelcu, 2013), it should be made an available option in students' learning repertoire. According to Kress (2000), some conceptual understandings cannot be expressed through language with the same impact as they are conveyed through imagery. Visual choice, as advocated by Sidelnick and Svodoba (2000), can be regarded as an individualised way to organise learning. Literacy pedagogy must allow for multiple modes of presentation (Kendrick & McKay, 2004) and being able to treat all modes of meaning as equally significant is taking a constructive step towards building a multi-modal approach to enrich learning (Kress & Jewitt, 2003).

Some Examples of Learners' Self-initiated Visuals

In a research project conducted by Bao (2017), learners were invited to write and draw about their dreams or main concerns in life. The drawing shown in Figure 12.1, by Landy, a 15-year-old student from a middle-school English class in China, is an annotated story of how humans have destroyed the living environment over the last four decades. The sketch comes in four panels, representing four gradual stages in the development of the story.

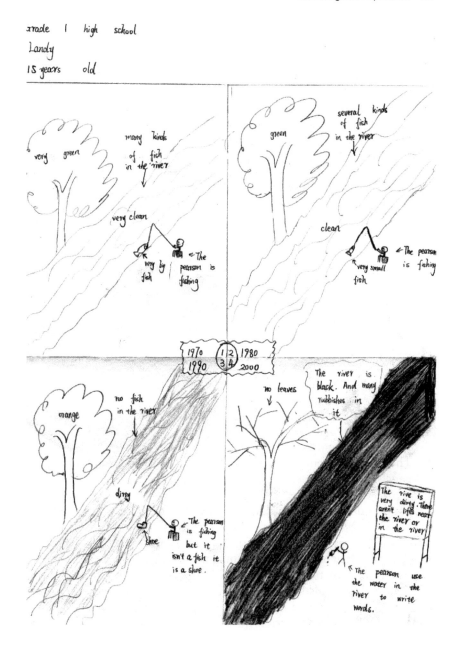

Figure 12.1 'The environment story'. Source: Student drawing (Bao, 2017: 33)

As is visible in Landy's drawing (not reproduced in colour here, but anyway drawn largely in monotone), in 1970, the tree, apparently symbolising a forest, was 'very green'. The river was 'very clean', with 'many kinds of fish' in the water. The person sitting on the river bank with his fishing rod was catching a 'very big fish'. By 1980, the environment had became less wholesome: the tree was now just 'green' and the river merely 'clean'. The kinds of fish had decreased and the person could catch only 'a very small fish'. By 1990, the situation had become worse: the tree was now orange, the river dirty, there were no more fish, and the person trying hard to fish ended up getting a shoe. By 2000, nature had been utterly ruined: the tree was bare of leaves and the river had turned into mud due to excessive rubbish; all the fish had died and the person ironically dipped his brush in black water as ink for writing. These scenarios contain an advanced level of complex thinking, as analysed below.

- There is a causal relationship between humans and the environment, between human needs and natural resources, between humans' mistakes and negative responses from nature, as well as between humans' destruction of nature and its consequences.
- There is a glaring contrast between the artist's humour and the sad reality.
- The development of actions is framed in respective components, namely the tree, the river, the supply of fish and the person's action, each of which is a story in itself, yet together they form the whole theme.
- The development of moods changes gradually from a positive initial state to the negative ending in a logical, dramatic manner.
- There is consistency in size, layout and components across the four panels.

Landy's drawing works as a narrative tool. A narrative, as defined by Malchiodi (1998: 43), is 'a story or a recounting of past events, a history, statement, report, account, description, or a chronicle'. With minimal writing, the drawing takes a dominant role in indicating a complex, advanced range of tasks, such as asserting a position, expressing views of the world, demonstrating logic and solving a social or psychological problem. It is also noted that each component in the drawing provides a different kind of information through the language of metaphors and symbolisation.

Studies of meaning making in children's drawings have noted students' ability in developing sequences (Einarsdottir *et al.*, 2009), among other skills. Although Boyden and Ennew (1997) contend that drawings often function as the basis for discussion, the student has shown that drawing can be the main discussion in itself rather than merely serve as a stimulus. Landy's work also presents a system of symbolisation, where the tree stands for the forest, the river indicates water supply, the character denotes the human community and the act of fishing characterises basic human needs. These elements not only tell us about the student's perspective but, more importantly, they allow us to look into the author's mind and follow her thinking process.

In a second example (Figure 12.2), Angela, a 14-year-old Chinese student, uses her imagination in a creative way that stretches her thinking beyond the everyday world and she shares a fantasy story. The character comes from outer space and his interaction with the Earth seems unique and amusing.

In this story, Alf, a young alien spy, comes to the Earth in a UFO called 'con-purposes'. When flying over a museum, however, the spaceship suddenly drops to the ground and the alien is captured. He gets locked up in a case to serve as an exhibit for entertaining visitors. The drawing reveals two important abilities, namely, to adopt terms used by Kendrick and McKay (2004: 122), 'imagined identity' and 'metalinguistic awareness'. Not only does Angela invent a mythical alien who is not part of her life

Figure 12.2 'The alien'. Source: Student drawing (Bao, 2017: 40)

reality, but she also displays the ability to formulate tones and emotions that make her characters more believable. Such metalinguistic features are evident in the alien's confidence as a spy, his sadness when captured, and the museum visitors' excitement on viewing the new exhibit in a glass case. Additionally, Angela attempts to develop vocabulary in her own way, which are 'Alf' and 'con-purposes', and she also creates characters' speech, such as 'I want to be [a] spy' and 'he look[s] like cool!'

With innovative ways of telling stories, these personalised visuals are worth embedding in coursebook activities for learners to enjoy, comment, interpret and relate to their own thinking. It is through such interaction with virtual peers that learners can feel their creative expression is welcome and will develop the confidence to play with their imagination. Research shows that self-initiated drawings allow learners to exercise the ability to build sequence, develop a reasoning procedure, create logic and solve problems (Bao, 2017). Without such graphic thinking-aloud, one might not be able to construct meaning so efficiently. The literature also indicates that drawing encourages a different kind of intelligence (Brier & Lebbin, 2015), including greater awareness of detail (Baldwin & Crawford, 2010), comprehension of feeling beyond words (Kantrowitz, 2012), hypothetical exploration skills (Brier & Lebbin, 2015) and the ability to collect multi-sensory cues (Willis, 2012). These extensions of learner competence should not be restricted by a conventional classroom that involves students mainly in the written word and through many uncreative textbook pictures.

Arguably, such activities will also allow the teacher to see learners' thought, attitude, behaviour, preferences and interaction styles. In a study which explored student perceptions of their teacher, Weber and Mitchell (1999) found that a large number of drawings depicted the teacher as someone invariably talking in front of a blackboard or from behind the desk, rather than socialising with students. This response shows how students recognise the typical teacher, reveals what most teachers do and provokes further thoughts on the need to make teachers less boring. In another project, by Bao (2015), many students' drawings portrayed the teacher as a giant, standing next to students, who were shrunk into min-iatures. This narrative suggests a relationship in which the former held far more power than the latter. Such spontaneous output provided by students is so genuine and thought-provoking that they are valuable substance for classroom discussion.

Through self-driven drawings, learners form a reasoning procedure and graphic work is a way of thinking aloud for meaning construction. This understanding is manifest in a research study conducted by Helm and Katz (2001) in which a four-year-old child drew images of shelves to assist her own thinking and to explain to others how she made them. As research has demonstrated, complex thinking ability in learner visuals should inspire materials writers to come up with activities in which there is a problem to be solved. Some examples would be how to wash a gorilla, how to build a tree-house and how to save a bicycle that has fallen into a river. Once given such a task, students can develop their own solution and draw it in pictures.

Proposed Activity Models for Learners' Creative Participation

This section recommends three types of task which I have piloted in the classroom in various countries and which have generated enthusiastic, creative responses from learners. The first model invites learners to complete a scenario or find the hidden story. The second provides a structure for story-making through both visuals and words. The third supports learners in reviewing previously learned vocabulary and in using it in a new context. The activities in this discussion are examples to demonstrate the models, based on which course writers might like to consider creating similar tasks.

Activity 1: Reveal the hidden story

The first activity is called 'Reveal the hidden story'. It introduces to the class the drawing segment shown in Figure 12.3, which can be presented on a PowerPoint slide or printed out as a handout for students.

What are these people doing?

Figure 12.3 Reveal the hidden story. Source: Dat Bao's drawing (Bao, 2010: 61)

The picture is deliberately left unfinished, to stimulate the viewer's imagination. Learners work in groups to share ideas and complete the scenario. The pedagogical aim of the task is to engage students in an amusing reflection on life experiences. Figure 12.4 shows some examples of responses from the classroom, each of which represents a snapshot of a story developed by learners. Together with their image presentation, learners also provide a title, a plot, a set of characters, a problem or conflict, a solution, a short dialogue, an ending, a follow-up picture if necessary and the moral of the story. These elements are provided in a framework as a metacognitive strategy that guides story construction and

Figure 12.4 Learner responses to 'Reveal the hidden story'. Source: Dat Bao's drawings based on classroom discussion

presentation. The discussion also involves peer questions, new possibilities and additional elements such as social context, animals, object items, time and atmosphere.

From a learning perspective, this collaborative process requires learners to exercise creativity, explain tension, write amusing dialogues, interpret behaviour, express emotions and exchange views on gender relationships. In an international classroom, the activity might stimulate individual and cultural reactions to the way men and women might behave in learners' contemporary society. Some topics and issues created by learners include, for example, dating, marriage, verbal argument, fighting for food, a singing contest, brushing teeth, domestic division of labour, planning a trip, going to the dentist, practising pronunciation and so on.

From a social-affective perspective, perhaps the most remarkable part of this process is that almost all learners who engage in the activity feel the urge to capture the hilarious side of life and come up with a witty comedy to entertain one another. In this way, the class is filled with laughter every time a story is shared. To make all of the above happen requires some degree of pedagogical imagination on the part of materials writers so that a picture does not have to equal one idea but opens new doors to multiple meanings. After all, the value of a coursebook visual should be measured not by how splendid the image looks, but by how far it engages learners, how much learning it generates and how effectively the cognitive, metacognitive, kinaesthetic, social-affective and sociocultural domains in the learner's mind are triggered.

Activity 2: Contextualising grammar

This task, which is called 'If I was/were', aims to promote learners' creativity and self-expression. To begin with, learners are given the cartoon shown in Figure 12.5 to read for enjoyment. Later it also serves as a template for them to draw their own fiction.

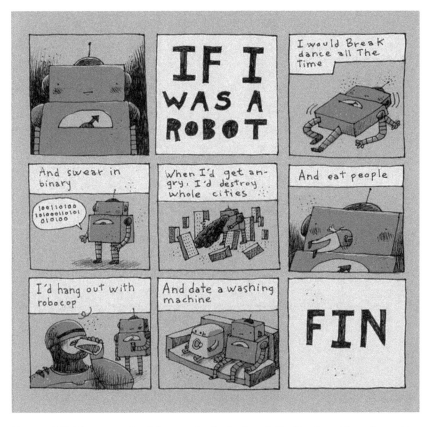

Figure 12.5 'If I was a robot'. Source: *Funky Junk* website. Retrieved from https://www.funnyjunk.com/funny_pictures/1236258/If

Based on that template (Figure 12.6), learners are invited to construct their own story. The activity can be performed individually or in small groups. The stories are later presented to the class, to another individual or to another group. This process can generate a follow-up discussion with comments and questions. The class might like to vote for the most thought-provoking and entertaining piece of work.

Figures 12.7 and 12.8 are example of learners' responses from the actual classroom. The respective texts are reproduced below:

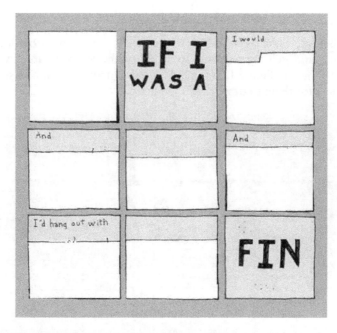

Figure 12.6 'If I was a...' template. Source: Dat Bao's adaptation of Figure 12.5

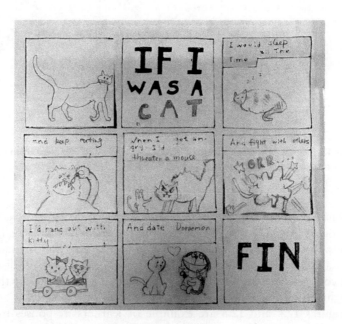

Figure 12.7 'If I was a cat'. Source: Student drawing

Figure 12.8 'If I was a witch'. Source: Student drawing

If I was a cat, I would sleep all the time, and keep eating. When I got angry, I'd threaten a mouse. And fight with others. I'd hang out with kitty. And date Doraemon.

If I was a witch, I would scare people. And I would cook any food with magical power. When I got angry I'd ride a broom at hig[h] speed. And break some mountains. I'd hang out with Harry Potter. And date a handsome vampire.

The visual template serves as a self-scaffolding tool that stimulates learners to come up with fictional ideas and weave them into their own design. Although guidance is provided, learners can exercise the freedom to find their own topic, practise a syntactic structure, contextualise language use, play with imagination, conceive communication among characters, relate compatible elements, develop logic, have fun, share stories with classmates and integrate the four macro skills. During presentation, individuals have a chance to state what else they would do if they were the chosen characters. This follow-up discussion might generate more creative options and language practice can be stretched in individualised, innovative ways.

Activity 3: Translating images into words

A third activity, called 'translating images into words', helps learners review previously learned vocabulary by putting words into context. Learners are invited to draw tiny images within a text to replace words that they wish to revise, as shown in Figure 12.9. The task can be performed in groups. Each group creates a text comprising both pictures and words. They then invite another group or the class to read the text aloud. Every time readers encounter an image, they will need to speak the appropriate word. You can try reading the visual reproduced in Figure 12.9.

Figure 12.9 Relationship scenario, with translation of images into words.
Source: Dat Bao's drawing (Bao, 2010: 62)

The activity not only elicits vocabulary but also contextualises learning through follow-up tasks. For example, after studying the text shown in Figure 12.9, learners can develop the boyfriend's perspective within the same story and imagine how he might talk about the girl. They can also build multiple scenarios, such as a counselling session, a family role-play with parental involvement, a set of email exchanges with friends, a discussion in a lonely-heart column in a popular magazine, among others. The activity covers many learning functions, including problem-solving skills, interpersonal strategies, intrapersonal issues, writing in different genres, dialogue writing, role-play improvisation, emotional expression, decision justification, anticipation of reactions, sharing advice and so on.

The activity taps into the complexity of real-world situations where a wide range of language skills and social communication abilities are involved. Pedagogically, learner drawings not only generate creative ideas and language use but also need to promote the integration of the four macro skills alongside many social skills that students will need to engage in authentic communication. These tasks can lead students to generate something different from the everyday textbook, inspire creative effort, experiment with methods of conveying ideas, develop divergent thinking, promote awareness of social problems and facilitate value judgement.

Conclusion

This chapter has recommended ways to bring learners' worlds into the classroom for individualising materials content. The suggested models not only tap into the social context where learners live but also make their inner self more visible when individuals contribute to the classroom process with their own wisdom, imagination and personality. It is the balance between relevance and originality that is hard to achieve but once accomplished will have the power to lift learning quality to the next level. Commonsensically, drawing is a literacy strategy that serves to manipulate words and an optical channel in the brain that helps restore the flow of ideas. From an economic perspective, owing to learners' contributions to materials, resources will be richer, ideas will be more diverse and the cost of coursebooks will be lower. From an innovator perspective, since there have been commonplace, similar ways of exploiting visuals in commercial coursebooks, it is about time for learners to embed their fresh, different voices into ELT materials so as to keep the everyday classroom process from being repetitive and predictable.

Drawing, as a tool for self-expression, however, does not have to be a stand-alone resource but can serve, in Vygotsky's (1962) view, as graphic manifestation that informs writing in a dialogic process. Gardner (1980) believes that the mixing of visuals and words represents complex conceptualisation. Other scholars also indicate the positive impact of learners' drawings on cognitive competence (Piaget, 1956), language development (Kendrick & McKay, 2004) and on the strengthening of writing abilities (Adoniou, 2013, 2015). If we see learning as a lifelong process, drawing in the classroom can start any time, even with learners of young age. As children grow, they adjust to the demands and priorities of their social environment, which might lead to a change in perspective (Adi-Japha *et al.*, 2010). If educators do not nurture young learners' artistic expression, these skills may perish over time and weaken their imagination.

References

Adi-Japha, E., Berberich-Artzi, J. and Libnawi, A. (2010) Cognitive flexibility in drawings of bilingual children. *Child Development* 81 (5), 1356–1366.

Adoniou, M. (2013) Drawing to support writing development in English language learners. *Language and Education* 27 (3), 261–277.

Adoniou, M. (2015) English language learners, multimodality, multilingualism and writing. In J. Turbill, G. Barton and C. Brock (eds) *Teaching Writing in Today's Classrooms: Looking Back to Look Forward* (pp. 316–332). Norwood: Australian Literacy Educators' Association.

Altun, F. (2015) The use of drawing in language teaching and learning. *Journal of Educational and Instructional Studies in the World* 5 (4), 91–93. Retrieved from http://www.wjei s.org/FileUpload/ds217232/File/10a._altun.pdf.

Anglin, G.J., Vaez, H. and Cunningham, K.L. (2004) Visual representations and learning: The role of static and animated graphics. In D.H. Jonassen (ed.) *Handbook of Research for Education Communications and Technology* (pp. 865–913). New York: Simon and Schuster.

Arif, M. and Hashim, F. (2009) *Young Learners' Second Language Visual Literacy Practices*. Oxford: Inter-Disciplinary Press.

Baldwin, L. and Crawford, I. (2010) Art instruction in the botany lab: A collaborative approach. *Journal of College Science Teaching* 40 (2), 26–31.

Bao, D. (2006) Developing materials for local markets: Issues and considerations. In J. Mukundan (ed.) *Readings on Materials II* (pp. 52–76). Selangor: Pearson Longman.

Bao, D. (2010) The teaching of language through interactive cartoons. *Education Technology Solution* 34, 60–62.

Bao, D. (2015) Images of dreams and hopes: Hmong and Yao primary students in Northern Thailand. In J. Brown and N.F. Johnson (eds) *Children's Images of Identity: Drawing the Self and the Other* (pp. 169–180). Rotterdam: Sense Publishers.

Bao, D. (2017) Learner drawing as connected with writing: Implications in ELT pedagogy and materials development. *European Journal of Applied Linguistics and TEFL* 6 (1), 27–47.

Barry, A.M. (2001) Faster than the speed of thought: Vision, perceptual learning, and the space of cognitive reflection. *Journal of Visual Literacy* 21 (2), 107–122.

Boyden, J. and Ennew, J. (1997) *Children in Focus: A Manual for Participatory Research With Children*. Stockholm: Radda Barnen.

Bradshaw, A.C. (2003) Effect of presentation interference in learning with visuals. *Journal of Visual Literacy* 23 (1), 41–68.

Brier, D.J. and Lebbin, V.K. (2015) Learning information literacy through drawing. *Reference Services Review* 43 (1), 45–67.

Brinton, D.M. (2001) The use of media in language teaching. In M. Celce-Murcia (ed.) *Teaching English as a Second or Foreign Language* (3rd edn) (pp. 459–475). Boston, MA: Heinle and Heinle.

Canning-Wilson, C. (1998) Visual support and language teaching. *TESOL Arabia News* 5 (4), 3–4.

Canning-Wilson, C. (2000) Practical aspects of using video in the foreign language classroom. *Internet TESL Journal*. Retrieved from http://itestlj.org/articles/canning-video.html.

Canning-Wilson, C. and Wallace, J. (2000) Practical aspects of using video in the foreign language classroom. *Internet TESL Journal* 6 (11), 1–36.

Carney, R.N. and Levin, J.R. (2002) Pictorial illustrations still improve students' learning from text. *Educational Psychology Review* 14 (1), 5–26.

Clark, R.C. and Lyon, C. (2004) *Graphics for Learning: Proven Guidelines for Planning, Designing and Evaluation Visuals in Training Materials*. San Francisco, CA: Pfieffer.

Cox, S. (2005) Intention and meaning in young children's drawing. *International Journal of Art and Design Education* 24 (2), 115–125.

Einarsdottir, J., Dockett, S. and Perry, B. (2009) Making meaning: Children's perspectives expressed through drawings. *Early Child Development and Care* 179 (2), 217–232.

Fang, Z. (1996) Illustrations, text, and the child reader. What are pictures in children's story-books for? *Read: Horizons* 37, 130–142.

Gardner, H. (1980) *Artful Scribbles*. New York: Basic Books.

Goodnow, J. (1977) *Children's Drawing*. London: Open Books.

Grave, D. (1983) *Writing: Teachers and Children at Work*. Portsmouth, NH: Heinemann.

Helm, J.H. and Katz, L.G. (2001) *Young Investigators: The Project Approach in the Early Years*. New York: Teachers College Press.

Hendricks, S. (2015) *Speed Drawing for Vocabulary Retention*. Retrieved from http://ameri canenglish.state.gov/files/ae/resource_files/53_1_teaching_techniques_speed_drawing_vocabulary_retention.pdf.

Isenberg, J.P. and Jalongo, M.R. (2001) *Creative Expression and Play in Early Childhood* (3rd edn). Upper Saddle River, NJ: Merill.

Jacobs, J.S. and Tunnel, M.O. (1996) *Children's Literature, Briefly*. Englewood Cliffs, NJ: Prentice Hall.

Jung, C.G. (1939) *The Integration of the Personality*. Oxford: Farrar and Rinehart.

Kang, S. (2004) Using visual organizers to enhance EFL instruction. *ELT Journal* 58 (1), 58–67.

Kantrowitz, A. (2012) The man behind the curtain: What cognitive science reveals about drawing. *Journal of Aesthetic Education* 46 (1), 1–14.

Keddie, A. (2000) Research with young children: Some ethical considerations. *Journal of Educational Enquiry* 1 (2), 72–81.

Kendrick, M.E. and McKay, R. (2004) Drawings as an alternative way of understanding young children's constructions of literacy. *Journal of Early Childhood Literacy* 4 (1), 109–128.

Kress, G. (2000) Multimodality. In B. Cope and M. Kalantzis (eds) *Multiliteracies: Literacy Learning and the Design of Social Futures* (pp. 182–201). London: Routledge.

Kress, G. and Jewitt, C. (2003) Introduction. In C. Jewitt and G. Kress (eds) *Multimodal Literacy* (pp. 1–18). New York: Peter Lang.

Malchiodi, C.A. (1998) *Understanding Children's Drawings*. New York: Guilford Press.

Mannan, A. (2005) *Modern Education: Audio-Visual Aids*. New Delhi: Anmol Publications.

Mason, J. and Urquhart, R. (2001) Developing a model for participation by children in research on decision making. *Children Australia* 26 (4), 16–21.

Mayer, R.E. and Moreno, R. (2000) Engaging students in active learning: The case for personalized multimedia messages. *Journal of Educational Psychology* 92 (4), 724–733.

McDermott, G. (1974) *Image in Film and Picture Book*. Athens, GA: University of Georgia.

Mukherjee, N. and Roy, D. (2003) A visual context-aware multimodal system for spoken language processing. Retrieved from http://web.media.mit.edu/~dkroy/papers/pdf/mukherjee_roy_2003.pdf.

Neale, B. (ed.) (2004) *Young Children's Citizenship*. York: Joseph Rowntree Foundation.

Nedelcu, A. (2013) Analysing students' drawings of their classroom: A child-friendly research method. *Revista de Cercetare și Intervenție Sociala* 42 (1538-3410), 275–293.

Newkirk, T. (1989) *More Than Stories – The Range of Children's Writing*. Portsmouth, NH: Heinemann.

Piaget, J. (1956) *The Child's Conception of Space*. New York: Macmillan.

Saracho, O.N. (2012) *Contemporary Perspectives on Research in Creativity in Early Childhood Education*. Greenwich, CT: Information Age Publishing.

Saracho, O.N. and Spodek, B. (2013) *Handbook of Research on the Education of Young Children* (3rd edn). London: Routledge.

Schaenen, I. (2013) Hand-I coordination: Interpreting student writings and drawings as expressions of identity. *Qualitative Report* 18 (12), 1–24.

Shrosbree, M. (2008) Digital video in the language classroom. *Jactcall Journal. Selected Papers* 4 (1), 75–84. Retrieved from http://journal.jaltcall.org/articles/4_1_Shrosbree.pdf.

Sibley, A.G. (1957) Drawing of kindergarten children as a measure of reading readiness. Master's thesis, Cornell University, Ithaca, New York.

Sidelnick, M.A. and Svoboda, M.L. (2000) The bridge between drawing and writing: Hannah's story. *Reading Teacher* 54 (2), 174–184.

Snelson, C. and Perkins, R.A. (2009) From silence film to YouTube: Tracing the historical roots of motion picture technologies in education. *Journal of Visual Literacy* 28 (1), 1–27.

Stoller, F.L. (1992) Using video in theme-based curricula. In S. Stempleski and P. Arcano (eds) *Video in Second language Teaching: Using, Selecting and Producing Video for the Classroom* (pp. 25–46). Alexandria: Teachers of English to Spears of Other Languages.

Sulzby, E. (1990) Assessment of emergent writing and children's language while writing. In L.M. Morrow and J.K. Smith (eds) *Assessment for Instruction in Early Literacy* (pp. 83–109). Englewood Cliff, NJ: Prentice Hall.

Tomalin, B. (1991) *Video, TV and Radio in the English Class: An Introductory Guide*. London: Macmillan.

Vygotsky, L. (1962) *Thought and Language*. Cambridge, MA: Harvard University Press.

Vygotsky, L. (1978) *Mind in Society*. Cambridge, MA: Harvard University Press.

Watkins, J.K., Miller, E. and Brobaker, D. (2004) The role of the visual image: What are students really learning form pictorical representations? *Journal of Visual Literacy* 24 (1), 23–40.

Weber, S. and Mitchell, C. (1999) *Reinventing Ourselves as Teachers: Beyond Nostalgia*. London: Falmer Press.

Willis, J. (2012) Brain-based teaching strategies for improving students' memory, learning, and test-taking success. *Childhood Education* 18 (23), 310–315.

Wyness, M. (2000) *Contesting Childhood*. London: Falmer Press.

13 Bangladeshi EFL Teachers' Views on the *English for Today* Textbook

Mohammod Moninoor Roshid, Md Zulfeqar Haider and Hosne Ara Begum

Textbooks play a significant role in language teaching and learning. They are viewed as the second most important factor in foreign language learning classrooms, after the teachers (Riasati & Zare, 2010). However, textbooks are not without their limitations. The purpose of this chapter is to critically evaluate *English for Today*, a textbook that has recently been introduced for teaching English at the secondary schools in Bangladesh, and to contribute to existing debates.

Bangladesh belongs to the outer circle of Kachru's (1992: 356) three-circle model of world Englishes. As a former British colony, Bangladesh has a long tradition of using Anglo-centric English coursebooks, mostly written and edited by native speakers of English. However, since Bangladesh's independence in 1971, there have been attempts to produce local textbooks. Since 1972, all textbooks, including textbooks on the English language, were produced centrally by the then Bangladesh School Textbook Board, which was later restructured as National Curriculum and Textbook Board (NCTB), the sole, state-run authority for developing, publishing and distributing the secondary-school curriculum and textbooks. The textbooks published by the NCTB are now being used in all the government-approved secondary schools throughout the country as the only instructional materials for TEFL. In 2013, the NCTB introduced a new series of English textbooks, titled *English for Today*, for learners in grades 6–10. These textbooks were published to reflect the spirit of Bangladesh's first ever education policy, adopted in 2010. These books are expected to address the national curriculum goal of developing the communicative competence of secondary school learners by following the communicative language teaching (CLT) approach.

In English language teaching, textbooks are considered an appropriate guideline for non-native English teachers for teaching English (Williams,

1983). Textbooks influence both what teachers teach and how they deliver the content (Akbari, 2008: 647). Considering the significance of textbooks as instructional materials, it is necessary to assess the extent to which current textbooks facilitate the achievement of curriculum goals and objectives and how useful they are to teachers and students. However, until now, almost no research has been conducted to explore the effectiveness of the English textbooks currently used in secondary school classrooms in Bangladesh. This study has made an attempt to evaluate the *English for Today* textbook for grades 9 and 10, used in secondary schools in Bangladesh, retrospectively through the voice of teachers as a key agent of implementing textbooks in classrooms.

Textbooks are prevalent forms of instructional materials that play a vital role in the teaching and learning of a language. They provide the basis of an instructional programme and are regarded as the heart of education because students and teachers largely depend on them (Sarem *et al.*, 2013). The standing of textbooks as instructional materials, particularly in language classrooms, is well recognised in the literature. Textbooks play critical role in English classrooms all over the world (Dendrinos, 1992; Hutchinson & Torres, 1994) because they are usually designed to improve learners' linguistic and communicative abilities (Sheldon, 1987). No teaching–learning situation is complete until it has its own relevant textbook, which, in fact, works as agent of change (Hutchinson & Torres, 1994). Moreover, students' progress and achievement can be readily measured if they use a textbook (Haycroft, 1998).

Ur (1996) has pointed out a number of advantages of using textbooks in language teaching. For instance, textbooks (a) provide a clear framework for teachers and students about their destination, (b) serve as a syllabus that includes language content, (c) provide ready-made texts and tasks, (d) are the cheapest way of providing learning material for students, (e) are convenient packages whose components are bound in order, (f) are useful guides, especially for inexperienced teachers, and (g) provide autonomy, as the students can use them by themselves to learn new material, and to review and monitor their own progress. Without textbooks it is probably more difficult to teach English. Accordingly, the success or failure of an English language teaching programme largely depends on textbooks (Mukundan, 2007).

Despite all the advantages that textbooks may offer, problems can be caused by poorly written and designed textbooks. For example, issues might arise from contents that incite gender bias or gender inequality (see Carrell & Korwitz, 1994; Florent & Walter, 1989; Gupta & Yin, 1990). There are authors who consider the target language culture as a vehicle for target language teaching (Alptekin, 1993; Prodromou, 1998). Richards and Renandya (2002), cited in Sarem *et al.* (2013), have pointed out a number of possible weaknesses of language textbooks: textbooks may (a) fail to present appropriate and realistic language models, (b) propose subordinate learner roles, (c) fail to contextualise language activities, (d) foster inadequate cultural understanding, (e) fail to address discourse competence, (f) fail to teach idioms, (g) lack equity in gender representation.

A textbook is not merely an instructional material but also has considerable professional, financial and political significance (Sheldon, 1988). Considering the importance of a textbook in the teaching–learning process, it is crucial to design a suitable textbook that effectively addresses the needs of learners and serves the purpose of an English language programme. Textbooks should promote pedagogical and cultural values and also need to be economically viable. In doing so, the evaluation of textbooks is imperative, and that can be done in different ways. In materials evaluative research, most projects are based on checklists and scholars' views, some on users' perceptions, experience and reflection. We postulate language teachers are well placed to evaluate a textbook, as they are important agents in introducing textbooks to students in classrooms. In fact, language teachers not only need to know how to use the textbook but also need to know how useful the book is (Williams, 1983). Like teacher-based retrospective evaluation, qualitative content analysis can be another way to evaluate textbooks. Considering this viewpoint, the mixed-method study reported in this chapter offers a retrospective evaluation of tdhe locally developed *English for Today* textbook for classes 9 to 10 in terms of the views of the teachers who use the book in the classroom. Simultaneously, qualitative content analysis has been adopted for triangulating the study. The findings of this study may help provide useful, systematic and contextual insights into the various aspects of the *English for Today* textbook for grades 9 and 10. The insights gained from this study may have implications for getting the best out of the textbook in the classroom, as well as for revising the existing book or even designing better ELT textbooks in future.

The chapter proceeds with a review of literature to summarise the core features of a textbook that need to be considered in an evaluation. It then gives a brief account of the historical developments and current state of English language teaching and textbook reform in Bangladesh. Thereafter, the chapter presents the methodology of the research and discusses the findings.

Literature Review and Conceptual Framework

Over the last three decades, a number of studies have evaluated textbooks or coursebooks used in different countries at different levels. Those studies have produced numerous checklists, guidelines and frameworks for evaluating textbooks (e.g. Cunningsworth, 1995; Sheldon, 1988; Skierso, 1991). Sheldon (1988) provides a textbook evaluation framework that takes into account rationale, physical characteristics, appropriateness, authenticity, cultural bias, educational validity and layout as some key criteria. Williams (1983) developed a scheme for ESL/EFL textbook evaluation with a set of linguistic, pedagogical, general and technical criteria. These criteria led to the formulation of four core assumptions (i.e. methods of teaching, guidance for non-native speakers of English, needs of learners, and relevance to sociocultural environment) that provided the theoretical grounding to formulate an initial checklist for textbook evaluation. Prior to that, Daoud and Celce-Murcia (1979) proposed an evaluation checklist for textbooks consisting of five major elements: (a) subject matter, (b) vocabulary and structures, (c) exercises, (d) illustrations and (e) physical make-up.

More recently Mukundan *et al.* (2011), based on their focus group study, developed a tentative checklist for textbook evaluation and classified the evaluation criteria in terms of general attributes and learning–teaching content. According to the checklist, general attributes include criteria such as relevance to syllabus and curriculum, methodology, suitability to learners, physical and utilitarian aspects and efficient outlay of supplementary materials; on the other hand, the evaluation criteria within the learning–teaching content are the four language skills – vocabulary, grammar, pronunciation and exercise. However, despite the existence of so many frameworks or guidelines developed for textbook evaluation, there are still questions regarding those frameworks and guidelines.

Apart from linguistic and pedagogical aspects, integrating culture is seen as an important agenda of ELT that is transmitted through textbooks. The intercultural awareness and communicative competence of the learners are developed by introducing the cultures of different countries and regions in textbooks (Juan, 2010). However, the important question is, what aspects of culture are usually taught or need to be taught through English textbooks? In response to this question, Saville-Troike (2003) argued that it depends on the social context in which the target foreign language is learned and used. It is usually observed that the 'Anglo-American' culture is becoming dominant as the target language because most of the materials used in teaching English are produced by British or American experts and native speakers of English. According to Kramsch (1993) the teaching and learning of culture in many language classes are often reduced to 'the four Fs' – 'foods, fairs, folklores and statistical facts' (as cited in Juan, 2010: 318). Byram (1993) developed a comprehensive list of what cultural contents should be taught through ELT and suggested eight areas: (a) social identity and social group (social class, regional identity, ethnic minorities); (b) social interaction (differing levels of formality; as outsider and insider); (c) belief and behaviour (morality, religious beliefs; daily routines); (d) social and political institutions (state institutions, health care, law and order, social security, local government); (e) socialisation and the life cycle (families, schools, employment, rites of passage); (f) national history (historical and contemporary events seen as markers of national identity); (g) national geography (geographical factors seen as being significant by members); (h) stereotypes and national identity (what is 'typical' or symbolic) (Byram, 1993: 5–10).

However, the question of whether a textbook really fosters and develops cultural awareness of English learners largely depends on the nature of the book. According to Juan (2010), if a textbook is systematic and comprehensive, it is likely to promote cultural input. Nevertheless, cultural teaching is almost absent if a textbook is rigid. Therefore, it is necessary to assess whether the English textbooks used in Bangladesh are effective instruments for generating cultural awareness and developing intercultural communicative competence among the learners. Hence, this research also seeks to explore the cultural facets covered within the *English for Today* textbook.

The studies mentioned above identify some core principles to be considered for making textbooks suitable for English language learning and teaching. In order to be effective, textbooks need to contain authentic language and texts, a wide range of topics, unbiased cultural facets, teaching–learning contents such as language skills, vocabulary, grammar, pronunciation and exercises, and so on. In addition, aspects such as suitable and appropriate teaching approach, activities, physical makeup and illustration also reflect the standard of a textbook. In this light, a conceptual framework (see Figure 13.1) was developed for evaluating the *English for Today* textbook. The six important criteria integrated in this framework are: linguistic, sociocultural, pedagogical, technical, general and output. While linguistic criteria include vocabulary, rules of words and sentence formation, linguistic semantics, pronunciation and spelling, sociocultural criteria embrace the representation of sociocultural facets and values such as local cultures, international cultures and target cultures.

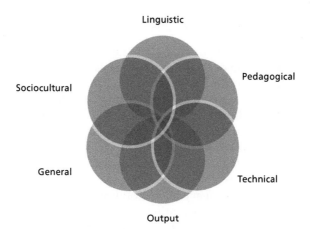

Figure 13.1 Conceptual framework for the *English for Today* textbook evaluation

Pedagogical principles involve the teaching–learning practices, whereas technical criteria are concerned with the quality of printing, illustration and makeup. General criteria comprise topics covered in the textbook, and output reflects the overall learning outcomes of English language teaching. Needless to say, these criteria are closely interconnected and collectively determine whether a textbook is effective.

As teachers are the main players for implementing textbooks in classrooms, they are likely to be able tell whether a textbook is effective or not to achieve the goal of English language learning and teaching, whether students enjoy the textbook or not, and whether the contents, tasks and activities included in textbook are appropriate to the learners' level and interests. Therefore, it is worthwhile to take into account the views of the teachers who are actually using this book in classrooms. The aim of this research is to explore Bangladeshi EFL teachers' perceptions of the *English for Today* textbook, and to identify to what extent their perceptions are aligned with the contents of the book. Accordingly, the study addresses the following research questions:

- How do secondary school EFL teachers of Bangladesh perceive the *English for Today* textbook?
- Do the teachers' perceptions of the textbook vary with regard to their demographic characteristics, such as gender, training and teaching experience?
- To what extent do the perceptions of the teachers align with the contents of the textbook?

In order to address the above research questions, the study adopted a mixed-methods approach. Before turning to discuss the methodology of this study, however, we need to understand the background of the *English for Today* textbooks in Bangladesh.

Background to the *English for Today* Textbooks

Textbooks are the only learning materials available to most Bangladeshi school learners. All the mainstream secondary schools in Bangladesh follow a centrally developed curriculum prescribed by the NCTB, which is also responsible for the writing, publication and distribution of textbooks in the country. Bangladesh, being a densely populated country, has a huge number of students enrolled in secondary schools and *madrasas* (Islamic schools). Hence, the job of publishing and distributing the textbooks for all subjects for all students is an enormous task for the government. In 2015, about 326 million textbooks for all subjects were distributed among 44.4 million students in primary and secondary schools, including those from *madrasas* and technical education (Azad, 2015). This massive effort each year reflects the government's commitment to free education for all school-aged children.

The government of Bangladesh has so far been successful in printing and publishing a huge number of books each year and distributing them among students free of cost, but the quality of these books has been questioned. The national education policy adopted in 2010 reiterates the government's strong commitment to free and quality education for all school-aged children. That policy was developed following the spirit of the first Education Commission of Bangladesh, which was formed immediately after independence. The First Education Commission, known as the Qudrat-E-Khuda Commission, recommended for a 'pro-people, modern and science oriented' education policy for the people of the new nation (Ministry of Education, 2010: 2). The policy reiterates earlier commitments to access to quality education for upgrading the living standards of the people of Bangladesh. The policy called for a uniform curriculum to be followed in all primary and secondary institutions. Moreover, it stressed the need for writing and publishing new textbooks following the newly developed curriculum and syllabus. The aims and purpose of preparing new textbooks are stated as follows:

> While preparing the textbooks, it will be kept in mind that education must be related to real life and inspire the students with patriotism and the spirit of our liberation war and further facilitate the development of thinking ability, imaginative capability, inquisitiveness and creativity of the learners.(Ministry of Education, 2010: 69)

In 2012 the NCTB published a set of new books for all subjects to be taught at secondary level. As part of the initiative, a set of English textbooks titled *English for Today* were published following the recommendation of the new curriculum that came into being in 2011. These books were written and edited by Bangladeshi ELT teachers. The panel of writers for each book included senior ELT experts from the English/ELT departments of different local universities, English language teachers and teacher trainers from the government colleges and teacher training colleges (TTCs) and practising English teachers from secondary schools. The textbook for grades 9 and 10 was written by a panel of ELT teachers and experts from schools, colleges and universities. The book targets students aged 15–16 who go to mainstream schools and *madrasas* all over the country.

The new *English for Today* series of textbooks were developed following a set of underlying principles specified in the new curriculum document produced by the NCTB. These principles are in line with the general objectives of learning English at grades 9 and 10, which emphasise the teaching–learning of English as a skills-based subject, so that learners can use English in their real-life situations. The objectives of teaching–learning English at grades 9 and 10 are clearly spelt out in the NCTB curriculum document, as follows (National Curriculum and Textbook Board, 2012: 74):

- to acquire competence in all four language skills – listening, speaking, reading and writing;
- to use the competence for effective communication in real-life situations at pre-intermediate level;
- to acquire necessary grammar competence in the English language;
- to develop creativity and critical thinking through the English language;
- to become independent learners of English by using reference skills;
- to use language skills for utilising information technology;
- to use literary pieces in English, both for enjoyment and for language learning;
- to be skilled human resources by using English language skills.

In addition to these general objectives, the NCTB curriculum also sets a list of comprehensive guidelines for the writers of English textbooks. The guidelines lists a set of instructions for the potential textbook writers, covering a wide range of issues, such as the content, teaching–learning approach, possible selection of topics/themes, level of difficulty, presentation style, and so on. These guidelines stated in section 14 of the curriculum document include the following (National Curriculum and Textbook Board, 2012: 87):

1. Textbooks should reflect social and moral values and the spirits of our Liberation War. Materials should be sensitive to issues on gender, cultures, colour, race, religion, ethnic groups etc.
2. Topics and themes should be interesting, realistic, and suitable for learners' age and cognitive level.
3. Topics/activities should be chosen to achieve the objectives and learning outcomes of the curriculum.
4. Topics should properly address all learning domains (cognitive, affective and psychomotor).
5. The textbooks should contain authentic texts as needed, and language appropriate to different contexts and cultures.
6. Instructions should be brief and written in simple English.
7. The textbooks should include a variety of activities to provide adequate exercises on four language skills.
8. The textbooks should provide opportunities for learners to learn and practice social interactions through dialogues.
9. Some language games, puzzles, mini dialogues may be used as exercises for developing language skills through fun and entertainment.
10. Grammar items should be provided in context in a systematic and graded way.
11. At each level new vocabulary should be introduced. Vocabulary introduced in previous classes should be revised.
12. Stress and intonation marks should be shown in the examples and sample texts.

13. The textbook should be attractive and colourful. Illustrations (charts, maps, photos, drawings, diagrams etc.) should be relevant to the contexts/topics.
14. The sound symbol chart should be provided in the Teacher's Guide.
15. A section on sample classroom instructions (such as for greetings, starting a lesson, common Wh/Yes-No question, monitoring students' activities, checking answers, simple social English) should be provided in the Teacher's Guide.
16. The textbooks will create opportunities for sound and pronunciation practice as through listening texts with tasks.
17. Phonetic symbols are not to be used in the textbooks for learners but should be explained in the Teacher's Guide.
18. Writers must acknowledge the sources of their collected or adapted materials.

ELT materials in Bangladesh: Past and present

Bangladesh, being a former British colony, has been strongly influenced by an Anglo-centric textbook culture in the field of English language teaching and learning. In fact, there was a strong presence of typical British English contents, including great literary texts of classic British (and a few American) authors. In fact, the English textbooks published for the Bangladeshi school learners in the 1980s were dominated by the works of many British and American sort-story and non-fiction writers, novelists, playwrights and poets. One could hardly find a Bangladeshi school or college leaver in the 1980s who was not familiar with the names of O. Henry, the popular American short-story writer, or Somerset Maugham, the British playwright, novelist and short-story writer. Until the mid-1980s students in Bangladeshi schools had to memorise the poems of Wordsworth, Shakespeare or Longfellow as part of their English lessons. There were also grammar and composition books known as 'English Second paper' which were written in the tradition of widely used and popular British grammar books written by Wren and Martin, J.C. Nesfield and Raymond Murphy.

A major breakthrough was marked in the late 1990s when the English Language Teaching Improvement Project (ELTIP), a UK–Bangladesh joint funded project was launched, with a view to bring qualitative change to English language instruction at Bangladeshi schools. The ELTIP had a textbook development wing that produced a new series of textbooks titled *English for Today* for grades 6–12. The books were written by a group of Bangladeshi ELT practitioners under the guidance and technical assistance of a British ELT expert. Those books introduced communicative contents and skills-based lessons for the first time. Famous literacy pieces were not featured, and nor were typical grammatical definition, explanations and exercises, and written composition that was meant only to be memorised by the students.

The current *English for Today* NCTB textbooks have been written following the same communicative language teaching approach evident in the previous textbooks. These books were written after 15 years of introducing CLT in Bangladesh. The new *English for Today* for grades 9 and 10 has a focus on both communicative tasks and grammar exercises. While the books written in the 1990s totally abolished the explicit teaching of grammar, the newly written *English for Today* series included selected explicit grammar-based activities in some of the lessons. Another important aspect of the new *English for Today* textbooks is the inclusion of more communicative test items as part of the exercises set at the end of the lessons. However, it is not well documented how English teachers perceive the new EfTs. Since the *English for Today* textbooks are centrally prescribed by the government of Bangladesh, teachers just have to use them in the classroom and accordingly they should be used judiciously (Williams, 1983).

Methodology

The purpose of this study was to investigate secondary English teachers' perceptions of the *English for Today* textbooks, which is the only teaching material used by all secondary school teachers throughout Bangladesh. The project aimed to get a collective view of a large body of the secondary teacher community, rather than the subjective views of individual teachers, so that the study would produce comparable and generalisable results. Nonetheless, it was important to examine the teachers' perceptions of the subject matter and information reflected in the textbook, and this necessitated a qualitative approach. Thus, the study employed a mixed-methods approach that embraced both quantitative and qualitative enquiry. The research design involved a questionnaire survey of 100 English teachers and a qualitative content analysis of the *English for Today* textbook.

Participants

The research participants were male and female secondary English teachers with diverse levels of education, teaching experiences and professional training (Table 13.1).

Data-collection tools

To record teachers' perceptions, a questionnaire was developed with 38 statements about the *English for Today* textbook for grades 9 and 10. The participants were asked to respond to each statement on a five-point Likert scale. Statements were allocated to each broad criterion as specified in the conceptual framework developed for this study. These areas were:

Table 13.1 Demographic information of the participants

Demographic variable	Number of participants (*n* = 100)	%
Gender		
Male	83	83
Female	17	17
Education		
Bachelor degree and equivalent	59	59
Master's degree	41	41
Teaching experience		
Beginners	55	55
Experienced	45	45
Professional degree		
Yes	64	64
No	36	36
Training		
Yes	86	86
No	14	14

coverage of topics, tasks and activities, lexis and vocabularies, grammar, pedagogical approach and support, representation of sociocultural values and outcomes of the textbook (as specified in Table 13.2). In developing the tool, previous research (e.g. Mukundan *et al.*, 2011; Sheldon, 1988; Williams, 1983) questionnaires were reviewed. Some more context-specific statements were also included. The items used in the questionnaire were closed ended, so as to provide definite answers about teachers' perceptions. The quantitative analysis offered a meaningful summary of repetitive responses and reflected the common views of the teachers. Both descriptive (mean, standard deviation) and inferential analyses (*t*-test) were used to understand the teachers' collective views about the textbook.

The reliability of the tool was determined by examining the internal consistency of the scale items for the current study data set (see Table 13.2). Cronbach's alpha is a widely used method for measuring the internal consistency of Likert-type instruments. The 'Scale Reliability' command of IBM SPSS Statistics 21 was used to conduct the Cronbach alpha reliability test for the whole questionnaire as well as the sub-scales separately. The Cronbach's alpha can range from 0 to 1. The higher the alpha value is, the higher the reliability of the scale items is. Researchers have suggested that values between 0.70 and 0.95 are acceptable (DeVellis, 2012). As seen in Table 13.2, the Cronbach's alpha for the whole scale is 0.96. For sub-scales C, D, E and F, the Cronbach's alpha values are above 0.80 and below 0.90; for sub-scales A, B and G, the values are above 0.70 and below 0.80. These values lie in the acceptable range of 0.70–0.95. Thus, all the items in

Table 13.2 Cronbach's alpha values of the whole scale and its sub-scales

Linguistic and pedagogical components	No. of items	Cronbach's alpha
A. Topics included in the textbook	5	0.742
B. Tasks and activities used in the textbook	6	0.727
C. Inclusion of lexis and presentation	5	0.832
D. Presentation of grammar	5	0.801
E. Pedagogical approach and support	5	0.839
F. Representation of sociocultural values	8	0.872
G. Outcomes of the textbook	4	0.781
Overall	38	0.955

the scale are considered appropriate to measure the teachers' perceptions regarding the textbook under consideration.

Data analysis

Data were analysed using both quantitative and qualitative approaches. Data obtained from Likert scales were analysed using descriptive and inferential techniques. The mean perception scores (including standard deviations) of the participants were reported for each of the statements. Independent-sample *t*-tests were performed to examine the significance of differences in perception scores with regard to gender, training status and teaching experience.

Content analysis

The qualitative data for the study related to the content of the textbook *English for Today*. The aim of analysing the textbook content was to crosscheck teachers' views of the textbook collected through the survey. In analysing the textbook, a qualitative content analysis (QCA) was used. The goal of contents analysis is to provide knowledge and understanding of the phenomenon under study by making valid inferences from verbal, visual or written data (Downe-Wamboldt, 1992). QCA is a flexible approach to qualitative data analysis that reduces and summarises qualitative material, without reporting them in detail (Neuendorf, 2002; Schreier, 2012). In QCA, data codes are partly 'data-driven' and partly 'concept-driven' (Schreier, 2012). In light of the conceptual framework for the present study (Figure 13.1), a coding framework was developed and following the coding framework data were codified through close reading and re-reading of the textbook. After the initial coding, the codes were revisited and sub-themes were generated. From the sub-themes the main themes were developed. Finally, data were analysed, interpreted and presented thematically, maintaining the alignment with research questions.

Findings and Discussion

As the purpose of this research was to present the perceptions of the secondary English teachers of the *English for Today* textbook, this research focused on seven aspects of the textbook (as specified in Table 13.2). While presenting the findings of the study, these seven aspects of the textbooks evaluation have been considered and presented sequentially under sub-headings. The data presentation starts with discussion of teachers' overall perceptions of the textbook before the findings are considered thematically.

The perceptions of the 100 secondary teachers are summarised by reporting arithmetic means and standard deviations. Table 13.3 shows the overall mean perceptions in the seven areas of textbook evaluation. The teachers believe that the overall quality of the selected dimensions of the textbook are largely maintained ($M = 3.64$; $SD = 0.73$). Their preference was the most enthusiastic for the ways the tasks and activities are presented in the book ($M = 3.77$; $SD = 0.743$) followed by the representation of diverse sociocultural values ($M = 3.60$; $SD = 0.88$). Findings on other areas of book evaluation include usefulness of the topics ($M = 3.58$; $SD = 0.85$), pedagogical approach for supporting language learning ($M = 3.58$; $SD = 0.95$), indication of grammatical rules ($M = 3.56$; $SD = 0.87$) and sufficiency of vocabulary ($M = 3.56$; $SD = 0.93$).

Table 13.3 Secondary teachers' overall perceptions of the *English for Today* textbook

Areas	N	Mean	SD
Topics included in the textbook	100	3.58	0.85
Tasks and activities used	100	3.77	0.74
Inclusion of lexis and their presentation	100	3.56	0.93
Presentation of grammar	100	3.56	0.87
Pedagogic approach and supports	100	3.58	0.95
Representation of sociocultural values	100	3.60	0.88
Outcomes of the textbook	100	3.85	0.87
Overall	100	3.64	0.73

Note. *N* = number of teachers in the sample; *SD* = standard deviation

Linguistic evaluation (grammar and vocabulary)

The conceptual framework includes linguistic criteria for textbook evaluation that cover vocabulary, rules of words and sentence formation, linguistic semantics, pronunciation and spelling. However, in this research we focused only on grammar and vocabulary as two individual criteria because these are considered major elements of an English textbook. The quantitative findings indicate that teachers largely believe that the textbook appropriately portrays the grammatical rules. The data further tell us that the book incorporates a range of practice activities aligned with students' interests and level of understanding ($M = 3.68$; $SD = 1.15$), set in a meaningful context ($M = 3.58$; $SD = 1.17$), presented through familiar examples and simple explanations ($M = 3.55$; $SD = 1.10$), embedded in reading texts ($M = 3.54$; $SD = 1.28$) and implicitly embedded ($M = 3.46$; $SD = 1.11$).

As with the case of grammar, the quantitative findings reveal teachers' high level of contentment with the inclusion and presentation of new vocabulary in the textbook. As perceived by the teachers, the textbook includes a variety of new words that are presented in suitable contexts ($M = 3.75$; $SD = 1.14$) in a variety of ways ($M = 3.70$; $SD = 1.17$). It is also evident that a simple-to-complex approach is adopted to distribute the lexical items ($M = 3.53$; $SD = 1.16$) across the various lesson units ($M = 3.57$; $SD = 1.13$) and the new words are repeated in subsequent lessons ($M = 3.25$; $SD = 1.40$) in order to strengthen the meaning and use of vocabularies.

The content analysis indicated that in order to teach grammar in meaningful settings, a number of activities are included in the textbook. Among these activities are: completion of sentences based on reading text, matching columns to make sentences, filling the gaps in a passage with *will*/*would* and so forth. However, from the content analysis it appears that *English for Today* does not focus on teaching grammar explicitly. One reason for that might be that there is a separate book on English grammar and composition for students in grades 9 and 10 which is taught as 'English Second Paper'.

Likewise, for teaching vocabulary in meaningful contexts the textbook incorporates some vocabulary practice activities such as gap-filling with appropriate words from the box, finding the opposites of the given words and making meaningful sentences with the opposite words, writing/ inferring meanings of words from the context, filling in gaps with the appropriate verbs given in the box, matching words with meanings, completing passage with suitable words, and so on. These types of activities are provided in many lessons throughout the book. However, in order to retain and reinforce the new words, few instances of repetition of the newly presented words are found in subsequent lessons. This indicates that although the textbook is designed to teach new words to the learners, the lessons are not organised enough to give repeated practice of the new words through vocabulary recycle activities and this represents one of the weak aspects of the *English for Today* textbook. In addition, there is no clear list of the vocabulary items that have been covered in the previous grades. This finding reflects the limited number of direct vocabulary exercises. Moreover, phonetic transcriptions are not provided to show

how to pronounce words correctly. Similar trends were observed by Sarem *et al.* (2013) while evaluating the ESP coursebook in Pakistan.

Sociocultural representation

As discussed above, the transmission of cultures and awareness of cultural values through language teaching largely relies on the textbook. The teachers perceive that the textbook is largely satisfactory in terms of accommodating learning experiences that represent diverse sociocultural values. Teachers believe that the contents are largely appropriate to build learners' awareness regarding both local ($M = 3.71$; $SD = 1.12$) and international cultures ($M = 3.71$; $SD = 1.18$); at the same time a balance was maintained between the learning experiences of both cultures ($M = 3.72$; $SD = 1.16$). The teachers are of the view that the textbook contents encompass a range of sociocultural and religious contexts ($M = 3.66$; $SD = 1.25$) that are clearly comprehensible ($M = 3.67$; $SD = 1.21$). Moreover, the illustrations are perceived to be largely consistent with students' native culture ($M = 3.49$; $SD = 1.24$) and appropriate for knowing the target culture ($M = 3.46$; $SD = 1.2$). It is reported that the contents are free from gender, religious and ethnic biases ($M = 3.42$; $SD = 1.39$).

The above quantitative findings indicate that *English for Today* is a flexible textbook which is able to promote awareness of not only local culture but also the social values of international cultures, including that of the target language. Here, target language culture refers to English culture, but which English? Is it British English or American English – the two polarised forms of Standard English? The content analysis demonstrates that although the book is written in British English, it does not promote only British culture. Instead, it promotes both British and American cultures. Content analysis also revealed that among these cultural facets in *English for Today*, political (units 1 and 3), social (units 3 and 12), health and sports (unit 4), workplace or profession (units 3, 4, 9 and 10), population and health (unit 4), environmental (unit 5), people (unit 7), historical (unit 8) and technological (units 11 and 13) cultures are widely portrayed through various reading and listing texts. A suitable balance is maintained between local and international cultures. These cultural aspects are reflected through contents, pictures, words and texts. No contents and pictures reflect issues not deemed appropriate in a Bangladeshi social context. In addition, the textbook illustrates some culture-neutral elements which have been reflected in unit 14, in the lesson 'Pleasure and purpose'. This finding is in line with the cultural elements that Byram (1993) comprehensively and practically suggested.

Although the quantitative findings indicate teachers' positive perceptions of the appropriateness of illustrations, from technical point of view, however, the illustrations are found to be unattractive. They are mono-coloured pictures printed on low-quality newsprint. Even the textbook cover is very simple, a thin bi-colour page with simple illustrations. It is argued that students have their first impression of a book based on its physical appearance (Sarem *et al.*, 2013). Physical makeup and illustrations make a book interesting and motivating to learners. This finding is consistent with previous research conducted in different countries (Karimi, 2004; Maleki *et al.*, 2014).

General elements evaluation (topics covered)

Another aspect of the conceptual framework was a general element, which refers to the topics covered. The quantitative findings of this research indicate that the newly designed *English for Today* textbook covers a wide range of topics ($M = 3.52$; $SD = 1.12$) which are interesting and motivating for learners ($M = 3.43$; $SD = 1.23$) and suitable for the learners' age and cognitive level ($M = 3.82$; $SD = 1.23$). The topics were also reported to be suitable for promoting learners' critical thinking ($M = 3.36$; $SD = 1.20$) as well as useful for enhancing day-to-day communication ($M = 3.77$; $SD = 1.24$).

The above findings are supported by the content analysis, which revealed that a diverse range of topics are presented throughout the 74 lessons within the 14 units of *English for Today*. Each unit focuses on a broad theme and has several lessons relevant to the theme. The topics of the 14 units are: Good citizens, Pastime, Events and festivals, Are we aware, Climate change, Our neighbours, People who stand out, World heritage, Unconventional jobs, Dreams, Renewable energy, Roots, Media and e-communications, and Pleasure and purpose. Thus, the book has been structured in terms of diverse interesting themes/topics rather than the language features. However, each lesson has a specific language focus in terms of the four skills, vocabulary, grammar/structure and language functions. This finding is aligned with previous research where it was seen that a variety of different topics were presented in the ESP coursebook focusing on English for international tourism (see Sarem *et al.*, 2013). Such a variety of topics, on the one hand, are likely to provide general knowledge about different local and global issues that facilitates everyday communication; on the other hand, they may enlighten learners' attitude towards the world, life and human beings. Therefore, it can be said that the topics in *English for Today* were not randomly or haphazardly chosen, rather those were chosen to match the secondary English curriculum guidelines discussed above.

Tasks and activities

Teachers' perceptions indicate that the tasks and activities are accompanied by clear instructions ($M = 3.88$; $SD = 1.01$) and they leave opportunities for individual and cooperative learning ($M = 3.85$; $SD = 1.18$), are adequate, useful and interesting ($M = 3.81$; $SD = 1.10$) and are balanced for improving both the fluency and accuracy ($M = 3.80$; $SD = 1.04$) of learners. The teachers also largely believe that these activities and exercises encourage independent learning ($M = 3.69$; $SD = 1.20$) and emphasise the application of learning outside the classroom ($M = 3.57$; $SD = 1.31$).

The content analysis was consistent with the above findings and showed that the textbook incorporates a variety of activities, such as individual tasks, pair work and group work. This is in accordance with what the NCTB claims in the preface to the book: 'the book emphasises practising language skills through a variety of meaningful and enjoyable activities'. These tasks and activities usually facilitate communicative language learning. However, it is assumed that the tasks and activities cannot be performed well until they have been clearly explained. Since the instructions given in the book seem simple, easy and brief, the tasks and activities are probably clear to learners. The above finding contradicts some previous research. In evaluating the contents of an Iranian pre-university ELT textbook, Maleki *et al.* (2014) argue that their study identifies the inappropriateness of the activities and exercises in the book for communicative learning. Despite contradiction with earlier research in a different setting, the present finding suggests that the suitable nature of tasks and activities is likely to enhance the communicative competence of learners.

Pedagogical approach and support

It is argued that sound pedagogical approaches facilitate intake and acquisition (Masuhara *et al.*, 2008) of a language. The most obvious pedagogical concerns that interest us are whether the teaching approaches are learner-centred or teacher-centred, whether it is interactive or traditional, and whether it caters different learning styles or not. Teachers' perceptions suggest that the book offers a range of activities to support various language skills ($M = 3.75$; $SD = 1.11$) and different learning styles ($M = 3.70$; $SD = 1.12$). In addition, there are various situations/activities in the book that increase the possibilities for students' engagement, with reduced opportunity for teacher talk ($M = 3.60$; $SD = 1.32$) while leaving a wider scope for instructional adaptation by the class teachers ($M = 3.52$; $SD = 1.25$). Overall, the book has been designed to promote a learner-centred approach ($M = 3.31$; $SD = 1.29$). As discussed above, since the 1990s ELT instructions in Bangladesh have been based on CLT, which focuses on developing communicative competence through maximising learners' use of the target language.

The above findings are supported by the content analysis, which showed that throughout *English for Today* students are involved in learning activities through pair work, group work and individual work. As the textbook is full of many student-centred activities, students are supposed to get more time for practising the language than teachers to talk. Moreover, the textbook provides scope to engage students in a variety of activities. Some of these activities focus on a particular language skill (i.e. speaking) while some integrate two or more skills (reading and writing or listening and speaking). Some examples of these activities are: looking at the picture and discussing in pairs, making lists, answering questions, storytelling, discussing in a group, listen to a CD or a teacher and answering questions, filling the blanks with given words, matching, and completing sentences. The content analysis further showed that *English for Today* promotes a combination of learning styles, such as collaborative learning (sharing ideas), presentation, learning with fun, learning by doing, learning by seeing pictures, learning by reading, listening, comparing, surveying, inferring and so forth.

Outcomes of the textbook

Teachers' perceptions were positive regarding the overall outcomes of the textbook. The teachers believe that the textbook design is aimed at the learning outcomes of the NCTB curriculum ($M = 3.92$; $SD = 1.07$), it is helpful in developing learners' imagination and creativity ($M = 3.98$; $SD = 0.94$), and it assists in developing learners' communicative ability both locally ($M = 3.60$; $SD = 1.21$) and globally ($M = 3.91$; $SD = 1.22$). As seen above, the aim of English language teaching is to make the learners communicatively competent so that they are able to interact with people from diverse linguistic and cultural backgrounds. In achieving this aim, the curriculum emphasises developing learners' four language skills, and this is emphasised in the preface to *English for Today*: '...the **English For Today** [bold in original] textbooks have been developed to help students attain competency in all four language skills, i.e. listening, speaking, reading and writing'.

However, the content analysis demonstrated that the skills are not equally emphasised. The textbook focuses on speaking, reading and writing skills. Almost every lesson has one or more reading texts, speaking tasks and writing activities related to real life. Listening skills, however, are relatively disregarded. A similar finding is evident in the study by Sarem *et al.* (2013), who argue that the balance between skills development in their book was not appropriate to the learners and learning situation. While the textbook was dedicated to developing listening and speaking skills, reading skills were relatively ignored and writing skills were limited to only some units. Therefore, it can be assumed that if all skills of language are equally emphasised in *English for Today*, the teachers' satisfaction level would be much higher.

The content analysis further demonstrated that *English for Today* offers a number of avenues to exploit creativity in the language classroom and to promote critical thinking. Firstly, the book marks a shift in the convention of using highly Anglo/American themes and contexts for

English language instruction within a textbook. *English for Today* for grades 9 and 10 is written solely by Bangladeshi practising EFL teachers. As Pardo *et al.* (2004) observe, practising teachers had a chance to explore their creativity as innovative professionals by including them as textbook writers. In addition, the textbook incorporates a wide range of topics, such as citizenship education, climate change, world heritage, renewable energy, and media and e-communication, which are likely increase the creativity of learners.

Demographic variables and teachers' perceptions

The teachers' perceptions of the textbook were also examined with respect to gender, training/qualification and experience.

Gender and teachers' perceptions

This research considers gender a variable which is likely to influence the teachers' perceptions of *English for Today*. Table 13.4 shows the mean perceptions of the secondary teachers by gender. It is apparent that the male teachers recorded higher mean values than female teachers in all seven major areas of the textbook, although these differences did not reach statistical significance.

Table 13.4 Differences in the mean perceptions of male and female teachers

Major areas of investigation	Gender	N	Mean (SD)	Mean diff.	t value	p value
Topics included	M	83	3.59 (0.79)	0.06	0.270	0.79 ns
	F	17	3.53 (1.10)			
Tasks and activities	M	83	3.78 (0.71)	0.09	0.428	0.67 ns
	F	17	3.70 (0.90)			
Inclusion of lexis and their presentation	M	83	3.58 (0.90)	0.13	0.538	0.59 ns
	F	17	3.45 (1.10)			
Presentation of grammar	M	83	3.59 (0.87)	0.14	0.598	0.55 ns
	F	17	3.45 (0.88)			
Pedagogical approach and support	M	83	3.59 (0.94)	0.10	0.387	0.70 ns
	F	17	3.49 (1.03)			
Representation of sociocultural values	M	83	3.64 (0.86)	0.20	0.874	0.38 ns
	F	17	3.43 (1.0)			
Outcomes of the textbook	M	83	3.86 (0.89)	0.03	0.150	0.88 ns
	F	17	3.82 (0.78)			
Overall	M	83	3.66 (.69)	0.12	0.604	0.55 ns
	F	17	3.54 (.89)			

M=male; F=female; N =number of respondents; SD =standard deviation; Mean diff.=mean difference; ns =not significant.

Table 13.5 Differences in the mean perceptions of trained and untrained teachers

Major areas of investigation	Training	N	Mean (SD)	Mean diff.	t value	p value
Topics included	Yes	86	3.64 (0.83)	0.44	0.270	0.07 ns
	No	14	3.20 (0.87)			
Tasks and activities	Yes	86	3.79 (0.74)	0.19	0.428	0.39 ns
	No	14	3.61 (0.78)			
Inclusion of lexis and their presentation	Yes	86	3.60 (0.96)	0.23	0.538	0.39 ns
	No	14	3.36 (0.74)			
Presentation of grammar	Yes	86	3.57 (0.87)	0.09	0.598	0.72 ns
	No	14	3.49 (0.87)			
Pedagogical approach and support	Yes	86	3.63 (0.95)	0.37	0.387	0.18 ns
	No	14	3.26 (0.94)			
Representation of sociocultural values	Yes	86	3.70 (0.86)	0.72	0.874	0.004*
	No	14	2.98 (0.73)			
Outcomes of the textbook	Yes	86	3.94 (0.85)	0.62	0.150	0.013*
	No	14	3.32 (0.81)			
Overall	Yes	86	3.69 (0.72)	0.40	0.604	0.058 ns
	No	14	3.30 (0.66)			

M = male; F = female; N = number of respondents; SD = standard deviation; Mean diff. = mean difference; ns = not significant.

Training and teachers' perceptions

In Table 13.5, comparative views of teachers with and without a professional degree are summarised. The trained teachers have higher means than those without training. The differences in the mean perceptions between trained and untrained teachers are statistically significant for only two aspects of the textbook. The mean perceptions of trained teachers with regard to the representation of sociocultural values (trained $M = 3.70$, $SD = 0.86$; untrained $M = 2.98$, $SD = 0.73$) and textbook outcomes (trained $M = 3.94$, $SD = 0.85$; untrained $M = 3.32$, $SD = 0.81$) are significantly higher than those of untrained teachers. However, for the other aspects, no significant differences are found.

Teaching experience and teachers' perceptions

Comparative views of experienced and inexperienced teachers are summarised in Table 13.6. The mean perceptions of experienced teachers are generally found to be higher than those of the beginners in all the selected areas except two, namely presentation of vocabulary and indication for pedagogical approaches. However, teaching experience does not have any significant influence on their perceptions regarding the *English for Today* textbook with respect to the selected language aspects.

Table 13.6 Differences in the mean perceptions of experienced and inexperienced teachers

Major areas of investigation	Teaching experience	N	Mean (SD)	Mean diff.	t value	p value
Topics included	Beginner	55	3.55 (0.83)	0.07	0.40	0.69 ns
	Experienced	45	3.62 (0.87)			
Tasks and activities	Beginner	55	3.72 (0.68)	0.09	0.58	0.56 ns
	Experienced	45	3.81 (0.81)			
Inclusion of lexis and their presentation	Beginner	55	3.60 (0.86)	0.09	0.50	0.62 ns
	Experienced	45	3.51 (1.0)			
Presentation of grammar	Beginner	55	3.52 (0.84)	0.09	0.53	0.60 ns
	Experienced	45	3.61 (0.90)			
Pedagogical approach and support	Beginner	55	3.59 (0.91)	0.04	0.19	0.85 ns
	Experienced	45	3.56 (1.02)			
Representation of sociocultural values	Beginner	55	3.53 (0.77)	0.15	0.88	0.38 ns
	Experienced	45	3.69 (0.99)			
Outcomes of the textbook	Beginner	55	3.76 (0.81)	0.21	1.19	0.24 ns
	Experienced	45	3.97 (0.93)			
Overall	Beginner	55	3.60 (0.66)	0.07	0.49	0.62 ns
	Experienced	45	3.68 (0.80)			

M = male; F = female; N = number of respondents; SD = standard deviation; Mean diff. = mean difference; ns = not significant.

Conclusion

The purpose of this chapter is to report the collective views of the English teachers of the newly and locally developed and introduced textbook *English for Today*. In addition, the study explores whether teachers provide diverse observations on the textbook with regard to selected demographic variables, specifically gender, experience and training. In order to do so, the study has explored different aspects of textbooks to produce a conceptual framework which is assumed necessary to consider when a textbook for English teaching is evaluated. Overall findings reveal that, generally, the teachers have positive perceptions about the textbook from the perspectives of linguistic, pedagogical, technical, cultural and learning outcomes. Differences in their perceptions across selected demographic variables are mostly insignificant, with differences evident in only two contexts, based on training experience. The mean perceptions of trained teachers with regard to representation of sociocultural values and textbook outcomes were significantly higher than those of untrained teachers. However, regarding presentation of vocabulary and indication for pedagogical approaches, the beginner teachers had more positive perceptions than experienced teachers. The findings based on content analysis in a number of contexts contradict their views in some respects, which indicates that the teachers' perceptions to some extent are very subjective.

Developing an appropriate English textbook is a challenging task for non-native English experts. It requires time, energy and expertise, and special considerations. Since in Bangladesh, both teachers and students heavily rely on textbooks, the task of developing a textbook should be undertaken with great care. As the education system of Bangladesh is centrally controlled, unlike in many other countries, for teaching English at secondary level, Bangladesh does not need to select one or more textbooks from the enormous on the market. Instead, Bangladesh needs to justify and improve the locally produced textbooks to ensure their appropriateness from linguistic, pedagogical, general, technical and cultural points of view. The overall findings of this research, based on teachers' perceptions, suggest that the *English For Today* textbook is well designed and acceptable to teach English in Bangladesh. The book is likely useful to develop learners' communicative competence to meet both local and global communicative needs. However, the book is not free from limitations and there is still scope for improvement.

This research is a starting point for drawing general views of the teachers about the newly developed *English for Today* textbook for grades 9 and 10. The research did not explore the reasons for their views (which could provide an insight into teachers' classroom practice). Hence, further qualitative research could be conducted to explore teachers' views in greater depth. It would also be helpful to conduct retrospective evaluations of the dynamics of classroom practice and adaptation procedures. It could also be a methodological paradigm shift. The study findings indicate that while the task of ELT materials development is globally dominated by native speakers of English, materials developed locally by local experts are also worthwhile and able to fulfil local needs. On the one hand, *English for Today* can assist the accomplishment of the ELT objectives set out in the curriculum; on the other hand, it could be more culturally appropriate to teachers and students (Maleki *et al.*, 2014).

References

Akbari, R. (2008) Postmethod discourse and practice. *TESOL Quarterly* 42 (4), 641–652.

Alptekin, C. (1993) Target-language culture in EFL materials. *ELT Journal* 47 (2), 136–143.

Azad, A. (2015) New books, new class, new year. *Dhaka Tribune*, 2 January. Retrieved from http://archive.dhakatribune.com/bangladesh/2015/jan/02/new-books-new-class-new-year.

Byram, M. (1993) Language and culture learning: The need for integration. In M. Byram (ed.) *Germany: Its Representation in Textbooks for Teaching German in Great Britain* (Vol. 3-16). Frankfurt am Main: Diesterweg.

Carrell, D. and Korwitz, J. (1994) Using concordancing techniques to study gender stereotyping in ELT textbooks. In J. Sunderland (ed.) *Exploring Gender: Questions and Implications for English Language Education*. London: Prentice Hall International.

Cunningsworth, A. (1995) *Choosing Your Coursebook*. Oxford: Heinemann.

Daoud, A. and Celce-Murcia, M. (1979) Selecting and evaluating a textbook. In M. Celce-Murcia and L. McIntosh (eds) *Teaching English as a Second or Foreign Language* (pp. 302–307). Cambridge, MA: Newbury House.

Dendrinos, B. (1992) *The EFL Textbook and Ideology*. Athens: N.C. Grivas.

DeVellis, R.F. (2012) *Scale Development: Theory and Applications*. Washington, DC: Sage.

Downe-Wamboldt, B. (1992) Content analysis: Method, applications, and issues. *Health Care for Women International* 13 (3), 313–321. doi:10.1080/07399339209516006.

Florent, J. and Walter, C. (1989) A better role for women in TEFL. *ELT Journal* 43 (3). doi:10.1093/elt/43.3.180.

Gupta, A.F. and Yin, A.L.S. (1990) Gender representation in English language textbooks used in the Singapore primary schools. *Language and Education* 4 (1), 29–50. doi:http://dx.doi.org/10.1080/09500789009541271.

Haycroft, J. (1998) *An Introduction to English Language Teaching*. London: Longman.

Hutchinson, T. and Torres, E. (1994) The textbook as agent of change. *ELT Journal* 48 (4), 315–328. doi:10.1093/elt/48.4.315.

Juan, W. (2010) A content analysis of the cultural content in the EFL textbooks. *Canadian Social Science*, 6(5), 137–144.

Kachru, B.B. (1992) *The Other Tongue: English Across Cultures* (2nd edn). Champaign, IL: University of Illinois.

Karimi, A. (2004) An evaluation of a preparatory English course, Books 1 and 2: An EAP coursebook evaluation. *FLT Journal* 73, 24–28.

Kramsch, C. (1993) *Context and Culture in Language Teaching*. Oxford: Oxford University Press.

Maleki, A., Mollaee, F. and Khosravi, R. (2014) A content evaluation of Iranian pre-university ELT textbook. *Theory and Practice in Language Studies* 4 (5), 995–1000.

Masuhara, H., Hann, N., Yi, Y. and Tomlinson, B. (2008) Adult EFL courses. *ELT Journal* 62 (3). doi:10.1093/elt/ccn028.

Ministry of Education (2010) National education policy 2010. Retrieved from http://www.moedu.gov.bd/index.php?option=com_content&task=view&id=338&Itemid=416.

Mukundan, J. (2007) Evaluation of English language textbooks: Some important issues for consideration. *Journal of NELTA* 12 (1–2), 4–80.

Mukundan, J., Nimehchisalem, V. and Hajimohammadi, R. (2011) Developing an English language textbook evaluation checklist: A focus group study. *International Journal of Humanities and Social Science* 1 (12), 100–106.

National Curriculum and Textbook Board (2012) *National Curriculum 2012: English for Classes VI–X*. Dhaka: National Curriculum and Textbook Board.

Neuendorf, K.A. (2002) *The Content Analysis Guidebook*. Thousand Oaks, CA: Sage.

Pardo, A.N., Báez, C.P. and Téllez, M.F.T. (2004) Key aspects for developing your instructional materials. *Profile 5* (1), 128.

Prodromou, L. (1998) English as cultural action. *ELT Journal* 42 (2). doi:10.1093/elt/42.2.73.

Riasati, M.J. and Zare, P. (2010) Textbook evaluation: EFL teachers' perspectives on 'new interchange'. *Studies in Literature and Language* 1 (8), 54–60.

Richards, J.C. and Renandya, W.A. (2002) *Methodology in Language Teaching: An Anthology of Current Practice*. Cambridge: Cambridge University Press.

Sarem, S.N., Hamidi, H. and Mahmoudie, R. (2013) A critical look at textbook evaluation: A case study of evaluating an ESP course-book: English for international tourism. *International Research Journal of Applied and Basic Sciences* 4 (2), 372–380.

Saville-Troike, M. (2003) Extending 'communicative' concepts in the second language curriculum: A sociolinguistic perspective. In D. Lange and M.R. Paige (eds) *Culture as the Core: Perspectives on Culture in the Second Language Classroom* (pp. 3–17). Greenwich, CT: Information Age Publishing.

Schreier, M. (2012) *Qualitative Content Analysis in Practice*. London: Sage.

Sheldon, L.E. (1987) *ELT Textbook and Materials: Problems in Evaluation and Development.* Oxford: Modern English Publication/British Council.

Sheldon, L.E. (1988) Evaluating ELT textbooks and materials. *ELT Journal* 42 (4), 237–246. doi:10.1093/elt/42.4.237.

Skierso, A. (1991) Textbook selection and evaluation. In M. Celce-Murcia (ed.) *Teaching English as a Second or Foreign Language* (pp. 432–453). Boston, MA: Heinle and Heinle.

Ur, P. (1996) *A Course in Language Teaching: Practice and Theory.* Cambridge: Cambridge University Press.

Williams, D. (1983) Developing criteria for textbook evaluation. *ELT Journal* 37 (3), 251–255.

Index